GROWTH THROUGH GRIEF

Tom Pisello

HIGHERLIFE
PUBLISHING & MARKETING

HigherLife Publishing & Marketing
  PO Box 623307
  Oviedo, FL 32762
  AHigherLife.com

ISBN 978-1-951492-74-8 Paperback
ISBN 978-1-958211-73-1 Ebook
LOC # 1-12768196541

Printed in the United States of America

10 9 8 7 6 5 4 3 2 1

This book is the result of the vision God gave Tom Pisello to provide a path of healing and relief to other widowers like himself. He has juxtaposed his own story along with those of other widowers next to the wisdom of many healthcare professionals to compile a unique help to the grieving heart. Everyone who grieves goes on their own journey. No two are alike. For the sake of readability and to prevent confusion, all the stories and information in this book has been written in third person, including Tom's.

DEDICATION

This book is dedicated to my beautiful bride, Judy, who will always be loved and missed, and our beautiful daughters, Sophia and Alaina, who reflect the way their mom raised them each and every day.

And to all who have experienced their own loss: prayers and peace as you take each day of your own grief journey, one at a time.

ACKNOWLEDGMENTS

This book would not be possible without the contributions of so many widower brothers who were willing to transparently share their stories—the good, the bad, and the ugly—as well as mental health professionals, experts, and spiritual leaders who freely shared their insight and advice to help guide and heal.

Thank you, Christopher Ice, Joey Pazzelli, Fred Colby, Terrell Whitener, David Brock, and Tim Ohai, for so openly and honestly contributing your stories.

Thank you to our experts, including Jon Thurman, Pastor Chris Wassermann, Carly Paige, Dr. Kirsten Carter, Mary-Frances O'Connor, PhD, and Pastor Joseph Thompson.

A special thank you to Helen Keeling-Neal, mental health professional, widow, and dear friend, who sat down with me for dozens of interviews to discuss everything from treatment options to dating again.

ACKNOWLEDGMENTS

CONTENTS

MEET THE AUTHOR

Tom Pisello is a widower and the father of two daughters. Tom lost Judy, his wife of nineteen years, in 2017 after her ten-year battle with cancer.

As a result, Tom founded Growth through Grief, a set of healing resources and a ministry through which he shares his personal growth through his grief, and helps other widowers with their unique healing process. Through his own journey, Tom achieved sobriety, lost sixty pounds, gained a growth mindset, rekindled lost faith, and is now sharing these hard-earned lessons along with the experiences of other experts and widowers in this book.

Prior to creating Growth through Grief, Tom was a successful entrepreneur, analyst, speaker, and author of the business books entitled *Evolved Selling* and *The Frugalnomics Survival Guide*. Known as "The ROI Guy," he is also the founder of the value, sales, and marketing consultancy and software firms Genius Drive, Alinean, and Interpose; a Managing VP of analyst firm Gartner; chief evangelist and sales enablement expert for Mediafly where he was the founder of the Evolved Selling Institute; and host of the popular revenue and sales enablement podcast, Evolved Selling.

Tom lives in the Flatiron District in New York City and Winter Park, Florida. You can find him most days writing from one of the local coffee shops, working out, spinning at a local cycle studio, or jamming as a keyboard player with his band Rock Mobster.

Chapter 1

HOW IT ALL BEGAN

TOM + JUDY

The Meeting

> FOR THE FIRST TIME IN MY LIFE I SAW THE TRUTH
> AS IT IS SET INTO SONG BY SO MANY POETS, PRO-
> CLAIMED AS THE FINAL WISDOM BY SO MANY
> THINKERS. THE TRUTH—THAT LOVE IS THE UL-
> TIMATE AND HIGHEST GOAL TO WHICH MAN CAN
> ASPIRE. THEN I GRASPED THE MEANING OF THE
> GREATEST SECRET THAT HUMAN POETRY AND
> HUMAN THOUGHT AND BELIEF HAVE TO IMPART:
> THE SALVATION OF MAN IS THROUGH LOVE AND
> IN LOVE. —VIKTOR E. FRANKL, *MAN'S SEARCH
> FOR MEANING*[1]

On a sunny October day in 2017, Tom's family's dear friend and kids' preschool school leader, Dr. Kristin Milson, breathed a tearful prayer to welcome everyone to Judy's Celebration of Life. Tom took the stage next, before a packed room of 300 neighbors, friends, and schoolmates.

Judy had lived her life by the mantra: "A life serving others is a life well lived," and the room was full of those she had befriended and helped: other moms, neighbors, and especially those afflicted with cancer.

Tom had spoken before much larger crowds in his business, but this was completely different. The community, family members, and especially his daughters were relying on him. He had to set the tone for this goodbye to his beautiful bride.

He began where it all started:

Before the arrival of their beautiful daughters, Sophia and Alaina. Before their home in Winter Park. Before creating their business Alinean together. Before cross-country and soccer. Before great vacations in Harbor Springs and Boulder and their

---

1   Viktor E. Frankl, Harold S. Kushner, and William J. Winslade, *Man's Search for Meaning* (Boston, MA: Beacon Press, 2006).

camp in Maine. Before school at All Saints, Park Maitland, and Trinity Prep.

Tom called Judy.

"Hello, Judy? This is Tom. Our friend Jan said that we should connect." An incredible journey can begin with just a simple call and a few words. For Tom, it was just in time.

He had just started his first company, jumping headfirst into the deep end. He was also recovering from a broken relationship, and really struggling to make meaningful connections with women again. In that moment, on that call, Judy was a breath of fresh air.

They talked for a really long time: About her new job at Disney as an Imagineer. About her digital marketing for the new Celebration development and the Disney Cruise Line launch. She had brains, talent, and dreams. Tom was instantly entranced.

After about a half hour of captivating conversation, he commented: "This blind date stuff is really awkward, huh?" Complete silence. When that friend told Tom to call Judy, she aparently neglected to tell Judy. Judy thought Tom was looking for a digital marketer position. She thought this had been a job interview, not one of romantic interest!

Crap! No wonder the conversation had gone so well!

Tom broke the awkward silence: "Sorry, I didn't mean to catch you by surprise. I thought this was a great conversation, and if you'd like to continue, I'd really like to meet you. Here's my number. Give me a call." *Suave, huh?*

Luckily, Judy had just left a long relationship herself. She had moved back to Florida and had a new job, a new apartment, and apparently a new sense of adventure. Even though she had determined to never go on a blind date, she too had enjoyed their conversation and was looking for meaningful connection. With a little encouragement from her friends, and one or two glasses of wine later, she decided to call Tom back.

A few days later, Tom waited anxiously, grabbing an out-side table at Pannulo's Italian restaurant so he couldn't miss her—and she couldn't dodge him! This was before social media platforms and dating apps, so they had absolutely no idea what the other looked like except for a description shared by their mutual friend, who unfortunately didn't have a photo of either one.

Judy walked up and time stopped.

Ripped acid-washed jeans and a tight peach sweater. Long auburn hair, and best of all, that great big smile. Before you even knew her, that smile communicated Michigan whole-someness and a heart full of kindness and giving. She reminded Tom of Melissa Gilbert from *Little House on the Prairie* series, but a grown-up, no pigtails version.

She was brand new, but familiar. Confident, she was not afraid to order garlic-laden *penne tufo* on a first date. Most of all, Judy felt like "home" to Tom. Comfortable in her own skin, she made those around her feel the same way as she listened attentively and seemed to truly care as Tom spoke.

What did she think of him? Later, Judy often reminded Tom about this first date: the obnoxious wraparound Oakley and Guido gold rope necklace Tom was wearing. She had con-fided to their mutual friend that Tom was a little "too nice." *Can you believe that?*

However, in the end, somehow Tom got her to look past all that. Before you knew it, their lives were entwined.

It was during a long walk, talking art and architecture, when Tom knew she was the one. He was head over heels in love. Their first house was on Lake Copeland in that same neighborhood, Delaney Park. Their first puppy, Software. After selling their first company, they would sail away into the sunset on their sailboat, Downtime.

Pretty soon after that first walk, they were floating on a cloud at the top of the Citrus Club in their first dance as husband and wife. And what a dance it was.

Tom wrote this poem for Judy and read it aloud to all those gathered to celebrate their wedding. He can still clearly remember how beautiful she looked that day.

Time without Memory

The world I dream of has no memory, only promise.

Memory, the secretary of time, lasts only one day,
Before being blindly obscured by each night's repose.
Who am I, where did I come from, where have I been?
All in a journal next to my bed, have I logged my story.

Each morning I read the testament to a life well-lived, but do not know firsthand.
There she is. That smile, those eyes
that I have only read about.
A fairytale princess come to life
from the pages of my own writings.
She is exploring her own story again today and has found me where I was left.

We embrace in a passionate kiss.
Timidly in the beginning, for although many in time, the first in our minds,
It grows to a numbing passion,
like only a first kiss can.

Unencumbered by a long life of greetings and farewells, of love's battles won and lost.
There is time enough to reacquaint,
to affirm our feelings in native dance,
To quench the passionate fires in our souls.
But not nearly the time to take for granted
the caring and commitment.
To not realize the beauty.
For renewed every day are the first fantasies,
hopes and desires.

Time without memory.
For this is the world I dream of.
I dream.

My Love Story: A Home with a Heart

LOVE IS PATIENT, LOVE IS KIND. IT DOES NOT ENVY, IT DOES NOT BOAST, IT IS NOT PROUD. IT DOES NOT DISHONOR OTHERS, IT IS NOT SELF-SEEKING, IT IS NOT EASILY ANGERED, IT KEEPS NO RECORD OF WRONGS. LOVE DOES NOT DELIGHT IN EVIL BUT REJOICES WITH THE TRUTH. IT ALWAYS PROTECTS, ALWAYS TRUSTS, ALWAYS HOPES, ALWAYS PERSEVERES. LOVE NEVER FAILS. (1 CORINTHIANS 13:4–8A)

Equal parts passion and adventure, there was nothing Tom and Judy couldn't do together. It wasn't perfect, but they were deeply committed. Since they married later in life, they wasted no time trying to grow their family. Tom didn't make this easy with the constant traveling his business demanded.

Before flying back home one weekend, Judy told him, "We need to talk." Tom knew she was unhappy about the little time they had together, so he was not expecting this conversation to be a pleasant one.

7

They grabbed a casual lunch, and Judy said, "It's time to talk." Taking a deep breath, she pushed something toward Tom on the table.

Instead of a painful discussion, she had joyful news. Tom looked down at a positive pregnancy test. The family they had both talked about since the earliest days of their relationship was becoming a reality. Before too long, and after twenty-four hours of labor, in which Judy wanted Tom out of her face and nearly bit his nose off, they were blessed with their daughter, Sophia.

Hand in hand around this time, they bought a small office and started a new business. Judy ran marketing and operations, and Tom handled the product, sales, and service. From the beginning, Judy was Tom's collaborator, confidant, and complement.

They both wanted a Spanish Colonial lakefront house. Blessed in business, they bought a vacant lot with a beautiful sunset view. Judy's passion for architecture and design was one of the first things Tom loved about her, and now she finally had a blank canvas for creation. Judy began designing an absolute masterpiece.

Their original home sold quickly, so they moved into a small rental, not knowing that those "temporary" confines would be their home for three years of design and construction. That wasn't the only surprise. They also welcomed a second daughter, Alaina, into the world.

Tom gave this poem to Judy the day he told her he loved her for the first time.

No Going Back

When I tell you I will be trembling,
In trepidation and delight.

The words need to be spoken.

They have formed an emotional tidal wave in my heart,
Though my head doubts the intelligence
of their consequence.
I still know that the feelings are true.

I imagine sounds and syllables moving through the air.
Words resonating in the night.

Never to be retracted. It is too late.
The doubts will be lifted and
you will know exactly how I feel.

What will you do?
Run and hide, retreat inside,
Speak with silence, respond in kind?

"I love you," he softly says.
"I love you too," her heartfelt response.
There is no going back.

*There are some souls that are entangled through several lifetimes,
through space and time. Judy and Tom were like that. Tom tried to
capture this dance with these words.*

Unbroken Circle

You were someone else the last time our eyes met.
An angel in heaven. It was you. I touched your soul.

Or was it your tears? My last breath, holding hands.
In faith. In love. In hope.

Or a hateful slap. A promise broken,
shattered in the dark.
Or another. A look back as I walked away.
Or a forgotten word, I never knew I didn't say.

Could it be this is a first hello, or the last goodbye?

All paths together we take.
This time, which is the one?

Gone Too Soon: Losing My Beautiful Bride, a Little at a Time

FOR BETTER, FOR WORSE, FOR RICHER, FOR POORER, IN SICKNESS AND IN HEALTH, TO LOVE AND TO CHERISH... (TRADITIONAL WEDDING VOWS)

TO LOVE AT ALL IS TO BE VULNERABLE. LOVE ANYTHING, AND YOUR HEART WILL CERTAINLY BE WRUNG AND POSSIBLY BROKEN. —C.S. LEWIS, *THE FOUR LOVES*[2]

"The world is our oyster" defined their first ten years. When you are blessed so much, it is easy to take it for granted.

The next ten years? A trial of sickness and recovery. A grind of rinse and repeat.

Soon after their youngest was born, Judy started to suffer from peripheral nerve issues and chronic fatigue. Sleep

2   Clive S. Lewis, *The Four Loves* (London: Collins, 1982).

deprivation from running after a toddler and caring for a new-born? This mystery illness took much of her energy just when their family needed it most. They pursued different tests, acu-puncture, and holistic healing—all to no avail.

One of the doctors finally ordered an MRI. It revealed what Judy had been trying to tell Tom from the first day they met: her brain was big. So big in fact that it didn't fit completely in her skull. She had a Chiari Malformation. Literally, the lower portion of her brain protruded out of the hole in the base of her skull. This pressing against her spine caused discomfort and fatigue now, but could worsen to paralysis or death.

Brain surgery was in order. The base of her skull needed to be shaved away to make room. With the muscles of her neck moved out of the way, Judy was literally a bobblehead post-sur-gery. Her sister, Jean, came to the rescue, staying by her side for the next two weeks. This became a blessed pattern that would unfortunately need to be repeated.

Breast cancer came next. A small lump was successfully re-moved just after her fortieth birthday. Minor and successful. Judy would later recount the doctors wanting her to go on es-trogen blockers to help prevent recurrence, but she didn't. She didn't want to go into menopause fifteen years early, and who could blame her? However, this became a source of deep regret later.

A few years passed and Judy and Tom and family were in one of their favorite places to escape the Florida summer heat: Colorado. They were getting their "mountain on" and spend-ing the summer in Boulder, visiting Tom's mentor Dan, enjoy-ing Boulder Creek, and hiking every day with the girls. They loved it there so much that somehow Tom convinced Judy of starting a new adventure. Before they left, they made an of-fer on an incredible mid-century modern, just steps up from vibrant downtown Pearl Street, and also made a call to their favorite Florida realtor to ready their home there for listing when they returned.

Unfortunately, the Boulder move wouldn't come to fruition. Just before leaving for this trip, Judy had her annual follow-up visit. Her radiologist recognized Judy's name and spent a little longer looking at the images. He met with them on their return with bad news. Tom remembers it like it was yesterday. A double mastectomy soon followed. A stage 3b diagnosis led to many months of radiation and chemo.

Judy's sister, Jean, was there again when it mattered most. Judy had an incredible inner circle of other breast cancer survivors surrounding her through the trauma, recovery, sickness, and hair loss. Wendy and Suzy had both been diagnosed around the same time; they provided support and shared the nightmare. There was also a broader group of moms affectionately known as Judy's Village. They blessed Judy and Tom greatly. Angels all.

Five years later, Judy and Tom were heading to Camp Huckins in New Hampshire to drop off their oldest at summer camp. Judy's hair had grown back, and their girls were maturing under Judy's incredible example and guidance. Tom was in Boston on business, and picked them up from the airport to make their way north for a short vacation in Maine before they dropped off Sophia in the White Mountains. As they drove, Judy asked why the highway signs looked so odd. Why were they double? She had vision and balance issues the whole trip.

Their primary physician and friend Tracy immediately ordered a brain scan, taking nothing for granted based on Judy's history. A day later, Tracy was waiting for them in their driveway when they returned home from the office. She sat them down inside and delivered the results. The news was devastating. A glioblastoma brain tumor. A GBM in Judy's mid-brain on her pineal gland. A completely different cancer. After five years, they thought they'd be in the clear. Tom certainly thought so.

The brain tumor was inoperable. It was pressing on Judy's ocular nerve even more now, and she wore an eye patch at all times. Her balance deteriorated soon after as the tumor grew, and especially through the radiation treatment. Judy struggled to walk, and eventually used a walker just to make it across the room. During a walk down to their dock on the lake one day, Judy collapsed, and they could barely get her back up to the house. Just forty-seven and suffering greatly, they needed another miracle.

And somehow, they got one. Radiation and chemo were enough to halt and then shrink the tumor. After some time, Judy was able to walk and function again. The girls had their mom back.

However, everything was not back to normal. Judy had significant trouble sleeping and binge-watched *Breaking Bad* and other movies all night long. Her pituitary gland and her source of melatonin had been compromised with the tumor and treatments, so her sleep-wake cycles and circadian rhythms were no longer the same. Through each cycle of sickness and recovery, Tom and the girls were blessed to have Judy with them still, but less of her returned. They were losing her a piece at a time.

Knowing their time might be limited, Tom and Judy booked a magical Christmas cruise in Europe: Budapest to Munich for just the two of them. This getaway was a long time coming, a renewal of their relationship. Afterward, they had the best family Christmas ever. Soon after that, they celebrated Judy's fiftieth birthday with a surprise party. Another magical evening.

Over the next few months, they sold their family home and downsized to make things more manageable. Settled, but in need of a break, they took a great family trip to the Florida Keys, and then headed north to drop both kids off at Camp Huckins in Maine once again. During a bike ride in

Kennebunkport, Judy got nauseous and struggled with balance and vision issues which continued throughout their time away.

Returning, they ordered up more tests, and the worst was confirmed. Tom had thought, based on the overwhelmingly positive response to prior treatment, that if the brain tumor came back, they could just "zap" it some more. But cancer doesn't work that way. Stop it in one place, and it can just reappear elsewhere. That's what it did.

The cancer spread to her spinal fluid. Additional chemo was ordered, and another painful battle began. Judy was a fighter. She wanted to be there to see our girls (now seventeen and fourteen) reach some critical milestones. Again, her sister was by her side, and Judy's Village rallied.

A hospital battle unfortunately turned into hospice care over the next three months.

After celebrating their nineteenth wedding anniversary, Tom and Judy ordered in from the Italian restaurant where they had that blind date way back when, and danced to their wedding song, "Just the Way You Are." Judy was able to celebrate their oldest daughter's eighteenth birthday with long hugs and incredible love.

Judy took her last breath in Tom's arms three days later.

This poem was written for Judy's Celebration of Life ceremony.

To See You Again

There's a hole where my heart used to be
Where the rain seeps in and drowns my will to live

Falling inside to heal, confident of the strength I'll gain
Only to find weakness is all that remains

And so I cry, and try, knowing that real love never ends
Our love will be reborn

Another time, another space, another place
I will find you and we will love again.

Widowers by the Numbers: Research on Grief and Loss

For men, healing comes from re-partnering. It is part of the process. Statistically, widowers marry in two to three years based on U.S. Census Bureau data. For women, they like to heal first and then re-partner. Women remarry somewhere between six to seven years. But men heal differently, and re-partner much sooner as a result.
—Carolyn Moore, founder of Modern Widows Club

Y ou are not alone. According to U.S. Census 2019, there are 3.6 million widowers in the U.S. alone, not counting those that are now remarried, which tends to happen rather quickly. The numbers also don't include those who have experienced the loss of their life partner, but weren't legally married. So overall, between 2-3% of the total U.S. population are widowers. In our own community, a widower's average age is fifty-seven which means many are still also working, raising children, and shepherding young adults.

In my own backyard in Central Florida, there are:

- Over 8,000 widowers in Orange County alone.
- Over 20,000 widowers in the greater Orlando metropolitan area.
- Over 250k widowers in the state.

Expanding this figure, we estimate that there are over 50 million widowers worldwide.

The Impact of Loss

The loss of a wife is an incredibly stressful event, and for those who suffered through a long disease, the stress started long before the actual loss. And that stress continues for many years afterward.

Just how much impact does the loss of a spouse have? According to research, losing a spouse is number one, tipping the scales at 100 stress points, exceeding *all* other hurts and losses.[3] Divorce rates at 73 points.[4]

The loss of a spouse doesn't just deal the stress of the direct loss. Many additional challenges manifest. These complications compound the grief and add up dramatically.

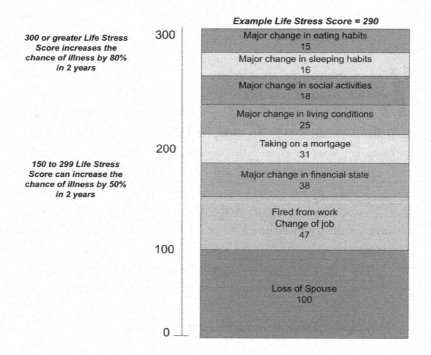

Example Life Stress Score = 290

300 or greater Life Stress Score increases the chance of illness by 80% in 2 years

150 to 299 Life Stress Score can increase the chance of illness by 50% in 2 years

300	Major change in eating habits 15
	Major change in sleeping habits 16
	Major change in social activities 18
	Major change in living conditions 25
200	Taking on a mortgage 31
	Major change in financial state 38
	Fired from work Change of job 47
100	
	Loss of Spouse 100
0	

---

3   T. H. Holmes and R. H. Rahe, "The Social Readjustment Rating Scale from the Journal of Psychosomatic Research," American Psychological Association (American Psychological Association), accessed February 28, 2023, https://psycnet.apa.org/record/1968-03998-001.

4   Ibid.

Stress points pile on top of one another. Many widowers struggle with career priorities which can lead to job changes or even loss, adding 47 more stress points. The loss of a late wife's income can pile on an additional 38 points. A move (or a major change) in living conditions (25), a loss of social activities (18), a disruption in sleeping habits (16), and altered eating habits (15) all compound.

According to the research, when the death of a spouse is combined with all these other factors, an accumulation of stressors can occur, impacting wellness and eventually causing disease.

Even in a previously healthy individual, the probability of illness increases 50% in two years when the stress points go past 150 points. Worse, when they exceed 300 points, there is an 80% chance of a health breakdown. Researchers have documented widowhood effects, confirming an increased risk in mortality and possible disability as well as, to no surprise, depressive symptoms.[5]

Consistently, the effects of losing a spouse are larger for widowers than widows, at least in the near term. Worse outcomes often occur for men because their wife was their "primary source of social support."[6] Husbands rely on their wives for their social lives, care, and well-being. Without their partner, widowers often become isolated, don't eat well, or exercise self-care. They also tend to self-medicate and suffer from depression. The research is clear. Trauma and stress from the loss

---

5   G.R. Lee and A. DeMaris, "Widowhood, Gender, and Depression: A Longitudinal Analysis," ResearchGate (ResearchGate), accessed February 28, 2023, https://www.researchgate.net/publication/249630598_Widowhood_Gender_and_Depression_A_Longitudinal_Analysis.

6   Allison R. Sullivan and Andrew Fenelon, "Patterns of Widowhood Mortality," The journals of gerontology. Series B, Psychological sciences and social sciences (U.S. National Library of Medicine), accessed February 28, 2023, https://pubmed.ncbi.nlm.nih.gov/24077660/.

of your spouse can impact wellness, and manifest in chronic illness.

In Tom's community, almost all widowers, especially within their first year, indicated that their grief greatly impaired their ability to work properly, and greatly affected their family life and social relationships. Additionally, these stressors were slow to recede: 40% indicated that their work, family life, and social relationships were *still challenged three years later*. Our widower's community named hopelessness as their top feeling, followed by overload, physical exhaustion, and loneliness.[7]

For example, Tom's once optimistic attitude for a bright future was replaced with doubt and hopelessness throughout Judy's illness and loss. Tom remembers the overload: trying to cope, planning a memorial while struggling with his business and finances, the kid's schedules, and the household—all of which Judy had managed. A persistent lack of sleep clouded that first year. Tom woke at the time of Judy's passing every night for months, which led to greater exhaustion.

Long before her passing, Tom's loneliness was extreme, which led him to get involved in a relationship after he lost her, way too soon.

When Tom and other widowers did their survey and looked at wellness traits, they wanted to know which ones took the biggest hits. They were confidence, self-image, and purpose.[8]

Men are the strength, the fixers, the solvers, but when it mattered most, none of them could save their wives. No one could have, but that doesn't mean they don't wear that robe of failure and shame anyway. Their once clear persona as husband,

---

7   That survey's list included Loneliness, Isolation, Fear, Indecision, Overload, Hopelessness, Depression, Anger, Physical Exhaustion, and Mental Exhaustion.

8   The options for current level of wellness choices were Happiness, Confidence, Positive self-image, Sense of purpose, Interest in self-care and health, Interest in interacting with others, and Interest in the future.

partner, and protector was now shattered, and their new purpose unclear, leaving them unsure.

Stress and this identity crisis impacted Tom's health. Over the course of Judy's illness, he had gained over sixty pounds, making him morbidly obese. A checkup soon after Judy's passing revealed extreme adrenal fatigue (long-term elevated cortisol levels took their toll). He was drinking heavily, especially during hospice. Tom worried he wouldn't be around to take care of his daughters. Chronic disease was in his future unless he got his shit together.

Tom needed to change his mind, body, and spirit in order to get there.

Twilight Prayer

Deliver, a safe place
From the nightmare, a dying breath

Find, these puzzle pieces scattered
Mend, this bleeding heart shattered
Lift, this prism of imperfection

Dance, a symphony,
Kaleidoscope into the twilight

The First Meeting of the Widower's Club

COMFORT COMES FROM KNOWING THAT PEOPLE
HAVE MADE THE SAME JOURNEY. AND SOLACE
COMES FROM UNDERSTANDING HOW OTHERS HAVE
LEARNED TO SING AGAIN. —HELEN STEINER
RICE[9]

Tom dove into his dinner without praying as he had yet to make that a firm habit. Thankfully, Joey held out his hand, reminding the group that sharing a few stories, laughs, and a good meal weren't our only goals.

At a high top table, in the middle of an eclectic hometown restaurant, five men had gathered. Each had lost their beloved brides—some just a few weeks ago and others a few years prior. They grasped each other's hands. Somehow they knew that

---

9   Helen Steiner Rice, "Helen Steiner Rice Quote," A-Z Quotes, accessed March 20, 2023, https://www.azquotes.com/quote/556657.

going forward, despite all their struggles, they were not alone. They had each other.

Having called the group together, Tom led the prayer: "Lord, thank You for bringing this group together. None of us asked to be a part of this club, and none of us would volunteer, but this is the journey You chose for us. We are grateful for the brothers You have gathered together, so we know we are not alone in this journey. We can rely on each other, and find our way from the darkness of loss into the light of Your love. Jesus, please help us to honor our late wives tonight, sharing stories of love and family. As we reminisce, let us not just gaze backward, but also look forward to what You have planned for us. May we be better fathers to our grieving children, better leaders to those who rely on us in business, and better friends to all who have helped (and continue to help) us, even as they are grieving too. Most of all, Lord, help us grow the way You intend, finding our new selves and future purpose. Amen."

Men are driven to solve problems, and seek to do so more naturally alone than as a group. They are strong and tough. They can handle it. They think like this: *We are, and we can.* But this journey is tough and they don't have to stay alone.

There are many in the unfortunate widower's brotherhood, who are going through the same loss, sadness, and trials, and have the same questions and concerns, and want to know "what's next." This prayer was appropriate for a very grieving heart.

As Tom started to work on his faith, he discovered that he was consistent in thanking God and asking for healing for those who were sick or suffering, but wasn't good at asking God questions. The concept of an actual conversation with God was foreign. This poem was his way of reconciling that shortcoming, trying to get into a habit of asking questions as part of their relationship. The questions were those he thought he should have asked followed by his interpretation of the answers God gave in return. These questions reflected his inner turmoil over the loss of the three most important people in his life—his mentor Dan, his dad, and his wife all within a short period of time.

Questions for God

Ask for Direction?
A straight line, bends

Ask for Strength?
Three whisper breaths, death

Ask for Grace?
A meditative prayer, pose

Ask for Why?
Two little girls still, love

Ask for Clarity?
Lucid dreams, sober

Ask for Healing?
A brother's hand held, firm

Ask for Forgiveness?
Hearts tears, shed

Ask, am I Worthy?
Full Surrender, Yes

CHRISTOPHER + MARY

Carrying on Despite Loss

> IT'S GOING TO GET BETTER. EVERY DAY CAN BE A
> LITTLE BETTER. —CHRISTOPHER ICE

Christopher Ice lost his wife Mary when she was fifty-four years old after thirty-two years of marriage and a five-year battle with breast cancer. They had seven children. Chris served as the CEO and President of Ava Maria University and the CEO of Catholic Charities of Kansas City-St. Joseph while handling family duties and trying to hold it all together. This wasn't easy. This is Chris's story of loss, healing, and purpose.

A Great Partnership

Chris and Mary met in college on her very first day there. Chris was a junior, and she was a freshman. Mary's mother noticed that Chris was wearing a Nebraska shirt, and said, "Hey, there's somebody here from Nebraska!" (They were in Kansas at the time.) Within four years, they were married and were married happily for thirty-two years.

Initially Chris was an assistant college baseball coach, and later began a long career in commercial insurance, moving up through the executive ranks. Being blessed with seven children became a challenge when higher positions in the company required more travel. Mary stayed home and cared for the kids, which allowed Chris to move ahead in his career.

Over twenty years later, Chris decided he wanted to spend more time with his family, so he stepped back and took a job with a university out of Ohio, and helped them build a fundraising division. This led him to becoming the leader of Catholic Charities, and eventually the president of Ava Maria University. Chris and Mary had the normal ups and downs and challenges, but they had a great partnership.

"Why Her, God?"

Cancer changed everything. Fortunately, Chris had already stepped down from his executive career, so he was able to take care of Mary in a greater way than before. The initial diagnosis was a shock. Mary had no family history of cancer. Not her mother, her sister. No one. She was under fifty, there were no markers, she never took a contraceptive, she never had an abortion, she exercised every day, she ate healthy, and she was not overweight. Mary did none of the major things that can lead to breast cancer. She had none of them. Chris's biggest question was, "Why her, God?" But there was no time for that.

Instead, it was time to help Mary with the medical labyrinth stretching before her. So much stuff comes at the cancer patient, especially when it's brand new. Chris's employer gave him the time to really focus on finding the right care. It's so important for the patient to have help navigating everything. Chris had to recognize that this was the area he needed to oversee. It was overwhelming to Mary. She couldn't understand it. All she heard was the "C" word, and shut down.

Initially, Mary went through sixteen rounds of chemo in 2015. She had radiation. She had surgery, the whole works. They thought they were in the clear at the end of 2016, and lived "cancer free" for a couple more years before it came back. It was really unexpected. The cancer came back in April of 2019, and they said it was a different kind. They were immediately catapulted into triggered survival mode.

Chemo was tough throughout. Mary had never put anything unnatural in her body, so at first she vowed not to use it, but then realized that wasn't an option. The poison took a toll on her physical and mental health. Her first four treatments were nicknamed "the red devil" because they were so bad. Red devil chemo just turned everything red and made her very sick. After the next round of chemo, they discovered that the cancer was now in her brain and removed a golf ball-sized tumor.

Chris had accepted the position as a university president at the time that included relocation, and the doctors assured them that Mary was going to be fine. Two weeks after the move, she wasn't feeling well. She was admitted and tests showed cancer cells within her spinal and brain fluids. She passed away within two days, leaving her family in shock.

They all thought she was going to get through this, or at least get more chemo and gain some time. Three to six months, maybe longer. No one thought they only had two days. They hadn't unpacked a single box.

Grieving Requires Time

After Mary's death, Chris dove into work. It was the start of the global pandemic, and there was a lot of pressure to make decisions immediately regarding the university opening and the kids getting back to school. Everything was crazy and haphazard. After stepping off the plane from burying his wife in Nebraska, the Board of Directors was already asking if they were going to keep the campus open or not and making plans for the next semester. Decisions had to be made.

Since Chris was on a six-week bereavement leave, he made the decision then, on faith, to keep the campus open. They planned to do lessons in person (as well as virtually for the immuno-compromised, or the concerned professor or student). The pandemic's impact was relentless, requiring hundreds of new decisions. As a result, Chris really didn't have time to grieve the way he needed.

Grieving requires time. Some people take six months, while others take years to recover. Chris had to throw himself into work so quickly that he hadn't had any time. Instead, he was trying to deal with great loss while he fathered his two youngest girls still at home and ran an entire university during an unprecedented pandemic. Even though he had a lot of support from the local community, it was difficult at best. When he saw the continued decline of his girls in respect to their trauma, he began to look for a less stressful job. He was able to step away from the university in July of 2021.

A Firm Foundation

God was Chris's foundation for keeping it all together. He knew God really was the Superpower He claimed to be, and that he was nothing without Him, so Chris's faith was his guiding light. He trusted God as his Creator—the one who loved him and his family. He trusted that their loss was meant to be, and had a purpose, even though he didn't know what it was. He trusted God's plan for mankind, firmly believing that his focus should be serving his family so they would be with Jesus in heaven. *That's where we're going to live in eternity*, he thought. *Our life here is just a speck of dust in the light of eternity.*

It's true that Mary got there much quicker than Chris would have desired, but once that happened, he chose to rely on God. Even though he didn't like the circumstances, he had to say, "Okay God, this is Your will." No one likes suffering, but that suffering helped Chris grow in a deep way. In the end, it caused him to completely reassess his life. Was he doing more for the university than his own family? Family was supposed to come first. Was his faith strong and was God first in his life? His daughters were young: eleven and fourteen at the time of Mary's passing. It was time to step back and help them—and his other children too. Just because they were older didn't mean they didn't need their dad too.

He found that each one of his children was in a different part of the grieving process. This continues. Two years after losing his mother, Chris's nineteen-year-old son commented, "Sometimes it only feels like she's been gone about five months." When he comes home from college, he has to reprocess things that maybe the girls had already gone through, or aren't needing to process at that time.

Grief is unpredictable. That's where faith played a significant role for Chris. One moment, you're fine and the next you glance out a window or at the TV and you're instantly drowning. Chris just kept praying and never stopped. His faith has been the anchor in the midst of the chaos.

Many years before, Chris had read Dr. James Dobson's book *When God Doesn't Make Sense*. The book was about why God doesn't step in and fix every problem and rescue us from every tragedy in life. He now recognized that reading that had prepared him to some extent in dealing with his loss. Much of life is about the decisions and choices we make, and God allows us complete freedom. He loves us so much that He lets us make our own choice—even if it is walking away from Him.

Failing and Remembering

So, Chris focused on his kids, trying to relate to them the best he could. He understood that his earthly fatherly role was important. It set the stage for how his kids would relate to their Father in heaven, and he knew that he was to give them the same freedom God gave him. When his kids got into trouble, he gave them advice, but he didn't force them to make the decisions he wanted them to make. His children had to learn to make decisions and deal with the consequences, for good or ill. Chris had watched some of his children suffer in that respect, but they were growing. God the Father allows us to do the same darn stuff, so we can grow too.

God lets us fail. He lets us love. He lets us go awry sometimes, so we can learn a lesson, so we can relate to our own kids or those around us. Chris's goal with his children was to give them a strong foundation when they were young, teaching them to maintain a prayer life and rely on God and Scripture. This is true for every faith. Parents can lay a firm foundation, and if a child strays, hopefully they will return. Some of Chris's children did come back to their faith in God. Possibly it was Mary's passing that was the catalyst for them to return to their Christian roots.

Chris also reminded his girls to not stop talking about Mom. He talks about her all the time, recalling the great memories, and laughing. It's important to speak about the one you think of so often. There is a thin veil between heaven and earth. The soul and the body are connected as one while we live on earth. When the body dies, our soul and spirit continue on, and never stop, so Chris and his family honor Mary's memory. She continues to be a central part of who they are as a family, even today and especially on holidays.

Mary homeschooled all of the kids to a certain age, so she was a big part of their lives. They all have wonderful memories, especially on holidays, so they still include her in them today.

On her birthday, they prepare her favorite meal for the family, and then serve a dessert she would never eat. Mary didn't like sugar, so it's fun to laugh, knowing "Mom would never eat these brownies" as the whole family devours them anyway.

Mother's Day is more difficult, especially because everybody's celebrating their mothers. Chris's daughter was asked if she wanted to make something for her mom at school. That was hard. To help, Chris asked all the kids to send texts sharing a favorite Mom memory. This helped them celebrate her life the best they could.

When Chris took a long look at his life, he realized that the long illness had taken a physical toll as well. When Mary was ill, Chris had gained a lot of weight. His time had been dominated by work and hospital visits, so he'd eaten on the fly most of the time.

During the pandemic, Chris was often hiding out in Mary's room, lucky to have a doctor that allowed him to be with her. That meant he was eating the hospital food that came to her room. (The cafeteria was out too as Chris was locked in the room, so Mary shared her food if you can imagine that.)

Afterward, Chris started exercising and reading again to get his body and mind back in order. Working out, diet, and order and structure, along with counseling and faith were all key components to growing again. In the beginning, Chris focused on going to church, praying each day in the morning and the evening, and trusting God first. The physical and mental parts came later. At first, he was flooded with a lot of anxiety and stress from trying to balance so many things.

People they knew served them meals for months. Everybody needs the benefits of such a community. Even though they'd only been there for a short time, people embraced them, wrapping their arms around Chris and his family. Today Chris is thirty pounds lighter, a good feeling. His girls are happier too because they see Dad being healthier, so they are less worried about being left alone.

Leadership through tragedy amidst all the fireworks of disease and loss was challenging. You still had to calmly make decisions and listen to the facts. Chris learned firsthand that while leadership took strength, it also took understanding that he wasn't on his own and needed to rely on God. Everyday, as bombs went off all around him and his family, he still had to decide whether to move his troops forward, hold them steady, or retreat. Many lives were at stake.

He learned to slow down as a result. He often thought of Winston Churchill, hiding out in the bunker and making decisions—not running out in front or standing on the front lines. It would have been stupid to expose the one making all the decisions like that. Instead, he stayed safe and made hard decisions as calmly as possible, even when London itself was under attack. Churchill was a great example of leadership through tragedy and turmoil. Chris did his best to make decisions thoughtfully, so they were not knee-jerk reactions.

Additionally, Chris was part of a group of six other men that walked with him through the whole tragedy. The men prayed and provided Chris with support. They called frequently, even setting up conference calls and meetings. Being in a men's group with these company leaders helped Chris reflect on his challenges and what to do about them. One of them had a wife who had cancer, so they talked together about some of the challenges he had gone through, and that helped guide Chris on his own journey.

Over time, Chris saw the light at the end of the tunnel. He knew in his heart that things were going to get better. Initially he walked in a dark cloud most of the time, but as he focused on the light in front of him, it lessened. He saw that there were people that wanted to help him and opened the door to them. This was important. When you're going through hard things, you sometimes don't want to be around people, but Chris learned to let them in, and that helped. They are showing forth the grace of God as they serve you. At some point in the future, it will be your time to be the servant and give. It helped Chris to receive their gifts and allow people to receive grace for their generosity.

The Top 5 Wrong Ideas People Have about Widowers

- Widowers will shake it off and don't need help.
- A quiet widower is a healed widower.
- Widowers will grieve for a year and be fine after that.
- Widowers need to get "back in the saddle" as quickly as possible.
- A widower's grief will eventually fade away.

Living Your Reality in 1.5 Second Increments: A Past, Present, and Future Perspective

REALIZE DEEPLY THAT THE PRESENT MOMENT IS ALL YOU HAVE. MAKE THE NOW THE PRIMARY FOCUS OF YOUR LIFE. —ECKHART TOLLE, *THE POWER OF NOW: A GUIDE TO SPIRITUAL ENLIGHTENMENT*[10]

BEGIN DOING WHAT YOU WANT TO DO NOW. WE ARE NOT LIVING IN ETERNITY. WE HAVE ONLY THIS MOMENT, SPARKING LIKE A STAR IN OUR HAND— AND MELTING LIKE A SNOWFLAKE. —SIR FRANCIS BACON[11]

As you look at how your life's advances, neuroscientist and author Moran Cerf believes that reality unfolds in tiny 1.5 second increments. That's how long he estimates it takes for your physical experience to be realized, understood, and processed, both consciously and subconsciously.

Most people don't live in this reality. They're not optimizing these 1.5 second clock ticks. Instead, they get hung up in

---

10   Eckhart Tolle, "A Quote from the Power of Now," Goodreads (Goodreads), accessed March 20, 2023, https://www.goodreads.com/quotes/50295-realize-deeply-that-the-present-moment-is-all-you-have.

11   Francis Bacon, "A Quote by Francis Bacon," Goodreads (Goodreads), accessed March 20, 2023, https://www.goodreads.com/quotes/128825-begin-doing-what-you-want-to-do-now-we-are.

their past and lost in their stored memories, which are often compressed and inaccurate—memories that can be changed and shaped in the present. If they're not doing that, they're thinking about their future, trying to use their current sliver of reality and knowledge of the past to make predictions about a future of which they know nothing. In the mix, people often yield to fear, anxiety, and stress.[12]

Your Past

Many get hung up right here.

To hold onto your huge store of memories efficiently, the brain uses shorthand: a story about the experience. This story is formed around a collection of 1.5 second sensory experiences of your current reality *plus* whatever sense you have of yourself at the time. Think of this sense as a picture of your psyche and its emotional point of view. The narrative stored in your memory will be dramatically different *according to how you feel* at the time the memory is stored.

That means that when you recall these memories, they are not just logical thoughts that you consider calmly. No, they are strong emotional reactions—sometimes positive because you felt well and happy at the time and sometimes negative because you were hurt and in pain.

In the case of grief, that last fight, regret, or image can weigh so heavily on your present that you can experience those similar emotions in the present as if the event was actually

---

12 Moran Cerf, "How to Bend Reality to Your Will and Become Un-stoppable: Mora...: From Robbing Banks to Earning a PhD in Neuroscience, Former Hacker Moran Cerf Has Unique Perspective on What Makes People Tick. in This Episode of Impact...: By Impact Theory," Facebook, accessed March 20, 2023, https://www.facebook.com/ImpactTheory-Show/videos/how-to-bend-reality-to-your-will-and-become-unstoppable-mora/1931861280399115/.

happening all over again. A lot of Tom's memories that he was replaying over and over regarding Judy were negative, reflecting the hurt and sadness he felt in his grief. He often saw himself helping the hospice nurse change and prepare her dead body for transport a little after she passed. Was this sad memory accurate? Because these events were stored shorthand as a story, his memory probably was not accurate. It was tainted by the mental lens he had at the time. He had been exhausted and feeling defeated. He'd just lost the battle, and through this lens he stored a lifeless, broken, scarred, and heartbreaking final image of Judy.

Looking back, the hospice nurse had needed help, but she also wanted to help Tom, not scar him for life (although he did have post-traumatic stress disorder (PTSD) symptoms regarding this for some time). The nurse had wanted him to realize something very important: This body was not Judy. Judy's beautiful soul had already departed and moved on. She was no longer sick and scarred, but restored to her inner beauty and light in a much better place. Tom's final image was not a beautiful one, but Tom could change that.

Memory can be reframed.

You don't have to be trapped in sad and traumatic memories forever. Memories are plastic, meaning you can recall and reshape their stories. If you've ever been to therapy, this will sound familiar. People are often helped by recalling the past and then by learning how to retell, recast, and replace that memory with a different, more positive perspective. According to some studies, doing this a few times will effectively reprogram the story and your mind.[13]

---

13   Gina DiGravio, "How the Hippocampus Influences Future Thinking," Neuroscience News (Boston University Medical Center, December 5, 2016), https://neurosciencenews.com/future-thinking-hippocampus-5680/.

So if there is a particular memory that is bothering you, is there a way to see it more positively?

Is there a way to forgive (or ask for forgiveness) about past events to replace guilt and regret with peace? Is there a way to transfer the burden of a memory to Jesus and store this transference as a part of the memory, making it lighter and easier to bear? Anytime you have an overwhelming burden from your past memories, you can cast that burden on Him. This process can change your past perspectives more quickly and permanently, and make all the difference.

Your Present

As you live your 1.5 second realities, you are shaping and storing new memories about those experiences.

The narrative that you tell yourself about yourself is vital as it shapes the way your new experiences will be stored. If you tell yourself a negative story about your struggle—one full of sadness, loss, victimhood, and inferiority, you are reinforcing those negative feelings in your new memories. And it doesn't stop there. As you recall the old memories, your current point of view can also impact how you update the story and replace those past memories, but not for the better.

Your negative self-thoughts and image reinforce and impact how you store current events, shaping a devolved narrative on those precious memories from the past. The best thing to do is reform and change your self-image, tamping down the negative thoughts.

As you grow in the Spirit, your current narrative should reflect His grace and His love He places on you and in you. So as you work on your current narrative, remember that any negatives will infiltrate your current and past memories, while positives will reinforce them and create peace and joy.

Your Future

To keep safe and optimize outcomes, the mind forms predictions about the future. These predictions are a story we tell ourselves about what will or might happen in the future.

It's all conjecture based on the current sliver of reality you have right now: your view of your self, what you have learned, plus your inaccurate and compressed past memories. Part of the midbrain, the hippocampus is vital in helping humans form memories, but also plays an important role in imagining the future. It helps construct possible future events in particular, and directly leverages your stories of the past to influence your forward-looking thoughts about the future.

Your current perspective and memories of pain and grief are easily projected into perceived future scenarios, as if the future will be similar to how you are looking, acting, living, and feeling today. We've all been there: we imagine what the future might hold around a particular scenario, forming story after story about the possible outcomes.

A common "future-scape" for Tom was seeing himself at home at night, alone, thinking about how empty the house was. This scenario produced more lonely forward-looking thoughts, projecting his current loneliness into the future where it morphed into a firm knowing that he would never be able to have another partner like Judy. He would *always* be alone and unhappy.

Many of the scenarios people forecast fuel fear, angst, and anxiety—all of which feel realistic and true, when in reality, *these predictions are only imaginary*. This anxiety and fear of the future affects not only your current mood, but can also cause you to act irrationally, dismissing help, making poor choices, or jumping at opportunities you shouldn't out of fear or desperation.

Realizing how your past narrative and current self-image impact your future is an important first step. You can use this insight to recognize that your projections can be distorted. Instead of doing this, you can reimagine the narrative you want in a more positive light (changing your future self-image first), which changes the potential outcomes.

Beyond this, don't forget to remember that you are in His hands. God already has plans for your future, and knows your best next step.

Your Right Now

Your life unfolds—
1.5 second consciousness
Marching forward, the arrow of time

Looking back, stories from your imagined reality
Captured through a lens of Self, distorted
Retold and shaped to fit a narrative
Sometimes productive, often times second-rate

Leap forward anxious
Future scenarios pondered
Possibilities and hurts
Outcomes, concerned frozen

We only have right now
To live fully in this precious clock tick moment

To retell ourselves of the past
Narrative, cast in a better light of forgiveness and grace
Placing the burdens on Him

To avoid future angst,
To know we are in the good hands
of He who has what is our best next.

JOEY + GIANG

You Don't Have to Go through This Alone

GRIEF AND HEALING IS *NOT* A LINEAR PROCESS.
—JOEY PAZZELLI

Joey Pazzelli lost his wife, Giang ("Yan," rhymes with "Can"), mother of their two college-aged daughters in the fall of 2021 after a two-year battle with colon cancer.

They met on a blind date. Well, they were *supposed* to meet that way. An old friend planned the date, and Joey readily agreed after seeing a picture of an absolutely beautiful woman. A double date was set for the following weekend.

A Blind Date

However, the night before that, Joey was downtown at a popular bar. As he casually scanned the room, a girl caught his eye. She seemed familiar and he was racking his brain for a long time trying to remember where he had seen her. It finally dawned on him that she was the girl he had a date with the next day!

Generally a shy guy, he wasn't sure how to approach her. Finally, he walked over and said, "You don't know me, but we're supposed to go on a date tomorrow!" At first, she thought he was trying to pick her up, but eventually, Joey said, "No, seriously. You know my friend Robert. He and his girlfriend arranged a double date with us tomorrow night." Understanding dawned.

They spoke for a long time, finding common ground almost instantly. Encouraged, they wrapped it up after deciding to seriously spoof their friends with a proverbially disastrous blind date the next evening.

The next night, Joey arrived early and listened as Robert went on and on about how sweet Giang was and how much he would like her. Joey played along. When Giang came, Joey formally shook her hand. They didn't talk much over dinner, and later, after going to a club, chatted sporadically. The atmosphere was rather chilly. Eventually, Joey leaned close to Robert and said, "Hey, can we go home now?" Robert was stunned as Joey shared how Giang just wasn't his type, and this was a disaster. Robert was extremely apologetic; he thought they'd really hit it off.

Finally, they all left. As they were walking outside, Joey and Giang suddenly turned and thanked Robert for arranging this supposedly blind date. After relating how they met the night before and hit it off, they said, "Thanks! We've got it from here!" They were so blessed by how God put them in each other's path.

Giang was the daughter of a three-star general from South Vietnam, and her mother was even stricter, if that can be imagined. A traditional Asian family, you didn't just walk and become part of their circle, and you also didn't casually ask to date (or marry) their daughter. Not in her family. So it took a lot of time, but eventually they married and had two daughters.

Joey was Italian and Giang Asian, so both valued family a great deal. Before they had children, they traveled together and enjoyed each other. When they decided to have children, it took them a few years to get pregnant. After the first, the second came almost instantly. They called them Irish twins because they were only seventeen months apart. Joey worked from home most of the time, and Giang stayed home too. This gave them plenty of family time and they were very happy.

"Come Here"

Around the time their oldest was looking at college, Giang went in for a physical after experiencing some intestinal issues. She left for the appointment and a little later the phone rang. Inexplicably, Joey's heart sank. He answered casually, but Giang's reply was terse and unforgettable: "Come here."

Fortunately, the doctor's office was close. Joey raced over and was immediately escorted into an exam room with Giang and the doctor. The doctor was trying to console her. They all began to pray immediately. The doctor thought they were looking at a form of cancer, but needed more tests. That ushered in their two-year battle against colon cancer, which included chemotherapy and radiation. Throughout the entire two years, they never got the cancer in remission.

Giang always handled herself with class and dignity, and had a high pain threshold, but she didn't get a reprieve. Joey and Giang went to multiple hospitals, taking part in a series of clinical trials, always chasing the right treatment. It turned out to be fortunate that the onset of her cancer occurred during COVID-19 because Joey's job allowed him to work virtually. Additionally, his vice president told him to take the time he needed with his family, and be there for them, which helped them immensely.

At the same time, their children were home from college and high school because of COVID-19, so they had time to be close in those final months. They look at that as a blessing. As things progressed, the pain Giang suffered went from awful to unimaginable.

Even though they had a large sphere of friends, there was a period in the last six months in which Giang saw no one. People were curious, and some never understood the extent of what she was going through, and where she was in the process. Even in the last few months when they knew they were losing the battle, they never gave up hope. They never stopped praying. They never stopped focusing on the next thing.

Joey was the fighter in Giang's corner, saying, "Honey, if this doesn't work, I'm here to pick you up. It's my role to be here for you. To be the guardian. To be the explorer. To be the fighter. All you have to do is heal: heal your mind and your body, and we're here as a family to love you, so you can fight with all you've got." And so they were able to surround her and do that, but in time, the cancer began to take over and her body began to fail. Nevertheless, her spirit never gave up and never faltered. In the last few weeks, they battled it out at home and in hospitals, trying to mitigate the pain. At the last hospital, Giang looked at Joey peacefully and said, "I'm done. I want to go home." Joey knew at that point that they were very close, so he took her home.

They had a candlelight vigil for their friends, who visited outside their home so Giang could see their support, and so they could share their love and support for her. Joey called family members from California and the D.C. area. One by one they began to arrive. They played beautiful spiritual music and surrounded Giang with candles all around.

Messages flowed in from friends and family, and they shared them and prayed over her. As they tried to relieve Giang of the pain, they began to increase the pain medication, and Giang began to drift off and lose consciousness, but she still held onto her family's hands until the very last moments. They are moments Joey will never, never forget.

Unprepared

Even though Joey had always been a believer in Christ, he had fallen far away from church, and wasn't secure in his faith when Giang got sick. He certainly was not prepared to face the trials that descended upon them when Giang was diagnosed.

Shortly after the diagnosis, a friend of Giang's and Joey's began to pray for Giang, and brought Joey's request to his men's group. These guys didn't know Joey from anyone, and his friend continually shared how this group prayed for his family regularly, often relating how one of the group said good things about Joey's family. Over time, this care and attention from a bunch of unknown guys drew Joey to them. He thought it would be good to get closer to the group and understand what they were about. He knew he had something missing in his life. Perhaps this would help him deal with his new situation.

The battle Giang and Joey were in caused them both to question their faith. In this kind of situation, a person could do one of two things: turn and run away from God or drop to your knees and ask for help. Joey did just that. He went to God, praying, "I don't know how I'm going to get through this, but I know that with Your guidance, You're going to find the way to get me and my family through it all—together and intact."

So Joey turned inwards toward his faith and upward towards God, and this men's group helped center him. After joining the group, Joey began sharing what he faced in life as the others did and they continued to pray for his family. This was good for Joey in many ways, not just in the battle he was immediately facing. As he drew closer and closer to these men, the light of Christ and his faith grew noticeably.

Eventually, Joey attended a weekend gathering, during which he really poured out a lot of the things he was facing. He laid bare his soul. It was nine months prior to losing Giang, and just after his father had passed away at ninety years of age. His father had led a full life, and Joey had given his eulogy, but he'd been so wrapped up in his personal fight at the time that when his father got sick and passed rather quickly, he had not really had the time to mourn him and go through the grief of losing him. The men's group allowed Joey to open up and visit what he had not resolved over his father's passing.

The group also helped Joey realize that even before he'd lost Giang, he was already experiencing grief. That was how a battle like this worked. This opened his eyes to an experience in the Lord that he hadn't had in being raised Catholic. Their meetings were quite different than a traditional mass. Music played and there were altar calls—a calling to the front, to which Joey felt compelled to respond. As he was prayed over for the things they were dealing with, he and his family were strengthened. One particular night, so many men laid hands on Joey as they stood in a circle that he had a breakthrough. He closed his eyes, lifted his arms, and began to seek and pray fervently for guidance as a father, as a husband, and for strength to help Giang through this. In that moment, Joey felt love and strength from above like he had never felt before.

As he stood there, arms outstretched, Joey knew he wanted to recommit with his family and friends as his witnesses. He was recommitting his life to be a better husband, father, and friend.

He felt the Holy Spirit enter into his heart and soul in a new way. Shortly thereafter he scheduled a formal ceremony at the church. Giang was very weak at this point, but they got her there and she was able to witness his baptism. This time of recommitment to Christ before his family was a turning point for Joey that led him into a stronger place in the Lord that he still enjoys today.

About a month after Giang passed was the toughest time for Joey. His daughters were still at home because of COVID-19. One night as he was walking up the stairs to go to bed, he heard his oldest daughter sobbing, so he opened the door, and said, "What is it? How can I help?" She was actually having an anxiety attack, but was almost frozen.

It turned out that when she heard Joey's footsteps coming up the stairs, it made her think of her mom. In Giang's last months (when she could make it up those stairs), she would always stop and spend time with her, and they'd often just hold each other. When she had heard Joey walking, she knew that she would never have that again. A rush of emotions had overwhelmed her instantly.

All Joey could do was hold her and try to comfort her, while trying to comfort himself at the same time. He struggled to understand what he needed to do as a parent to help his children through this unimaginable situation. His daughter asked questions he couldn't answer. Joey began earnestly praying that God would bring him those answers.

And God did not disappoint. As he sought Him, God gave Joey peace. He knew that God would put people in their path at the time when they most needed them. He knew God was going to do things to help them through the process. He didn't know how, but he knew it was going to happen.

The very next morning Joey got an early phone call out of the blue from his vice president. They didn't normally talk on a regular basis, and the man told Joey that he sensed that he might be having challenges. He told Joey that there was a gentleman who had rejoined the company that had lost his eleven-year-old son to an extremely rare brain-eating amoeba attack. A simply horrible story, he said the man had gone through a lot of healing, and as a result, joined his church and now actually oversaw a GriefShare support group.[14] He asked Joey if he was interested in it, and Joey immediately said yes.

Joey had just gone through the most difficult night of his life as a parent and knew he needed help. God had put this right in his path. He immediately called the man, and they spoke for hours. Both cried. He had lost his son nearly eight years before and still dealt with grief, so Joey saw right away that it was not going to go away overnight. It was a process. Everyone healed differently. There was no exact method or formula.

Help through People

Joey found that his healing came through multiple bonds and friendships: this dad, the GriefShare group, his men's Bible study, a widowers' group, and lifelong friends. All of that was helping him through this process.

He was blessed. He was not alone. God was with him the whole time. Members of the church were too. The Bible study group was praying over him and his family every week. The knowledge that he was in community comforted him, but it also opened the door to something else.

---

14 GriefShare is a biblically-based, Christ-centered support ministry dedicated to helping people of all ages process grief. For more information, go to griefshare.org.

Joey realized that as he was being helped, he was also helping others. It happened in a variety of ways. One guy dropped a book off in an effort to help Joey, so they grabbed coffee. Joey actually ended up helping him in the end, encouraging him in his faith, which was just what the guy needed.

When you reach out for help, sometimes through sharing your own experiences, you help the other person too. And vice versa. It is through this social healing that both grow, so part of the healing process is helping others. Once Joey recognized this, he began to do this more intentionally.

He changed his social media so that his spiritual beliefs were more prominent. In sharing his faith in Jesus, others began to respond, letting him know how he touched them. God's grace began to flow between Joey and others, changing his relationships. Joey was never religious. He simply wanted to do what Jesus asked people to do: love each other and let Jesus's grace flow from him to others.

He also began to pay attention to his physical and mental well-being. We are made up of mind, spirit, and body, so we all have to heal *all of those parts* to be well again. Joey began going to a spin class a few days a week. This positive forward movement helped.

Joey knew he couldn't love others without loving himself first, so he had to learn to love himself again. This was not selfish. Focusing a little on himself made him better for others. He had to be there for his children most of all. Giang had done an amazing job raising their daughters, and he was glad they were in their late teens and early twenties instead of younger. They already had core values and strong foundations, but they still needed his guidance as a father, and they definitely needed to see him heal and grow in a healthy way, so Joey worked on setting a better example of spiritual, mental, and physical health. They saw him getting back into the gym. They saw him refocusing his mind and doing some things differently than he had before. He began reading more and educating himself about healing and the grief process. He tried to expand his current knowledge base and think differently.

The Curse of Time and PTSD

Joey had spent the last thirty years completely immersed with his family. Suddenly that had all changed, and he was feeling the "curse of time." Overwhelmed initially, he began to think about how to change some of his interests and focus, so his time was used more productively. However, this resolve didn't happen overnight.

In the beginning, he just did his best to get through a day, but the nights proved to be most challenging. He often woke in a frenzy, as if he were still looking for the next thing to help Giang, awakening to the fact that it was all over. His mind was flooded with a barrage of regrets: What should he have done or done differently? But then he'd realized he no longer had the ability to do anything differently. These nightmares were a constant.

Not able to sleep well, Joey fell into a strange cycle: sleeping a few hours, and waking, his mind racing. He tried many methods to get to sleep and sleep better. He read more and said concentration prayers to calm his mind when he woke in the middle of the night. Not a believer in medication, he did try some to help, but wasn't personally at peace using them. He wanted other means.

Joey had never been clinically diagnosed with PTSD or received professional counseling, but when he looked at his symptoms, he knew he was probably suffering from that. He'd been through an intense battle and often found himself in "fight mode" now for no reason. He was still facing the same emotions and experiences he had when Giang was alive as if they were occurring in real time.

Like many PTSD sufferers, Joey found real relief through yoga. Designed to help the mind, body, and spirit connect, yoga helps the body overall. It increases your mobility and strength, but the toughest part of it is the last part in which it focuses and exhausts you to allow your mind to relax. Lying perfectly still on your mat, you're supposed to let your mind free, escaping into meditation as you finish.

This was the hardest part for Joey. Being able to free his mind meant turning off the noise, the regrets, and the anxiety. When he first started, his mind just jumped to Giang's last days. It took a long time to find peace.

As time progressed, Joey understood that grief and healing was not a linear process. Books exist that outline steps, but Joey's healing didn't work like that. Instead, he often felt that he took a few steps backwards at times. Sometimes he had bad periods of time. One of his faith leaders urged him to not let his bad moments make bad days. It was important to recognize it for a bad moment, but not let it dominate the day or the week.

Joey decided to visit his homeland and had always enjoyed opera, so in honor of his upcoming trip to Italy, he found a romantic opera to listen to on a long drive across Florida. He could have taken the interstate, but felt the need for some restful time alone. He turned on his music and took the path less traveled, turning this way and that on country roads. What an experience! The music and the scenery allowed him to reflect and it became very emotional. Halfway across the state, a song Giang always loved sung by Italian tenor Andrea Bocelli played. It was called "A Time to Say Goodbye." As the music poured over his soul, Joey cried and sang, belting out every note in the car. Midway, the song just stopped.

The next song that came up was "Claire de Lune," Giang's second-best favorite. He hadn't planned this. Joey didn't know how that soundtrack had come together as it did, but the change turned that emotional moment into laughter. He pulled over, sensing Giang's presence all around, and said. "Thank you, Giang, for doing this. Thank you for stopping me in my tracks and pulling me out of those tears. God is great. You're still around me. You're still with me and I love you for that."

Sometimes the past just invades the future.

Sobriety from Grief with Tom Pisello

GOD, GRANT ME THE SERENITY TO ACCEPT THE THINGS I CANNOT CHANGE, THE COURAGE TO CHANGE THE THINGS I CAN, AND THE WISDOM TO KNOW THE DIFFERENCE. —REINHOLD NIEBUHR, THE SERENITY PRAYER[15]

It had been a long night for Tom, perhaps the longest of his life. After saying goodbye to Judy around two a.m., and helping the nurse prepare her lifeless body for transport, they carried her away, passing the Dale Rogers sculpture in his courtyard, a Japanese symbol for honoring those who had died. It was as if that statue had been placed there, knowing this would be the place from which Judy departed. There are no accidents in God's plans.

Tom's buddy, Gerald, greeted him the next day with a couple of wine bottles in hand. He wanted to be sure Tom wasn't alone. Tom appreciated Gerald's fast New Zealand wit even now. As they had many times before, they opened a bottle and got lost in conversation, laughing and remembering countless good-time stories of Judy and their kids growing up together. One bottle turned into two, three, and four, as Tom drank away the reality of his partner leaving too soon.

He woke the next day with quite the headache, but also a struggling business that needed his attention, friends who wanted to know he was okay (and who themselves needed some comfort), and most especially, two daughters who needed

---

15 Reinhold Niebuhr, "Reinhold Niebuhr Quotes," BrainyQuote (Xplore), accessed March 20, 2023, https://www.brainyquote.com/quotes/reinhold_niebuhr_100884.

to know he was there for them, even though the pillar of their young lives had been taken away. He could barely function. Later, he didn't know how he even got out of bed that morning to face anything.

At some point that day, he realized just how broken he had become over the past twelve months. Losing his dad to lung cancer in April and Judy in October, had overset him. He felt defeated. He was overweight. His faith, shaken. Before this, he had been drinking heavily every weeknight, and even more on weekends. He was short-tempered, self-medicated, and checked out.

He needed to not rinse and repeat in alcohol again. Instead, he needed to move forward. He didn't want to forget or ignore his loss, but he also needed to show his girls and himself that there could be rebirth and renewed purpose from tragedy.

Giving Up to Grow

That last binge with his friend was a welcome escape from the pain of the night before, but Tom didn't need to escape any more. He needed to face his new reality. He vowed right then and there that he had taken his last drink the day before. *He had to embrace his grief through sobriety.*

He began that first full day without Judy and drinking by making the bed, something he could only remember helping with a few times in his entire married life. It felt incredible to accomplish something new, a small step forward in this first new day. Committing to doing things that he took for granted before, this was a great way to make it harder to crawl back in bed again later if he felt the need to escape. From that day on, every day began the same: Tom made the bed—even in hotels.

Tom focused on accomplishing goals and replacing bad habits with positive ones through willpower. His friends made fun of his monastic nature at times, but his new focus served him well. In college, he quit drinking in his junior year to raise his grades and compete with the foreign nationals, who were total academic machines, so he knew he could do it again. Except now, the stakes were even higher.

Many people that are self-medicating through the sickness or grieving process may want to quit in time, and have possibly even tried, but return to the bottle soon after. In truth, real help does exist. Therapy and Alcoholics Anonymous have a proven track record in having a positive impact on turning lives around.

Tom was able to change without a program, leveraging a growth mindset and embracing the fact that he no longer drank as his go-forward story. Whenever he wanted a drink, he told himself that story. Whenever anyone offered him a drink, he told them he didn't drink, and was quick to explain why: "I lost my wife recently, and was medicating heavily during the process, so I definitely needed to stop drinking altogether."

Sobriety is more accepted nowadays. Often when Tom shared his story, others reciprocated with their own or told him how many years they had been sober. Most appreciated Tom's openness and vulnerability. As a result of this recent cultural shift, more non-alcoholic and mocktails are being offered on menus and at events, as more and more people have chosen to live without alcohol.

Today Tom still hangs out with friends who drink occasionally—those that have one glass of wine in the evening or a couple of beers watching the game. Although he gets ribbed from time to time, his friends don't take issue with his choice. Tom wasn't just having that one glass in the evening or while watching football. His alcohol was consumed alone, not socially, and had become self-medication. Alcohol meant he got drunk often, and that had no place in a healthy lifestyle.

Tom 2.0: Advancing Day by Day

Tom's first day of not drinking turned into a second and third. He replaced his time with alcohol with exercise. It is vital to replace the old negative habits with positive ones. This could mean walking, reading, exercising, painting, playing an instrument—anything that could occupy the time you would normally be drinking. Not unexpectedly, Tom began feeling better almost immediately since his body didn't have to work so hard to process and remove all those toxins. He consciously made a note of the change to help his future motivation.

When he went to a friend's house, he brought his own big water glass with lemons or limes in it to make him feel like he was drinking. He kept that water glass in his hands so it was always full, and not available to accept wine or anything else someone might pass his way. "Here, see, I already have a drink! Thank you!"

He avoided going to bars, where the sole purpose was to drink; and when he had to meet someone in a bar, he ordered water with lemon and lime, always keeping the glass in his hand. Even though it was "bad luck" to toast with just water, the alternative was worse, so he lifted his water glass with a big *Cento anni!* (100 years of good luck), his Italian *salut*.

A week or two into the process, there were further improvements. He felt better as his gut regained balance. As the bacteria in his digestive tract was slowly restored, his acid reflux disappeared.

Within a month, he had dropped ten pounds. The workouts helped, but he had been working out a decent amount before that, so his weight loss was primarily from avoiding empty drink calories, especially sugar. Margaritas and amaretto slushies hadn't done him any favors.

He also noticed that he snacked less. When he was drinking, he'd usually grab some charcuterie, crack open a bag of chips, or some other unhealthy snack and indulge. Either the alcohol boosted his appetite or discouraged his self-control. He wasn't sure which, but now empty calories, sugars, and snacks were no more. After a couple of more months and with a notable calorie reduction and a big boost to his metabolism, he had lost another twenty pounds.

It's not just your thoughts informing your actions. Your actions determine your thoughts.

Five years later, Tom is sixty pounds lighter and a good amount is lean muscle mass. He is the most physically fit he has ever been. None of it would have been possible without giving up alcohol and achieving sobriety as his first substantial step forward to improving his body and clarifying his mind.

As Iron Sharpens Iron: The Power of Peer Sharing

AS IRON SHARPENS IRON, SO A FRIEND SHARPENS A FRIEND. (PROVERBS 27:17 NLT)

FOR WHERE TWO OR THREE ARE GATHERED TO-GETHER IN MY NAME, I AM THERE AMONG THEM. (MATTHEW 18:20 CSB)

THOUGH ONE MAY BE OVERPOWERED, TWO CAN DEFEND THEMSELVES. A CORD OF THREE STRANDS IS NOT QUICKLY BROKEN. (ECCLESIASTES 4:12)

COMFORT COMES FROM KNOWING THAT PEOPLE HAVE MADE THE SAME JOURNEY. AND SOLACE COMES FROM UNDERSTANDING HOW OTHERS HAVE LEARNED TO SING AGAIN. —HELEN STEINER RICE[16]

---

16   Helen Steiner Rice, "Helen Steiner Rice Quote," A-Z Quotes, accessed March 20, 2023, https://www.azquotes.com/quote/556657.

ove, Faith, Hope, and Joy: Tom's friend, Danielle, had
four different necklaces made, a single word on each, and
gave them to four close friends, symbolic of the bond they
shared. This gift reinforced their spiritual sisterhood, a tribe of
four women who regularly shared their struggles, much-needed hugs, support, and advice. Their regular meetings strengthened them as they helped each other through the daily trials
and tribulations of relationships, loss, careers, parenthood, and
more.

This group of very smart, creative and successful women
wore these special necklaces at all times to remind them that,
no matter what was going on in their lives, they each had a
"sister" that would always be there for them. It was their tribe.

Brotherhood Uncommon?

The differences between Dani's tribe and Tom's men's group
was stark.

Tom had lunch with one of the founders of his Bible study,
who admitted that even after five years of leading the gathering, it was still hard for *him* to share openly and freely. In
fact, most of those that attended regularly listened intently, but
didn't really open up the way the women did. Even though we
met twice a week, most of us didn't share our worries, trials, or
lessons learned.

On one particular day, when lunch arrived at the table,
Tom reached for the leader's hand to pray. The man pulled
back swiftly, commenting that "that was different." The same
thing happened when Tom tried to hug him. His initial knee-
jerk reaction was not one of closeness and caring, but one of
perceived vulnerability and unease. This is an example of the
challenges most men face in building a brotherhood.

Raised by a U.S. Navy veteran, this Bible study leader recently recounted how men just didn't hug and most certainly

didn't hold hands. Discussing these challenges, he spoke respectfully about his dad who never taught him how to share his feelings. He'd also never been taught how to swallow his pride and admit that he might not have all the answers. His favorite quote from his father was: "You don't ask for help, but if anyone asks you for help, you better be sure to be there and deliver." It was honorable to help others, but not receive it. What if you were the one who really needed help? What if you were grieving, lost, and struggling and needed support? Apparently, men were supposed to withdraw and deal with everything alone.

Many men have grown up just like this leader. Shaped by fathers of the Great Generation, the survivors of two world wars, they were raised to be tough. They were taught to "suck it up" or "shake it off" when they fell down. They were never encouraged to hug it out or shed tears together over a situation.

Men learned early not to share their feelings or problems. They were taught to be noble and help others wherever and whenever they could, but they were also taught to stuff their emotions and solve their challenges on their own. Just like their fathers, they'd been raised with capital punishment and criticism rather than hugs and words of encouragement. Most of all, their dads taught that despite how hard anything might hurt, big boys don't cry.

As a child, Tom had a bad bicycling accident, flying over the handlebars of his ten speed onto his elbow. He slowly hobbled home. Sitting on a chair in the dining room, his arm felt like it was bent ninety degrees, but it was clearly straight and misaligned. He knew it was broken. He cried, screaming out loud, begging his parents to take him to the hospital. The pain was intense. His dad replied, "Stop all this drama and crying!" Then, he told his mom to get some ice because it would be OK. Tom's arm began bleeding as the broken humerus poked out. It was clearly a compound fracture. Even then, it took several more "suck it ups" before his dad took him to the emergency room, perhaps just to stop the blood. He wouldn't want to ruin the carpet. His dad wasn't insensitive because he was cruel. It was simply a reflection of his Brooklyn upbringing.

When Tom compared notes with others, he found that this was not an uncommon experience. Most men he knew had been trained to be lone wolves in every way—friendship, business, even faith. *Men didn't share their feelings with other men*. It was hard to be transparent and vulnerable. It was hard to hold another's hand in prayer or hug. Surrendering and seeking help from God was also a challenge. After being strictly trained to be strong, why would they bother *anyone* for help to solve their problems?

However, wolves that hunt as a pack are much more effective than the one that hunts alone. The pack can bring down much larger prey and fend off threats in harmony. The benefits found in brotherhood were great, but they were almost unnatural to most men.

Tom's friend, Jon Thurman, shared this: "Most men spend their life's energy on who they're not—living in fear of being found out—not of having done some egregious wrong, but by incongruence: that the guy they see each day in the mirror is not the same guy others see. It's like being chased by a lie you can't outrun, or worse yet, running in a race with no finish line. Is it any wonder why men live such exhausting lives?"

The Need for Brothers

Unlike the widows he knew, Tom felt alone as he grieved, even though he had friends who were always there for him. They *just didn't talk* about his issues. Having never experienced loss themselves, they had a hard time knowing what to say. Time with them helped; it was good to know people cared, but he still felt alone. Tom had been thoroughly indoctrinated to rely on himself and remain that way. Alone.

Tom knew this wasn't productive. About four years after Judy's passing, he was introduced to another widower by a friend who recognized Tom needed help. Tom was more than ready to finally address his postponed grieving.

After that first coffee meetup, they gathered a few other young widowers and began meeting monthly just to talk casually. Their purpose was not to vent, but simply gather in their "knowing": knowing that they had all experienced similar loss, and were struggling to honor their late wives, raise their children, and rebuild their lives, finding new purpose in this 2.0 version of themselves.

As they gathered the fourth time, Tom was apprehensive about what would be discussed, but still looking forward to it. Happily, the awkward greetings, prayer, and careful sharing of their earlier meetings gave way to comfortable exchanges, deeper dialogue, and comforting embraces this time.

Although they didn't share necklaces, and none of them would have volunteered to repeat the experiences that made them eligible for the group, they all felt reassured and empowered because they were part of it. At a local pub, they talked about recent trips with their children, tributes to their late wives on Mother's Day, and how they were slowly healing and creating lives beyond their loss.

As Iron Sharpens Iron?

Whenever people gather, they often quote this verse: "As iron sharpens iron, so a friend sharpens a friend" (Prov. 27:17 NLT).

Tom had always accepted this verse at face value, but digging deeper, quickly realized that rubbing iron against other iron didn't actually sharpen it. Instead, it produced heat from the friction and sweat from the exertion. His meetings with various men didn't sharpen them as they wanted unless some other key elements were present, just as sharpening iron required more than other iron. Sharpening stones of a harder substance with varying levels of grit are required to sharpen iron. They had to be rougher to provide the initial shape, and later, more and more refined (eventually with diamond dust), to create a finely honed, sharp cutting edge.

If iron is to be used to sharpen iron, a piece of iron can work its magic only if it is rougher than the other. A casual interaction didn't work; it required intense friction. Aside from textural differences, the correct pressure had to be applied to produce the desired shape and angle so as not to remove large swaths of metal, but turn it into a blade instead.

This was true of interactions too. You had to have a "rougher" person—one able to apply the right pressure at the correct angle. This meant relying on a brother who elevated others past superficial discussions about sports and the weather, and did not accept an "everything is great" response easily. That rougher person prompted deeper connection, asked tough questions, and jumped into the uncomfortable conversations necessary to navigate pain and promote healing.

It made sense that this was the only way Tom and his friends could transcend their stiff upbringing. They needed to create a real brotherhood to overcome their challenges. Beyond that, they needed to learn to rely on God and His unconditional love and support, so they didn't continue to "suck it up" and "dust themselves off" on their own.[17]

The Power of Brotherhood

Will I be accepted?
Fear of rejection, anxious

Gathering with my brothers
Pride and ego reign

Can I be truthful in my sharing—
Transparent and vulnerable
Or will I get hurt

Beyond the news and scores
Share my pain and sorrow

Raised to always help others
You don't ask for help yourself

Taught to keep it in, to myself
Handle it all on my own
Dust if off, suck it up

In this gathering I realize
There are others with shared experiences
Of suffering and loss
Of spiritual reliance
Of rebuilding and renewal

Of iron and strength I can rely on
To lift me from the mud
To guide my path, straight
To sharpen, cut through focus
To raise me, into the light

---

17   Carolyn Gregorie, "How Love Conquers Stress, According to Science," SUS (Huffington Post), accessed March 20, 2023, https://sus.org/love-stress/.

The Top 5 Myths about Grief

1. You must be stoic.
2. No one will understand your loss and sadness.
3. Grief follows a defined, linear process.
4. Grief has a defined schedule.
5. You will reach a point when your grief goes away.

Chapter 2

G.R.I.E.F.: HOW TO GROW FROM THE CHALLENGE

NOT ONLY SO, BUT WE ALSO GLORY IN OUR SUF-FERINGS, BECAUSE WE KNOW THAT SUFFERING PRODUCES PERSEVERANCE; PERSEVERANCE, CHAR-ACTER; AND CHARACTER, HOPE. AND HOPE DOES NOT PUT US TO SHAME, BECAUSE GOD'S LOVE HAS BEEN POURED OUT INTO OUR HEARTS THROUGH THE HOLY SPIRIT, WHO HAS BEEN GIVEN TO US. (ROMANS 5:3–5)

AFTER TRAUMA THE WORLD IS EXPERIENCED WITH A DIFFERENT NERVOUS SYSTEM. THE SURVIVOR'S ENERGY NOW BECOMES FOCUSED ON SUPPRESSING INNER CHAOS, AT THE EXPENSE OF SPONTANEOUS INVOLVEMENT IN THEIR LIVES. THESE ATTEMPTS TO MAINTAIN CONTROL OVER UNBEARABLE PHYS-IOLOGICAL REACTIONS CAN RESULT IN A WHOLE RANGE OF PHYSICAL SYMPTOMS, INCLUDING FI-BROMYALGIA, CHRONIC FATIGUE, AND OTHER AU-TOIMMUNE DISEASES. THIS EXPLAINS WHY IT IS CRITICAL FOR TRAUMA TREATMENT TO ENGAGE

THE ENTIRE ORGANISM, BODY, MIND, AND BRAIN.
—BESSEL VAN DER KOLK, *THE BODY KEEPS THE
SCORE: BRAIN, MIND, AND BODY IN THE HEALING
OF TRAUMA*[1]

The acronym GRIEF represents a framework for systematic healing to achieve peace and joy.

The definition of grief is "deep mental anguish"—especially caused by someone's death.

But that doesn't cover it. Its synonyms give us a better sense of how grief feels: agony, bereavement, discomfort, distress, gloom, heartbreak, misery, melancholy, pain, woe, regret, sadness, suffering, torment, wretchedness, unhappiness, heartache, affliction, and despair.

Losing a loved one sparks many of these feelings. It often feels like you are endlessly struggling to climb out of a deep and slippery hole, the worst you have ever known. A heavy load on your shoulders weighs each step—a backpack filled with hurt. You are just trying to get out of it with no destination in mind. However, you can't stay like this. You have to grow. You must find a way to *grow through grief.*

How do you begin to turn your grief and continual sense of loss and pain into something positive, not so you forget, but in an effort to find new purpose, peace, even joy again? They say "time heals all wounds," but it doesn't seem that way when you are living in loss.

As Tom puzzled over his life after Judy's passing and continued to meet with his widower brotherhood to discuss their challenges and growth, he found a pattern for growth in the word "grief" itself. Because of his engineering background, he couldn't have been happier!

---

1   Bessel A. van der Kolk, *The Body Keeps the Score: Brain, Mind, and Body in the Healing of Trauma* (New York: Penguin Books, 2014), 53.

He turned *grief* into **G**race, **R**eflection, **I**ntention, **E**levation, and **F**aith.

Grace Defined

THEREFORE, SINCE WE HAVE BEEN JUSTIFIED THROUGH FAITH, WE HAVE PEACE WITH GOD THROUGH OUR LORD JESUS CHRIST, THROUGH WHOM WE HAVE GAINED ACCESS BY FAITH INTO THIS GRACE IN WHICH WE NOW STAND. (ROMANS 5:1–2)

ACCEPT—THEN ACT. WHATEVER THE PRESENT MOMENT CONTAINS, ACCEPT IT AS IF YOU HAD CHOSEN IT. ALWAYS WORK WITH IT, NOT AGAINST IT. MAKE IT YOUR FRIEND AND ALLY, NOT YOUR ENEMY. THIS WILL MIRACULOUSLY TRANSFORM YOUR WHOLE LIFE. —ECKHART TOLLE, *THE POWER OF NOW: A GUIDE TO SPIRITUAL ENLIGHTENMENT*[2]

Time after time as Tom discussed his loss with others, guilt was expressed: Guilt about not being able to do enough to stop the pain. Guilt at not being able to heal the disease. Guilt about being a poor substitute for Mom now. Guilt about considering a new relationship and its timing. Guilt about not healing as quickly as others. Even guilt about going out and having fun or traveling. The list went on and on.

The world was tough enough without torturing themselves by pondering the past, present, and future, and dealing with a host of relentless regrets on top of perceived shortcomings and anxious fears. The first thing to do was stop. *Stop beating yourself up.*

---

2   Eckhart Tolle, "A Quote by Eckhart Tolle," Goodreads (Goodreads), accessed March 29, 2023, https://www.goodreads.com/quotes/853487-accept---then-act-whatever-the-present-moment-contains-accept.

To give *grace* means to give favor with no regard to whether or not it's deserved. It's showing goodwill and kindness.

Why not start the growth process by giving *yourself* some grace? Could you have done some things differently? Of course. This is a difficult journey, but no one can go back in time and undo (or redo) anything! It's over. You might be trying your darndest to make things better than they are or you might be walled off, resting, and giving yourself time.

The bottom line is to stop beating yourself up over all of it. It's not productive and imprisons you in a self-destructive loop of negative thoughts. It is time to break free. The regret loop can be difficult to escape. It's a constant emotional battle.

Looking at the biblical definition for grace expands the earlier definition. Grace is "God's riches at Christ's expense." It's a spontaneous gift from God: generous, free, totally unexpected, and undeserved that "takes the form of divine favor, love, clemency, and a share in the divine life of God."[3]

You must begin by removing the burden of debt you feel from the past, doubt about the present, and anxiety over the future by providing grace to yourself. Tom found the best way to achieve grace was by listing each of the areas he was beating himself up over. Then he sought God's help in overcoming each one.

He began with his regrets and guilt. It was a long list, but it's one worth giving a lot of thought to because once it is processed, there is real change. Dig deep and pull them out. Go through each item prayerfully, speaking out loud: "Lord, please forgive me for...."

After the past has been addressed, consider other negative areas: self-torture over the present, apprehensions about the future, and anything else that comes to mind, and ask God for

---

3   "Grace in Christianity," Wikipedia (Wikimedia Foundation, March 15, 2023), https://en.wikipedia.org/wiki/Grace_in_Christianity.

guidance on the best next step as you surrender your anxiety to His will. Receive His grace over your soul. With it will come peace as well as the ability to show grace toward others. Grace softens our lives, encompassing us with a much-needed sense of peace.

Reflection: Careful Consideration

> IF YOU GET THE INSIDE RIGHT, THE OUTSIDE WILL FALL INTO PLACE. —ECKHART TOLLE, *THE POWER OF NOW: A GUIDE TO SPIRITUAL ENLIGHTENMENT*[4]

Now that you have created some "space" with grace, it is time to think a little bit about what you have been through, and reflect on what it means.

Reflection is defined as considering the past, with an eye on how this may be used to shape the present and future. Going to a quiet place alone without TV or social media is a good idea. It's time to use the space you made for yourself with grace to think about what's happened and where it has taken you. Tom was lucky to have a dog named Ruby, a Shih-Tzu/poodle mix that required several walks daily. He often used this time for reflection, especially in the morning after his time with God.

He thought first about the past—stuff that still troubled him: potential shortfalls in his previous actions or in himself that he was fretting over. He did this, not in an effort to stir up and relive the negative, but to examine it. The key here is to try and remove yourself from the feelings attached to the situations, and observe the pain, sorrow, anger, and conflict

---

4   Eckhart Tolle, "A Quote from the Power of Now," Goodreads (Goodreads), accessed March 20, 2023, https://www.goodreads.com/quotes/50326-if-you-get-the-inside-right-the-outside-will-fall.

as though you were a third-party observer. He tried to look at it all from the outside as if he were a loving friend watching, trying to describe where he'd been and where he was now. The eyes of grace are so much kinder.

Tom began by listing the challenges he was still addressing. The first morning after Judy passed, he took that first walk with Ruby, looking into an abyss. She was gone, and it felt like someone had placed him on a tightrope above an endless black hole, removing his sense of balance along with the safety net. Judy had shaped everything in their home and social life, and was also instrumental in their business. Tom began to reflect, taking inventory, and starting really small so as not to get overwhelmed and shut down. This was an early list:

- Tom woke up and the bed wasn't made. Of course not—Judy did this diligently every day. An unmade bed is very comfortable to just crawl back into and hide. He made the bed.
- He had a bad hangover from his time with his friend Gerald. Several bottles of wine had been the exclamation point on his daily medication ritual of several margaritas or amaretto slushies for some time.
- Tom was at least sixty pounds north of healthy, and with his family's cardiac issues and his drinking, he was at risk, and his daughters needed him around now more than ever.
- He had to get back to work immediately just to keep the wheels on the company's bus and pay his employees. The thought of getting back on the road for customer visits and sales calls, and leaving his grieving daughters, weighed on him like lead.
- He kept replaying the sadness of Judy's passing—her last struggled breaths and the nightmare images of helping the nurse prepare her body for transport.

- He regretted how much resentment had built up between him and Judy over the past years: a mixture of her resenting the fact that she was sick and couldn't do all she wanted and his resentment that she was unable to do the things they loved to do together.
- Tom felt like a complete failure. He hadn't been able to fix this, and they had lost after battling it out for a decade.
- Tom had to face his daughters without any idea how to answer their questions. He didn't know how to make their world right again.
- Tom's faith was shattered. He'd asked God for answers and healing for Judy and his dad and neither had turned out as he wanted.

That was just the first day's reflection, but *what an important first step it was.* Over time, Tom's reflection time would have a sustaining impact on his ability to grow and heal. To make it more impactful, Tom intentionally writes about what he's experiencing and how it makes him feel. What are the effects of anger, sorrow, regret, and fear? What worries you? How do you see yourself? Writing it down is a powerful tool.

The brain stores all of this. If, as you recall pain, sorrow, regret, fear, and anger, you put it into words that reflect the stories you tell yourself, you can become much more self-aware. If you were a writer and were writing about yourself as a character in a story, what would the story be about? Where have you been? What worries you most about where you are today? Why do you feel as you do? Breathe life and understanding into the swamp that overwhelms you by putting it on paper, where you can trace each troublesome issue back to its point of origin and make better sense of it. Tom developed an evolving list of the challenges he still faced from the past and an inventory of what bothered him each day.

Not long ago he ran into one of Judy's radiologists at the gym. This guy had a lot of experience with those going through grief and the aftermath of loss. He succinctly provided the motivation as to why reflection is vital when he said, "After a person sustains a loss, there are two decisions: One, they can ignore what they went through—indulge in drinking, eating, cavorting their way, burying the pain, and not unexpectedly, beginning a downward spiral that doesn't end well, and those that reflect on what they have been through, making a conscious decision to learn from their horrible experience and become a better person because of it."

May you take that second path: reflecting and moving into Intention.

Intention: What Next?

WE CANNOT DO THE THINGS WE LONG TO DO, SO OUR TENDENCY IS TO THINK OF OUR DREAMS AND ASPIRATIONS AS DEAD. BUT GOD COMES AND SAYS TO US, "ARISE FROM THE DEAD." WHEN GOD SENDS HIS INSPIRATION, IT COMES TO US WITH SUCH MIRACULOUS POWER THAT WE ARE ABLE TO "ARISE FROM THE DEAD" AND DO THE IMPOSSIBLE.
—OSWALD CHAMBERS, MY UTMOST FOR HIS HIGHEST[5]

Now that you have looked back, it's time to glance forward, clarify direction, and set some goals as to where you would like to be.

Everyone comes to this next stage of the growth process with issues, but if all you do is focus on what is wrong with you, arriving at the obvious, accurate (and negative) diagnosis that you are broken, you'll never get anywhere.

---

5   Oswald Chambers, *My Utmost for His Highest: Selections for Every Day* (Grand Rapids, MI: Discovery House Publishers, 1995).

It is time to take responsibility for your own healing. This means not defining yourself by your loss and the past, but setting a new *intention* for change, improvement, and healing. This often requires that you stop identifying yourself as a victim, depressed and alone.

So what is this capital "I" Intention? Intention is the thought that results in purposeful action. It is a determination to act a certain way, and is often the subject of a prayer. Medically, intention refers to the process or way in which a wound heals.

Let's define it like this: with determination and prayer, you need to set your mind and actions on healing your wounds and growing from your experience.

First of all, picture a better future. You can't achieve what isn't imagined, so do that first. Even though you are still grieving, imagine a better future for yourself.

This imagined future can be one in which you have not forgotten your lost loved one, but don't hurt so much anymore. Instead, you are leveraging the loss for purpose. You can see yourself as happier, loving, and whole again. You have embraced your broken pieces, inlaying them with gold. You are stronger and even more beautiful than before—like *Kintsugi* gold-repaired pottery.[6] More on that later.

Picturing a better future is easier said than done. The brain is preprogrammed against change, even when the new state is substantially improved and beneficial. This is called the status quo bias, one of over 180 different biases that causes our brain to act differently than we expect. This is mostly because of the strong influence our subconscious, reptilian brain has

---

6   "Kintsugi," Wikipedia (Wikimedia Foundation, February 26, 2023), https://en.wikipedia.org/wiki/Kintsugi.

over the more logical, conscious (and larger!) part responsible for thinking.[7]

A person perceives any change from the current baseline (the status quo bias) as loss, even if the current state is sad and heartbreaking. This means that for every change ahead, you form an outsized perception regarding its risks compared to its potential benefits. Darn our primitive brains anyway! We'll revisit this bias again, but for now, let's see how to get past it.

Journaling *from the future* helps. Imagine yourself some three to five years from now. What would you be writing in your journal? What would you be doing, seeing, and feeling? Where would you be living? What would your family relationships look like? Do you have a partner and extended family? The key to vision journaling (and its ability to overcome the status quo bias) is to impart a degree of *specificity* to your future.

With a specific, solid vision for the future physically written down, your brain can begin to adapt to the ideas you wrote about. Our brains have an amazing ability to grow called plasticity. As you think about this progressive journey, you put on paper, and your brain will begin to change its mindset so you can realize these thoughts. Over the next few days, weeks, months (and even years), you now have a method to adjust your goals, and even advance them.

A growth mindset means continually assessing, adjusting, and building the vision as you grow. We can use the word *growth* itself to define what a person living this mindset looks like. They will:

- G – Gravitate to the challenges placed before them (as opposed to avoiding the issues).
- R – Retain a positive outlook despite future struggles and challenges (instead of focusing on the negative).

---

7   "Status Quo Bias," Wikipedia (Wikimedia Foundation, March 17, 2023), https://en.wikipedia.org/wiki/Status_quo_bias.

- O – Operate in a space just outside their comfort zone (rather than avoiding discomfort).
- W – Work diligently, taking self-disciplined steps towards improving their mind, body, and spirit, enjoying the journey and not just focused on the end goal (versus avoiding the effort and focusing only on the outcome).
- T – Take lessons from setbacks, mistakes, and criticism (as opposed to striving for perfection and not accepting feedback or acting just on negative experiences).
- H – Help others to succeed and find lessons and inspiration in the success of others (as opposed to feeling threatened by others' success), especially following the mantra whereby you should "plant trees under whose shade you may never sit."

As you imagine your future, you will continually face your grief and shortcomings, but the work accomplished, the lessons learned, will provide the momentum and fuel to achieve Elevation, the next stage in the process.

Elevation

GOD DOES NOT GIVE US OVERCOMING LIFE – HE GIVES US LIFE AS WE OVERCOME. —OSWALD CHAMBERS, *MY UTMOST FOR HIS HIGHEST*[8]

If you followed those steps, you are actively working on a vision for the future and are continually improving your mindset. With a clear goal and the right attitude as a foundation, it's time for action.

---

8   Oswald Chambers, *My Utmost for His Highest: Selections for Every Day* (Grand Rapids, MI: Discovery House Publishers, 1995).

Elevate is defined as lifting up to new heights. It is time to raise ourselves up to a higher level, higher than we have been before, step by step progressing to the new life you envisioned.

To do this, you need to make progress in three areas:
- Physical health – your body and fitness
- Mental health – your mind and thoughts
- Emotional health – your heart and spirit

When a bodybuilder wants to get stronger, they stress their muscles, breaking them down to rebuild them and make them stronger. Constructive stress needs to be applied consistently to body, mind, and spirit to achieve the elevation we seek.

The only way change can be truly instilled is if they become habits. Popular sources say it takes twenty-one days to form a habit, but studies say it can take an average of sixty-six days. For some study participants, habits were formed in as little as eighteen days, while others took far longer—over 250 days. The point is that it takes work to change.

Body First?

Tom started working on his body first, and it really needed it. He was at least sixty pounds overweight, didn't exercise, and had been drinking to excess for a long time to escape pain. After vowing to never drink again, and adopting a new narrative—*I don't drink anymore*—he turned to walking, then running, and eventually working out at the gym or spinning every day. His first relationship took place too soon after he lost Judy, but still helped him as she was a yoga instructor, spin leader, and trainer, who could see he wasn't going to be around much longer unless he made a real change.

The son of an Italian-American mom who had lovingly stuffed him from his youth, Tom's diet needed an overhaul too. His daughters worked hard to help him understand the changes he needed, and supported him on his new food journey.

They were also not shy in their comments. As a result, he was able to drop sixty pounds and keep it off, achieving a level of physical health he hadn't had since his much younger days.

However, the focus was not on weight loss, but on physical improvement. They were just byproducts of the new habits. The focus for Tom was on carefully considering what he did and did not put in his body, as well as what he did to strengthen his body. So to elevate the condition of your body, slow improvements are the ticket, not trying to become a perfect yogi, vegan, bicyclist, runner, or bodybuilder. Every new habit eventually has an impact, even the slow ones, and helps on the journey, elevating a person to peace and joy and renewed purpose.

Mind

Neuroplasticity refers to the brain's ability to modify, change, and adapt both its structure and function in response to experience. People can take advantage of this by fueling and reinforcing their growth mindset, and by fine-tuning their experiences. A therapist can guide the grieving individual on this path by helping formulate specific individual goals. The idea is to shed unhealthy habits and get rid of Autonomous Negative Thoughts (ANT): thoughts that are negative and random in reference to one's self. These new pathways guide the mind to grow continually, and effect real change.

Tom adopted and thought about the elements of a growth mindset which was a good first step, but he needed to *do* something about it. He needed to learn from experts to reinforce what he was learning. For this, he turned to growth mindset podcasts, listening when he walked his dog. He started with a variety of podcasts on improved attitude, exercise, diet, gut health, relationships, leadership, and more. He especially enjoyed hearing stories about super-performers, like James

Lawrence, the Iron Cowboy, who completed 100 Ironman competitions in 100 days[9] (after successfully doing fifty in fifty days in fifty states), or retired Navy SEAL Chief David Goggins, commonly known as "the toughest man alive."[10] Tom's favorite was the weekly interview show called Impact Theory hosted by Tom Bilyeu. Listening to a diversity of mind, body, and spirit self-improvement podcasts, videos, and books begins to reeducate your mind, and so, begins to change it, setting a mental habit.

Spirit

Spirit is defined as the nonphysical aspects of our being—the conscious, feeling entity within our minds that makes us uniquely human.

From a biblical perspective, a person's spirit refers to the part of man that connects and communicates with God. Our spirit points toward God connecting with His Spirit. Through this, we experience the joy, comfort, and peace of God's presence.

For Tom, working on his spiritual health began with prayer. When he examined his daily time with God, he saw that it was clearly unbalanced. Physically, he had advanced to daily workouts. Mentally, he was consuming growth podcasts and reading self-improvement books two to three hours a day. He quickly realized that spiritually, a few short prayers and occasionally reading a spiritual book wasn't enough.

A preacher's daughter that he knew called him out, "You work out hard and study hard, but you hardly work on your

9   Adam Skolnick, "'Iron Cowboy' Completes 100 Ironman Triathlons in 100 Days," nytimes.com, June 28, 2021, https://www.si.com/edge/2021/06/09/iron-cowboy-james-lawrence-completes-100-triathlons-100-days-video.

10   "David Goggins: How to Become the Toughest Man Alive," Constant Renewal, August 2, 2020, https://constantrenewal.com/david-goggins.

faith. What's up with that?" Sometimes an outside perspective is what you need. This one shook him. He had thought he was making such great progress, and he was, but if his life was like a three-legged stool, one leg was too short, throwing everything off.

"You really should swap your priorities," the preacher's daughter had continued, "Your spirit should actually come first, and be your focus. It should be where you spend the most time, versus like it is now—a token and an afterthought." She was right. Tom embraced the challenge.

In God's perfect timing, another friend gave him a Bible for his birthday, while another gave him *My Utmost for His Highest*, a devotional by Oswald Chambers. He was thankful to have these amazing faith-filled people in his life, and he got the message.

Over time, Tom advanced from a couple thankful prayers each day to consistent conversations with God. He slowly migrated from starting each day with email and social media to a Bible app. Instead of allowing someone else to set his agenda in shallow water, he began each day according to God's agenda at a much greater depth.

He started attending church again, beginning with one with great music, lights, and a dynamic preacher, but eventually switching to a worship venue which also had great music and a preacher he found more intellectual and inspiring. He had found a home.

Reading Scripture and faith-based books became as important to Tom as consuming podcasts and books on growth. He found mentors by joining a Bible study, one a friend was already attending. Tom had only attended youth group as a teen, so a Bible study was quite new. Diving into the Bible, Tom began learning about theology and enjoyed the insights of others in the group, as they shared their personal struggles and stories. This group was key in reinforcing his progress.

Faith: The Final Superpower

Trust in the Lord with all your heart
and lean not on your own understanding.
(Proverbs 3:5)

God is our refuge and strength, an
ever-present help in trouble. (Psalm 46:1)

There had been a time when Tom believed he could do it all
by himself. He was a successful and strong man, a systematic thinker and problem solver: the penultimate "control
enthusiast" in business and in life.

He had made significant improvements and found some
solace by diving into improving his body, and adopting an intense growth mindset, but it wasn't enough. He still felt the
gravity of his losses. After Tom had spent three years ignoring his spiritual needs, a Christian song randomly came on his
playlist one morning as he walked Ruby. It was Jonny Lang's
"Only a Man."

The words of that song broke through, to finally surrender
to He who could take away all the pain. Helping his mind and
body wasn't enough. He didn't need to be in control and able to
solve every problem and answer every question all by himself.
If he gave it all up to a Higher Power and surrendered, God
would take all his burdens. He could be redeemed by His grace.

Faith is defined as a belief in something for which there
may be no tangible proof, but we have complete trust and confidence and a strong allegiance to it anyway. We walk in faith.
The Bible defines *faith* best as "the assurance of things hoped
for, the conviction of things not seen" (Heb. 11:1 RSV).

Tom eventually came to view faith as the ability to lift up
his heart to God in complete submission, trust, and belief.
Surrender. In a recent service, his pastor Ron Smith said, "You

can't carry the weight of a tomb for your entire life. Give it to Him so He can carry that weight."

As he looked at the past four and a half years since Judy's passing, he realized that faith should have been in place already, but it hadn't been—not in dealing with the cancer or her death. He should have worked on faith first to support his body and mind. Instead he'd tackled them first.

Maybe he was staying true to his namesake: Doubting Thomas. Thomas had traveled with Jesus three years, hearing His wisdom and preaching daily, following His actions, witnessing many miracles including life from the dead. But Christ's resurrection had been another story. This time Thomas needed tangible proof. This was delivered and recounted: "Then [Jesus] said to Thomas, 'Put your finger here; see my hands. Reach out your hand and put it into my side. Stop doubting and believe'" (John 20:27).

Tom had viewed faith according to how he conducted himself—*how* he walked the walk in order to earn his space in heaven, not really understanding that his salvation could not be earned. He only had to believe; salvation was a gift.

> FOR IT IS BY GRACE YOU HAVE BEEN SAVED, THROUGH FAITH—AND THIS NOT FROM YOURSELVES, IT IS THE GIFT OF GOD—NOT BY WORKS, SO THAT NO ONE CAN BOAST. (EPHESIANS 2:8–9)

Faith was a relinquishing of his sin, his anguish, and his control. Faith became the final superpower in his recovery, and the most important piece of the puzzle, bringing him true peace and joy for the first time in his life.

You First

Work on you first.
Be the best version of what you want to be—
Heart, mind, body, and spirit.

You will attract the exact person you want, naturally—
Unplug, find space, discover faith, calm, breathe.

The Top 5 Darndest Things People Say to Widowers

- "How are you doing today?"
- "You'll feel better over time."
- "I lost my dog/cat recently, so I know how you feel."
- "She's in a better place."
- "Have you met anyone new yet?"

FRED + TERESA

Widower to Widower: Overcoming the Top Three Grief Challenges

How you feel is perfectly normal. You are *not* going crazy. —Fred Colby

Fred Colby is the author of the book *Widower to Widower*. He lost Teresa, his wife of forty-five years and mother to their two daughters, in 2015 to cancer.

Love at First Sight

Fred had been attending a community college on his third attempt to complete his education. He had a friend and they took turns hosting parties at each other's houses when their parents were away. Fred had met a girl in one of his classes and invited her to a big party they had planned. She and a group of her friends were on their way to Los Angeles for a bigger party, but said they'd stop by for a bit.

When they stopped by, Fred met Teresa. She was only there for a half hour, but he knew she was the one instantly. They were married a year and a half later.

What if Teresa had chosen to just go to L.A. and skipped his party? What if he hadn't returned to school that third time? No one can explain how these seemingly small decisions have such large impacts on people's lives, but they do.

After school they lived in San Diego, both working. Within three years, they had two daughters. Fred started working for nonprofits, primarily in fundraising, while Teresa left her job to volunteer in the schools. Both of their families were nearby and helped raise the kids. A great situation, the girls grew up and graduated from Mira Mesa High School.

Afterward, they moved to Oregon for three years, and then both daughters moved to Fort Collins, Colorado, and started having grandbabies. Fred and Teresa followed them to help.

One Good Week

In 2014, about a year before she passed, Teresa found out she had uterine cancer. Quickly, she went through the whole gamut: surgery, chemo, radiation. During the chemo, Fred knew something wasn't right. When he was at the hospital as she was getting chemo, others that were getting treated talked about having a good week or a bad week. A good week was one in which you recovered from the treatment, while in a bad week, it just dragged out for the whole time. Theresa only had one good week overall. Something was wrong.

Eventually she needed a blood transfusion. She walked in, but came out in a wheelchair. That night, she had a heart attack. At the hospital, they found that the cancer had returned full blast; there was nothing else they could do for her. Only then did the reality that there was no getting out of this hit.

Fred stroked her arm, put on some music, and told her it was okay to leave. Watching her pass away was the most painful single moment in his life. She passed away on June 30, 2015, and Fred was fortunate to be with her.

Fred was totally numb the first week. As though he were sleepwalking. Fred and his daughters arranged Teresa's celebration of life a week later. He was thankful for the way his entire family, including his sisters, gathered and helped at the time.

The Cabin

Afterward, he escaped to a cabin up in the mountains all by himself, taking as much reading material as he could find on grieving. He had no idea what to expect. However, he didn't find much specifically for widowers. He took what he could.

After arriving, Fred went outside and screamed. He screamed as loud and as long as he could. He was in pain like he had never been before. His stress, too, was at its highest level ever. He had to express it. Screaming helps relieve pain and stress, and it is most beneficial if done earlier rather than later. It is a good idea to let it out.

For the first six months, sleeping was Fred's biggest challenge. Many nights, he was lucky to get two hours. He was completely wrecked after he lost Teresa, and felt like he was falling apart all the time.

He discovered the author Eckhart Tolle at the time. He read what he wrote and listened to his podcast. Tolle focuses on living in the present, the here and now—not dwelling on the past or freaking out about the future. Tolle says that doing that helps a person manage their emotions better and facilitates their healing journey. Living in the past or the future retards healing.

Although he didn't know it, Fred's choice to seclude himself and scream and focus on processing his experience was not at all typical of men. Most men are afraid to be by themselves at this time, instead craving connection with others. Men also tend to get involved in new relationships sooner than women after losing their mate, and this might be part of the reason for that. Unfortunately, it is often too early for them to get involved with someone else romantically. They don't know who they are anymore.

Men often don a stoic mask, throwing themselves into their jobs or some other activity in an effort to lose themselves in busyness. They don't go to the top of a mountain alone. They don't scream. They don't stop. They don't weep—even though their world was just turned upside down. Fred knew he needed to just stop life for a while.

There were times during this early phase (and this is true of most widowers) when Fred honestly felt like he was losing his mind. This was what crazy looked like. He had no control over his thoughts. They went all over the frigging map. Half of his soul had been ripped away from him, and he didn't know who this new person was.

Often, he'd be walking down the steps and suddenly feel like he'd been punched in the stomach. He would collapse to the floor. Sobbing. Sobbing without tears. It was miserable.

Experiencing constant anguish and without much sleep, Fred was in a delusionary state after a while, unable to distinguish between the real and the unreal. That's a scary place. He yearned for his wife. He wanted her with him right now. He wanted to physically touch her; he was desperate for her, but he could not go on like that. He had to accept this new life.

Finding Support

As a man, he'd been raised to think, *Okay, I'll get another woman, I'll have somebody to hug, make love to, just touch.* If his wife had survived him, she would have had twenty close friends encircling and embracing her, loving her, touching her, and helping her feel less alone. Guys are different. Men are lucky if they've got one or two friends, and they don't particularly want to hug. Men just are not trained to do that.

That makes this harder and it feels weird. Men must learn how to ask people for support—to ask them to love them. Fred did that through social media posts on the same site his daughter had set up so her friends could say goodbye. Now he was using it to say hello. It really helped him stay in touch with everybody. They felt engaged with his story. He could share his progress as well as his issues. This platform for open sharing allowed him to remain connected with many he would have lost touch with otherwise. Some of them still call him today, so it was worth the effort.

Fred knew he couldn't go on in sadness. He had to figure out how to live again. He started by working out regularly every morning and every afternoon. Sometimes he'd also get out for a walk. He listened to meditation tapes or Eckhart Tolle before bed, and tried to focus on the present and stay in the now.

In dealing with his insomnia, he used melatonin for a time, but Fred did not like drugs so gradually cut back the dosage until he could sleep normally again. Many people dealing with loss find that they must physically exhaust themselves so they can sleep. Mentally, they must make sure they are listening to the right content, relaxing music, or something serene to lull them to sleep. Otherwise, sleep will remain elusive.

Over time, many feel as though they are stuck in their grief. Two, three years in, they feel frustrated that they still feel depressed or are easily triggered. They feel like they should have made more or better progress.

There are some common elements in those that feel stalled. One of the biggest is a separation from family and friends. It might be because they live far away or they're estranged, but if there's nobody to fall back on, everything is more difficult. Some literally drive away their friends and family. They can't handle the question 200 times a week: *How are you doing?* It's hard to accept; instead of maintaining their relationships, they withdraw.

Some have another issue: they're angry. They are truly pissed off. Perhaps, it began before they lost their wife. Perhaps not. The issue is that they're pissed off at everything. There might be a legitimate reason. They may have had bad care or a bad medication. There might be clear evidence of malpractice. Their question is different: *Should I keep pursuing this?* They have to choose to let it go if they want to move on and find happiness and real life again. Otherwise, they drag themselves through a mire of anger, frustration, and despair as they are forced to rehearse and rehash it for another two or three years. Going to court is a long process, so it needed to make a difference to be worth the effort.

Another issue that stalls people in their healing is alcohol and drug use. Fred had always had a few drinks a day, so now, he had to be really careful about taking that third one. After that third glass, he'd fall into the pity pit, whining about his loss. That accomplished nothing, and each time he did it developed the habit, trapping him further. Once he limited himself to two drinks, he was fine.

There was also a difference between drinking alone or with friends in a social experience. With others, talking and listening was a therapeutic experience. Staying home alone with a bottle of vodka was a whole other beast. Fred needed other help.

Therapy

Even though Fred had many friends, he was also private, so it was a real challenge for him to reach out and find a grief therapist. However, he recognized that he needed to talk to someone. He had never felt so crazy and unsettled in his life, and these weren't things he could talk about with family or friends. It was deep stuff that troubled him. Some of it was rooted in his past. Preexisting hurts are a big player currently. *Whatever wounds a person carries that they haven't dealt with will be aggravated by their loss.*

Seeing a grief therapist as soon as possible is the best course of action. Fred began seeing one within two months and was very grateful for the help he received. Fred found that the more open he was about his challenges, the better his healing progressed. He had to be willing to be open and transparent or they couldn't help him. This is true for everyone. It's also important to find a counselor with whom you feel comfortable. This is one time when shopping around is vital.

A good therapist doesn't tell you what to do. They advise you on how to make decisions and set and reach goals without being intrusive and bossy. It's actually important to find a therapist trained in grief rather than a general counselor or primary doctor.

There are exceptions, but a regular counselor is not usually well-trained about grief. Grief therapists are. They truly understand the unique challenges acquainted with grief and know how to help the grieving with all the weird issues they experience. This matters more than people might think. A general doctor or a psychiatrist might be quicker to prescribe antidepressants and might not possess the experience to explore more natural (and better) methods in dealing with the trauma sustained from dealing with death, especially if it happened over a long period of time. A grief therapist will know about tapping, *eye movement desensitization and reprocessing* (EMDR), art therapy, brain spotting, and a great deal more. They can suggest exactly which methods will help a person most, based on that individual's experience.

For instance, the seven stages of grief are often slapped on a widower. Because they are framed as "steps," the stages are often misunderstood, as though dealing with death is a linear process. It isn't. Death is linear. For the person that is dying, it is linear. It has an onset, a middle, and an end. It's not that way for everyone else involved. Grief does not progress from denial to anger to acceptance and so on, so a grieving person thinks, *Oh, I'm in the angry stage, next I will be* _____, but next, they're back to a different stage instead. They already feel like they are going mad, and likely grappling with a general sense of failure as well. Now they are also not grieving correctly. It's simply overwhelming.

A grief counselor would have told them that this was *not* going to be a linear process. They would have told them that it was unique—different for everyone. The counselor would also help them explore any underlying issues they had along with their grief, so they could begin to heal, now that they had been ripped in half.

It's a journey.

No Major Decisions

A host of decisions slam into you when you first lose someone close to you. It's best not to make any major decisions you might regret. This could be as simple as cleaning out your wife's closet and sorting photos or major, like selling your house or changing jobs. If a big decision is breathing down your neck, do your best to put it off. Just ask for a year. Most can deal with that. It's OK to step back and give yourself time.

As Fred spoke with his therapist, he had to deal with a sense of failure, and forgive himself. Fred's grief was compounded by regrets: *Did I find the best doctors? Did I get her to treatment fast enough? Why didn't we catch it earlier?* It was a long list.

If he went back even further, it sounded like this: *I should have been a better husband. I should have treated her better. I shouldn't have had that argument with her.* All those things.

Learning to forgive himself became a huge part of his healing process. When he learned to forgive himself *and* express gratitude for the relationship he had, he was tremendously relieved of those regrets. Dealing with those two things accelerated his healing, and eventually became a normal part of his thinking. This also helped Fred sort out his goals.

The most important thing he learned was that what he was going through was perfectly normal. He was *not* going crazy. He was going to be okay. He also learned that asking for help— and accepting it—wasn't just okay, it was the smartest thing he would have chosen to do. Today he tells others: "You may think you don't need help, but I'm here to tell you, you do. Go for it!"

"Getting Back Out There"

Fred missed his wife, and a lack of a partner is especially hard for a widower. They are accustomed to having a mate, and as mentioned before, tend to get involved romantically with a new partner faster than widows do. They want somebody they can share things with, and that they can touch and hold, someone supportive, as they have always had.

Guys don't generally have many close friends, so they're driven to find that companionship again. And then there's sex, which feels weird—almost like being a teenager again. It's scary physically as well as mentally. It's been a long time since they've been "out there."

Just like a teenager, once you start dating, you're back in that mode you experienced just after the loss. You won't be able to get sleep, and you're racked with anxiety over the new girlfriend or friend. Fred thought: *Am I saying (and doing) the right things? What would Teresa think? Would she be angry?* You don't know what's normal, and a lot of this is about returning to a new normalcy. But above all, Fred tells everyone this: "No matter what, *do not get married in the first year!*"

Remember—no major decisions. Fred has met *lots* of guys that are already in relationships or living with someone within three to four months after their wife has passed. These guys are saying, "This is it. This is my chapter two!" The truth is that they're not in a strong enough mental state to make that decision. At least fifty percent of those relationships fail.

It's true that there's a strong drive, even a need, for companionship. Fred decided to protect himself from being taken advantage of by some cute young gal with cleavage on the Internet, and learn to date again. Everything was different than it was before. Even the women were more independent and forward than before.

Fred began dating as though he were setting up an experiment: he wanted to learn how to date again, so he'd take one girl out and decide whether he wanted to see her a second time. He'd just have coffee or a glass of wine, and enjoy himself. He also put himself into social situations, joining a breakfast club for those 55 and over. There were eight women for every guy. The club helped him get used to talking to women again, to have a real conversation. He dated a few, and eventually dated the woman he is still with now—five years later.

There are many options for meeting people: coffee groups, exercise groups like yoga, or groups devoted to a particular hobby. The point is that you get out there and put yourself in social situations and meet people again, not romantically, but just for conversation.

There's no pressure with coffee and a casual meetup.

Using the Internet, a guy could have ten dates in ten days with seven different women. If you go that route, you can usually eliminate those that don't fit your criteria pretty easily. You have to answer the question: What am I really looking for? Do I want a new friend? Or something more?

Fred didn't want the girl that described herself as buff, ran up and down mountains, and worked out four hours a day. No, thank you. He eliminated the ones that didn't match his likes, and focused on the ones that seemed more feasible. However, this required that he knew what he wanted. A recently widowed person probably doesn't know that yet. One more reason to not get heavily involved with any one person too quickly. That's the risk involved.

So one of the things a widower must do is rediscover what he likes and doesn't like, what he values, what he wants to do next. *Knowing all that takes time.* Once again, at least a year. Having that base helps in dating because one can make sure there's some alignment. It's far too easy to be taken in by charm and beauty. That doesn't mean you have to only have platonic relationships during the first year, but it does mean that you're not over-committing. There's no reason to be in a hurry.

And the truth is that a new relationship can happen just as it did when you were much younger. That's how it happened for Fred. He'd seen his present girl at a few events, and one night they sat and talked a long time. When he left, he knew she was the one he was looking for, but he would not have known that for sure if he had not done his homework: been to a counselor regularly, focused on his healing, and allowed himself real time to process his life.

Lightning does still strike.

Change a Thing?

If you could see your whole life
From start to finish,
Would you change a thing?

Roll the dice,
Slow the rush.

Extend a hello,
Forget that goodbye.

Forgive all the wrongs
To do more rights.

Want less and give more.

Regret the choices or embrace the mistakes.

Forget the destination and just enjoy the climb.
Wrapped in love for yourself and the world around you:
No regrets.

Are You Enough?

Overcoming Self-Doubt and Gaining Confidence through GRIEF

SITTING THERE AND FOCUSING ALL YOUR BLAME AND TIME ON THE FACT THAT YOUR PERFECT PLAN...OR YOUR WORLD GOT THROWN UPSIDE DOWN, ACCOMPLISHES NOTHING—NOTHING.
—JASON REDMAN, NAVY SEAL AND AUTHOR[11]

THE LORD IS MY ROCK, MY FORTRESS AND MY DE-LIVERER; MY GOD IS MY ROCK, IN WHOM I TAKE REFUGE, MY SHIELD AND THE HORN OF MY SALVA-TION, MY STRONGHOLD. (PSALM 18:2)

A VICTIM MENTALITY LIMITS YOUR SUCCESS IN THIS LIFE. YOU KNOW, YOU WILL STAY WHEREVER YOU ARE, AND YOU WILL ACHIEVE THE LIMIT OF WHAT YOU BELIEVE.
—JASON REDMAN, NAVY SEAL AND AUTHOR[12]

SEEK HIS WILL IN ALL YOU DO, AND HE WILL SHOW YOU WHICH PATH TO TAKE. (PROVERBS 3:6 NLT)

---

11 "Jason Redman," Impact Theory, April 18, 2022, https://impacttheory.com/episode/jason-redman/.

12 Ibid.

"Feeling sorry for yourself is a waste of time and effort." Jason Redman shared on a poignant podcast about his long recovery from the wounds he sustained from machine gun fire in Iraq that almost took his life and ended his career as a Navy SEAL. Jason had to undergo thirty-seven surgeries, receive 1,200 stitches, 200 staples, and fifteen skin grafts.[13] It wasn't a pretty picture.

Although Jason's loss is different from what a widower experiences, it is still grieving. Jason is grieving from his physical scars, permanent damage, and the loss of his career and purpose. As Tom listened to him recount how he transcended tragedy, it gave him fresh perspective.

Tom was feeling sorry for himself in a big way. Some days were easy. This one was not. On his sunrise walk, the podcast reminded Tom that he needed to confront his self-pity head-on. Tom was surrounded by doubt and sadness. He was alone. He was parenting girls in a faraway college. He had just left his career behind him. He felt alone on a high wire, even though he knew he had a safety net with God.

He'd been to enough therapy sessions to know that these doubts were indications of issues from his younger years. He'd endured extreme bullying from peers and had never received the affirmations he longed for from his dad. Awareness didn't erase the scars and stop the triggering.

He continually asked himself if he were *enough*—as a parent, a partner, and a growth evangelist, his present vocation. Big questions.

For some, self-doubt results in a falling inward, suffering extreme sadness and depression alone. For others, it causes a gap in the psyche, followed by the pursuit of something, anything, to fill it. The bigger the self-doubt, the bigger the gaps,

---

13 "Jason Redman," Wikipedia (Wikimedia Foundation, December 7, 2022), https://en.wikipedia.org/wiki/Jason_Redman.

and the more extreme the patching. Alcoholic, workaholic, shopaholic: all of these were filling these gaps, but none of them would ever be enough.

After Judy's passing, Tom immediately threw himself back into work and then into a new too-soon relationship. However, now with his career in transition, work was no longer a refuge but a source of anxiety, and he was in between relationships. The yawning gaps were front and center.

Evolving from Self-Doubt

So how do you address the questions you might be having about your ability to cope and eventually improve? The GRIEF model provides guidance.

Grace: First, stop being so hard on yourself! Nobody is perfect, and there isn't a manual for how to handle everything being presented to you. Life is full of the unexpected. You are doing the best you can. Beyond grace for yourself, you can ultimately rely on the grace of God, His spontaneous, unmerited gift of divine favor in saving you, and His influence for regeneration and sanctification.

Reflection: A quick inventory is helpful. Reflect on how you got to these current feelings of doubt. Ask yourself these key questions:

- What are the doubts specifically?
- Where do you think they come from? (Sometimes they are rooted in your youth.)
- Are you indulging in "pursuits" like alcohol, drugs, overwork, or overspending to cover your doubts?

Intention and Elevation: You can following Jason Redman's advice, and move from self-doubt to self-improvement by planning a course and taking action to elevate yourself from self-doubt to confidence. These steps should include:

- Asking for forgiveness and grace specific to your perceived shortcomings. There is something powerful about actually speaking about them aloud to God.
- Forgiving those who may have hurt you in the past (they may be the original source of your doubt). It helps to journal this step and verbalize the forgiveness to God out loud.
- Getting yourself moving forward through exercise, which will improve your body, boost your confidence, and clear your mind.
- Beginning to address and overcome any indulgences and addictions you identified when you answered the questions above. Commit to redefining your story in the exact opposite direction, taking steps to change that. Don't just talk about your story; own it.

Faith: Finally, and most importantly, don't forget the importance of faith. Those first steps get you moving in the right direction, but it is too easy to fall into negative thoughts again without transitioning beyond the earthly traps into faith.

Transcending self-doubt permanently is extremely difficult unless you know you are loved intimately and completely just as you are by God. When we know we have His love and are in His good hands, we can rest, knowing our Father has a great future planned for us. This knowledge helps with dealing with sadness, depression, guilt, indulgence, and addiction.

Once we embrace His love and faith, and surrender to Him, we can really live the life He wants for us. He fills the God-shaped hole in our hearts, and comes alongside us in a big way, allowing us to grow again and solve our problems. Taking action yourself is a great step, but transcending reliance on yourself alone to trusting God can turn our good actions into permanent healing, and eventually, a permanent solution to our self-doubt challenges.

Your actions and faith combine, so that you will know, not just now, but forever, that "you are definitely enough."

Am I Enough?

To overcome my sadness
To put my shattered heart together again
To raise our girls alone
To experience another special occasion without tears

To face who I am without you
To come home to echoes and silence
To survive another night in an empty bed
To find another love again

To renew my faith through the suffering
To help so many, like you did
To accept that this is exactly how He wanted it to be

Am I really enough?
Through surrender and faith
I am enough in His eyes and find peace in His hands.

Who Am I Now? Grief and Your Identity Crisis with Helen Keeling-Neal

TAKE YOUR TIME, AND DON'T OVERTHINK IT. YOU WILL EVOLVE INTO A NEW PERSON. WE ALL DO AS WE GO THROUGHOUT LIFE. —HELEN KEELING-NEAL[14]

Helen Keeling-Neal is a nationally certified and licensed mental health counselor and marriage and family therapist. She also has personal experience with grief as her hus-

---

14 See https://growththroughgrief.org/episode-27-who-am-i-now-grief-and-your-identity-crisis/ for a full interview with Helen Keeling-Neal.

band, David, passed away when their children were only four and six years old. Tom talked with her often and this section is about how identity changes and the role it plays in the grieving process on the episode just cited.

Many who grieve the loss of a partner face a fracture of identity. It's not like changing a job in which you assume the identity of that job—a new job description, and carry out a new role. Loss has abruptly shifted your identity—socially, spiritually, physically, financially, emotionally, all of it, and there's no ability to transition into that—no matter how long a loved one has been unwell.

No matter what you've been through, there is no ability to assimilate a new identity until it's over. You go from being a husband, a spouse, to suddenly being a sole parent and single. Additionally, we see being single as bad. Coupleship is the ascribed goal of our culture. It's easy to see that. Couples can file joint tax returns and get breaks. Being married is also the approved state of being in the church. Older unmarried folk are looked at as incomplete. Being single is the loss of an accomplishment, both social and cultural, in the United States.

And then there's that piece in parenting: you've gone from being a dad in a couple to being a single dad, the sole parent. This is completely new and different.

All things considered, one of the biggest effects of loss and grief is not the fracture of the identity, but having to assume a different identity, especially against your will. This has been forced on you. Now you are assuming this identity you never desired. It can be far-reaching in roles too. If the one you lost was the caregiver and nurturer of the children, you must now take their place. That isn't normal for you. It's not an identity you've had before.

Suddenly you are the cook. Now you must be a food nurturer and creator of meals that are healthy and appropriate, but that's not an identity that you've ever had, so you're not only losing one identity that you know in the relationship you had as a couple, you're now forced to develop these new identities as well.

Grace for Life

This also catapults you into social situations in which you might feel even lonelier and more out of place. This is especially true of school situations and events. This is the time you must learn to choose to not set yourself up for a bad night. You don't have to go to every event. Choose which ones are most important to you and your family. Give yourself the grace to *not* do it all. You don't have to show up for everything the way your partner might have. It's okay to let some things slide.

You can't make up for the loss of a parent. No matter how hard you push through being uncomfortable, you cannot replace that parent; it is just not possible. It's not who you are. They were them. You are you. Your skill set is your skill set, and theirs was theirs.

All you can do is trust that you are doing your absolute best. Raising children alone is going to be very different than raising them as a couple. It can't be the same. And that's it.

Internal Grace

Getting into your head about all the ways in which you are inadequate won't help. That sets up unrealistic expectations that could never be met. We internalize all that and play that narrative inside our head, continually feeling guilty and not good enough. And again, if you didn't have a good relationship with your own parents, all this will be much, much worse.

In situations where you are the only single person among couples, it's important to talk about your spouse, and say things like, "You know what? _____ would have really loved this dish." It's important to say, "It's really difficult for me to be here without her, and I'm just gonna say that out loud because I love you guys, and I want to keep coming. I'm glad you keep inviting me, and I want to be able to talk about her."

On the flip side, many widowers feel as though they *must* stay alone. That's the depression part of grief. The stages of grief are denial, bargaining, anger, depression, and acceptance, and they're *never linear*. The loneliness fits in the depression piece.

However, it's also part of survivor's guilt. It is difficult to feel deserving of life when your spouse is not. Some people wish they would pass instead. They want to take that death on themselves, because they feel so guilty about being here now on their own, as if it were a big mistake that they made somehow. They feel unable to move on in life (not move away from the person they lost, but move on to continue living).

The presence of guilt may be one of the symptoms of a major depressive disorder, and could mean that that person is having a really difficult time. Once again, it's an indication that there are other layers of guilt and depression, compounding the grief which need to be explored, so they can heal.

Loneliness and self-isolation often occurs out of guilt. Life is just too hard. It is too difficult to interact. Maybe the surviving partner was the introvert, and the deceased partner was the extrovert, the social calendar person. That surviving partner may not even know how to reach out on their own.

Loss of Identity

In counseling, Helen talks about rocks and balloons: every rock needs a balloon, and every balloon needs a rock. So, if you're a rock and you've lost the balloon that got you up off the couch and out into social situations, you don't have the ability to do that for yourself, especially if you're weighed down in grief. This is where the support system is key.

In most cases, the deliveries of lasagna and stuffed shells go away after a few months. This is the time when church friends, social groups, and relatives really need to lean back in to see how someone's doing. In fact, it's vital because the truth is that after the first year, it can get worse. The end of year two can also be worse because the numbness goes away, and the feelings burst out. Introverted people don't typically share how they feel and are not strongly connected with others, so they especially need help. They're not going to naturally want a support system, but *everyone* needs one.

The first piece to this identity change is the immediate freefall into survival mode. You think:

Who am I now? How am I going to do this? This is on me. How am I ever going to do it? I can't do this alone. I was half of a strong couple leading _____, and suddenly I have to cook meals and go to school events and work! *How can I possibly do it all?*

Truthfully, the only way to handle it is to take on a piece at a time and ask for help. This is one reason that a support system is so vital. You have to learn to delegate and use your resources. If you have the funds, and you want to hire a meal service, you do that, and then you don't have to become a cook. If you need someone to take care of the PTA, you can recruit a friend's parent for that. Recognize that you cannot do everything; do what you can and ask for help with the rest.

Most of all, you need to be able to settle in and give yourself space to become who you need to be versus who you're expected to be (or think you should be). Everyone must define one's own identity. Men inherently take on their internalized identities: the hunter gatherer, slayer of beasts, and provider of meat. He who makes the money. He protects. He is in charge of fixing.

That's the role our culture assigns to men, and we tend to take on what's assigned. If you're the wage earner or the financial guy, you have to lower that element in importance. This can be another element of grief—a grief within a grief—having to let go of that.

Men actually grieve the loss of identity along with the loss of their spouse. Many have to make a choice between making a really good income or being present with their kids, and having a moderate income for a period of time until they are older. Many aren't willing to just hand their children off to babysitters all the time. They have to make that trade. Tom made the decision to not live financially well for a period of time. It was all part of choosing his identity at the time.

Many widows and widowers overachieve, trying to be both parents and a shining example for the community, being the sole parent, assuming every role, and taking it all on. Before you know it, the weight of all these different worlds and their expectations overwhelm you. It did for Tom. He was exhausted from all the different masks he was wearing, and all the balls he had in the air every day. The incongruity of it all really weighed on him. How did he get out of it?

Well, he had to say no. He had to thoughtfully say, *Look, I'm not going to take all this on. I'm not going to be guilted into it by my internal voice or external voices.* It is a great help to recognize that and begin to ask for help. However, only some men are skilled in delegating. Tom was not. Many women don't ask for help either. We're all wired to think we should be able to do it all ourselves. And the truth is: we can't.

The good news is that people are very loving and want to help. They really do. And when there's been a loss of this magnitude, people are just literally *waiting to be asked* to help. They offer help: "If there's anything I can do, please let me know." They mean it. So we must do the following: "Could you pick my kids up from so and so?" "Would you pick up a cake so we can take it to the Fall Festival?" "Would you come over and be with the kids while I go do _____?" People want to help, so take them up on it. There's that piece of giving and receiving;

it's one and the same. To deny either is to deny someone pleasure or joy. Letting people help you, helps them.

Finding 2.0

It takes time to discover who you are on your own. It would be fantastic if there were a special formula, a secret sauce, even a linear process to transcend to Ourselves 2.0., but there is not. Dealing with the internal issues is the important first step.

For Tom, he focused first on his health and wellness, getting rid of alcohol and doing some things differently. That was a great first step to cooking up the new Tom. Imagine this journey as if we're making a stew: there are pieces of you still there—who you were when your spouse was alive, then when they were sick, and then, now. It's all a smorgasbord. We don't totally give up everything regarding our original and transitional identities. We bring in the pieces that best serve us, and help us feel good about who we are today. For Tom, one of those things is being a high achiever, so he's helping people. He likes to help people, so he put together a grief group, which helps many men. This kind of group is excellent for anyone who has lost a spouse. He also picked up writing in his workplace again. All this doesn't necessarily happen quickly. We're all evolving identities over time.

Helen works with many retired people. They are working on transitional identities, not fractured ones. In retirement, the old roles go away. It's a whole other kind of loss. They wonder: *Who am I now? What should I do?* So there is no magic solution for any of this. It's just about putting one foot in front of the other and trying to be mindful and aware of what's going on— when to say no, and when to say yes.

There's three strands of a person that need to be worked on: body, mind, and spirit. And they're intertwined. If you get them working together, there's nothing that can break them when they're wound together strong. For Tom, the physical piece was the launch that gave him the foundation to go into the others; and for other people, it may be the emotional piece first, or it may be the spiritual connection instead.

We need to find a balance by taking those identity pieces and creating a cohesion that has a foundation of body, mind, and spirit to support the person. This helps you to move forward in life and deal with everything that overwhelms you. It helps you cope, so that everything gets a little less overwhelming.

Ego, Id, and Superego

Sometimes when we think of identity, we also think of ego. The term *ego* comes from Sigmund Freud's work. Freud believed that everybody was born with the *id*, the natural driver, the desires, the impulses, the "Gimme, gimme, gimme, I want it now" with which we're born. Around age three, the *ego* starts to develop the "voice of reason." Then around five, the *superego* develops; this is all the internalized information from parents, role models, culture, and society—and it's perfectionistic in nature: "Oh, no, you can't do that. That's terrible."

So on the one hand, the *id* says, "Oh, give me that whole entire piece of cake!" And on the other hand, the *superego* yells, "No! That's terrible! You can't have the whole piece of cake!" And there in the middle, the *ego* is supposed to mediate between the two. Those are the ego states, according to Freud.

Now pop culture has changed it a bit. If someone has a big ego, an overinflated ego, it means they're overconfident. They think too much of themselves. They are arrogant. If someone has a lack of ego, they might feel ashamed, embarrassed, and are likely to have low self-esteem.

When the ego is dominant that is considered a healthy ego state. In pop culture, when we think of that overinflated ego, it's because someone is likely indulging the *id* a little more.

So we see these maladaptive behaviors: going out and getting drunk, hooking up, that type of behavior.

Someone who seems have a big ego could also be covering how poorly they feel underneath, so they act with bravado. So we equate inflated ego states with *id*-ish behaviors, and low ego states with *superego* shaming and internalized behavior.

Understanding these three identity states is important, but the balance between them comes in time as you try to get a handle on this new identity. You're going to feel out of balance: angry for no apparent reason, overindulgent, afraid, ashamed.

People need to take their time and not overthink it. You will evolve into a new person. We all do as we go through life. So be kind to yourself. Give yourself grace and use the resources around you. Make a list of those people that ask what they can do to help, and take them up on it.

Exercise some self-care. After all, if you don't put your oxygen mask on first, you're not going to be useful to anyone around you. You do not need to take on all these other roles, and forget about yourself. There is space in there to put on your mask first.

I Am

This is how I was born,
    How I died.
This is where I learned,
    Where I forgot.
This is when I laughed,
    When I cried.
This is what I aspired to,
    What I became.
This is why I love,
    Why I hate.
This is who I am,
    I am.

TERRELL + ROBYN

The First 365: Surviving Year One to Grow Better Beyond

THERE'S NO RIGHT AND THERE'S NO WRONG WAY
TO SURVIVE THIS GRIEF JOURNEY.
—TERRELL WHITENER

errell Whitener is the author of *The First 365: Learning to Live After Loss* which documents the aftermath of losing his wife of over sixteen years, Robyn.

Terrell grew up in a household with his great-grandmother who lived to be 102. Robyn was her social worker.

One day about two weeks before her hundredth birthday, his great-grandmother dropped a spoon in the kitchen, bent to pick it up, and fell. She broke her hip, and ended up in the hospital. Now, we are talking about a lady who used to read the newspaper from the first to last page, and never missed a St. Louis Cardinals game on the radio. She lived on the second floor of Terrell's house completely on her own, and suddenly, this happened.

Terrell's father took care of his great-grandmother and they made all their decisions together. When she was in the hospital, it was determined that she would have to go to a rehab facility before she came home. His father communicated that to the family.

The whole family was on board to help. But for some reason, his father decided that when they had the planning meeting with the hospital that Terrell needed to be present. Terrell had been divorced for about a year at that time, and didn't understand why he needed to be there, but he showed up anyway. He thought that it was because he was so close to his great-grandmother, and maybe they needed him to convince her to go to the rehab. They did have a great relationship. Terrell told his dad that he could talk to her, but didn't need to go to the hospital to do it. Nevertheless, his dad insisted he come. He insisted.

Primary Contact

So he went. The moment Terrell walked in to the office, he knew what his dad was up to right away. On the other side of the room was this lady with a wonderful smile, who said, "I'm glad to meet you. I've heard so much about you!"

Now Terrell's father was not that kind of guy. He was not a matchmaker, but he was the most discerning person Terrell ever knew. His dad turned and said, "This is my son, Terrell.

From this point forward, he will be the primary contact for his great-grandmother." And that was that. The rest was history, as they say. There was no getting around the fact that Terrell was going to be seeing Robyn regularly from that time on.

The irony of it was that his father didn't live long enough to see them get married, but he knew he'd put them together. It's one of the many discussions Terrell plans to have with his dad in heaven, but he has no regrets.

He always describes Robyn as "a comet dashing across the sky of his life." She arrived at a pivotal point, and they were a team. Like all marriages, they had rough patches. Robyn wasn't exactly a picnic all the time, and she would probably tell you that neither was Terrell, but they were bonded together for over sixteen years. Terrell never met anyone that believed in him more than Robyn, and it was a time when he really needed somebody to believe in him.

Robyn had a highly responsible job. She was the Director of Social Services at a Missouri Veterans Home. She was very patriotic and believed in taking care of those guys. She believed they deserved the best care and should be treated with dignity,

She was a fighter, an advocate, and an amazing social worker. Often, when a person gives and gives and gives, something gets lost in translation. As a result, she didn't always take the best care of herself, and she wasn't always compliant about taking her blood pressure meds. Unfortunately, this led to three strokes over four days while visiting relatives.

On a scale of one to ten, Robyn's personality was an eleven and a half, but after the stroke, it was different. They were at a social gathering not too long after she returned to work and felt well enough to get out again. One of her friends pulled me to the side and asked, "So how is she really?" Terrell replied, "Remember how Robyn used to be that eleven and a half on a scale of ten? Well, it's like they pulled some curtains down, and now she's a five and a half." She was just a little bit quieter, and more introverted.

But Terrell learned how to crack the code. Finding that her mind worked faster than her speech, Robyn was always two words behind where her mind was, so Terrell did a lot of translating in the last nine years of her life.

In the last two years, she wasn't able to work anymore. Terrell used to tell her she had two jobs: to get well and show up. She always did show up. She fought the good fight. Robyn did not give up. Her body gave out. Terrell honors and loves her even more for the fight she fought.

The Next Two Years

Terrell knew Robyn for twenty-two years overall, and never realized how fortunate he had been and all that she had done for him until she was gone. Devastated, it wasn't long before he went to a grief counselor. This really helped. Terrell knew he couldn't manage alone, so he reached out early and worked with a grief counselor for more than two years. Over time, she's the one that encouraged him to write, saying, "I've never worked with anybody like you before! You need to write about this."

Terrell's grief counselor rescued him. Friends tried to understand and his family just wanted him to feel better. But for that to happen, he needed that honest broker, that person with whom you can say whatever you want and be who you are. That person who truly understood his battle with eyes of compassion, but also possessed firm guidance. That person that helped you paint inside the lines where you wish to be.

Over the years, Terrell has built up trust with his counselor. Through her help, he chose to go on with life. Statistics show that many people do not choose to continue living, but his counselor literally saved his life. Terrell believed that if a man's spirit is broken, it will kill him. He saw that possibility and didn't want that to happen.

The one thing that he determined was this: he was not going to fumble this, and mess up the wonderful life and wonderful person Robyn had helped him to become. He knew that if he didn't talk it out, he'd act it out. He didn't want to be that person creating collateral damage because they couldn't live right, so counseling made sense. Additionally, it helped to talk with someone objective about how much he missed Robyn. He carried that load alone as long as he could. Now, he had someone else to help carry all those packages of sadness and grief. This alone helped him immensely in his walk from pain to livability.

Many widowers do not seek counseling. Some may fear it or even look at it askance. This sometimes happens because they confuse grief counseling with psychiatry, which is completely different. Grief therapists are not medical doctors like psychiatrists, so they cannot dispense prescriptions. Drugs for depression and the like can only be prescribed by a primary physician or a psychiatrist; general therapists and counselors can't give drugs. Grief therapists rarely suggest them. Instead, they listen, explore, question, and encourage, which is exactly what is needed. The basis of your relationship with a counselor is trust. You have to find someone with whom you are comfortable and can speak to easily. That's what Terrell did.

Losing Robyn was different than any other loss Terrell had ever experienced. As her primary caretaker the last two years, they had fought the battle together. On one occasion when Robyn apologized for being sick, Terrell told her: "Sweetheart, from the very beginning of time, God decided that we would need each other for a time. It wasn't the trips, it wasn't the house, it wasn't all the good times—it was *this* time. God put me in your life and you in my life for this time. You just didn't get sick—*we* got sick, so you don't have to do this by yourself.

In fact, I'm not going to allow you to do this by yourself. I am with you in this valley, just like I was with you when we were on the top of the mountain."

A Cornerstone of Faith

Beyond counseling, Terrell's faith held him when he and the team of medical professionals did everything they could to save her, but finally did lose Robyn. Once he'd done all he could do, Terrell had to accept the Master's decision. He often said it this way, "I emptied the tank, and it was God's decision."

Terrell looked at Robyn as a gift God had given him at the exact, perfect time when he needed her. Now, God had reclaimed her. He reclaimed this prize. Was it a loss? Definitely. It was the greatest battle he'd ever fought. The greatest loss he'd ever encountered. There would never be another Robyn. Terrell didn't like God's decision, but he learned to accept it and understand it.

The last thing he would have wanted was to watch Robyn suffer. He loved her enough to let her go. That's what every grieving person has to do.

Throughout the entire time, Terrell's faith was his cornerstone. It's true that many widowers question their faith, feeling angry, even betrayed by God when faced with death, but Terrell was able to wade through this quagmire largely because of his prayer life.

Conversations with God are not one-sided, so Terrell continually poured his heart out to Him and listened to what He said in return. He found that God was more than up to the journey.

In the process, Terrell was transformed in his thinking and grew deeper still in his relationship with Jesus. Many love the Lamb of God, but don't want to live with the Lion of Judah. God wasn't just wonderful and full of gifts and prosperity; God also wanted to take him through the hard times. God didn't waste anything—not even tears. God was with him as he wept, and then took his tears and used the experience to help him grow.

When Terrell sought God about what had happened with his Robyn, God told him, "I'm not going to allow you to grow old with Robyn. That was never My plan for you. When I gave her to you, from day one, it was never your choice about when it would end. Robyn didn't belong to you, but she's always been Mine." Terrell had to accept that this was God's arrangement and He knew what He was doing. In all His majesty, God was not going to ask Terrell's permission. Never has and never will.

That's not to say that Terrell just accepted everything without question. He had plenty of questions. That's part of how he grew. As he sought answers to his discomfort and pain, God showed up and revealed new things about Himself and helped him grow in his faith. He wondered why God would allow him to be hurt if He truly loved him. He wondered why it had to be Robyn and not him. He wondered a lot of things.

But one of the really good things about a relationship with Jesus is that there is nothing you cannot take to Him, and when you do, He gives you peace. Little by little, Terrell's questions were met with God's peace.

Terrell understood that God did what He willed, allowing us to mature through our triumphs and through our trials. Just knowing this and trusting God in the process helped Terrell in profound ways. Faith is powerful.

Terrell knew that nothing he could do was going to bring Robyn back, so he focused on making the best of the life he had left. So when he felt angry or depressed, he took it to God and did his best not to park himself there too long. Those emotions were there for a season at times, but in the end, they were a waste of time.

Terrell focused on getting some joy out of what was left. Instead of blaming God for taking his wife (as many do), Terrell chose the path of honoring her with the days he had left. More than ever, he saw the importance of a strong and balanced walk with God, not one focused only on the good things He does and His love. God had been with him in tragedy and heartache and terrible pain. In many ways, that was most wonderful of all.

We learn a lot from those tougher moments and seasons.

Terrell didn't have a lot of regrets, only a few. When Robyn was alive, she'd said, "Terrell, when I get better, I'm going to show you Paris." There were two things she wanted to do: drive again and take Terrell to Paris. She'd never been that great of a driver to begin with, so Terrell had not planned to let her do that anyway, but they never made it to Paris, and he still has not.

He has thought about it, but in the seven and a half years since Robyn has been gone, he hasn't had the nerve to go to Paris. Because she would not be there, he's not sure he would have the courage to do it yet. It might be too much. Or it might not be enough. He wasn't sure. He always just thought they'd have more time together.

Like many others, Terrell got involved with a really nice young lady way too soon. It might have gone differently if he'd not gone so fast. It was just nine months after Robyn was gone. Way too early for him. He just wasn't ready. After that relationship ended, and for the next five years, he didn't date at all. He felt lonely every day, but he healed and got used to being by himself and comfortable being him. He created his own space and lived his own life at his own pace.

In time, God gave him another unexpected gift. Soon to be engaged, he'll be moving to where she lives. Because she is twenty-two years younger than he is, his family thinks he's nuts but they love him.

Today

Terrell continues to walk trusting God with respect to His choices and His decisions. He found that accepting Robyn's passing as God's will was a much better choice than suffering in silence over something he could not change anyway. He also recognized how important prayer and counseling were in this walk called life: if you hurt, you should be able to be honest. You should be able to say, "I'm hurting and I need help."

He believes that those who want to do penance need to see that they are making that choice. Self-imposed suffering is not going to twist God's arm to come and get them any earlier than the date already set for that. If people choose the self-pity route, God will allow them to go there. He will not prevent that.

One of the greatest gifts God has given people is free will. One of the worst gifts God has given people is free will. It's what we do with it that matters, so if God ever asked Terrell how he had loved others during his life, he did not want to answer that he just stopped living when he lost Robyn and had stopped loving too. That wasn't a good answer.

The truth was that Terrell's life had been blessed by Robyn. He had loved her deeply and they'd stuck together. What kind of a person would choose to not go on now? He also had a renewed perspective on death. It was a little less scary to him now. He thought, *If she could do it, I should be able to do it.*

Overall, Terrell came to some hefty conclusions. His advice to others is this: "Be patient with yourself. Be loving to yourself. We have no control over the amount of time we have left. God did not leave you here to punish you. The quality of your life is built on the foundation of being loving to yourself, having grace for yourself, and loving and serving others. Trust God as you go through this process. Ask for help when you need it. Prayer really helps, so find something you believe in. If you look in the mirror, and the person staring back inspires you to move forward, do that."

The truth is that there's no right or wrong way to survive this grief journey. Don't look at others and think, *I should look like them. I must not be doing well.* Waking up is something, so just make today a little bit better than yesterday.

One last thing: become the curator of the memories you have for your spouse. Don't let anybody else be the curator of the museum of your love.

A Prayer to Last

Give us this day our music
And forgive my past
Deliver me to happiness
And make it last.

The Brain on Grief

TRAUMA IS NOT JUST AN EVENT THAT TOOK PLACE SOMETIME IN THE PAST; IT IS ALSO THE IMPRINT LEFT BY THAT EXPERIENCE ON MIND, BRAIN, AND BODY. THIS IMPRINT HAS ONGOING CONSEQUENCES FOR HOW THE HUMAN ORGANISM MANAGES TO SURVIVE IN THE PRESENT. TRAUMA RESULTS IN A FUNDAMENTAL REORGANIZATION OF THE WAY THE MIND AND BRAIN MANAGE PERCEPTIONS. IT CHANGES NOT ONLY HOW WE THINK AND WHAT WE THINK ABOUT, BUT ALSO OUR VERY CAPACITY TO THINK. —BESSEL A. VAN DER KOLK, *THE BODY KEEPS THE SCORE: BRAIN, MIND, AND BODY IN THE HEALING OF TRAUMA*[15]

INTENSE EMOTIONS ACTIVATE THE LIMBIC SYSTEM, IN PARTICULAR AN AREA WITHIN IT CALLED THE AMYGDALA. WE DEPEND ON THE AMYGDALA TO WARN US OF IMPENDING DANGER AND TO ACTIVATE THE BODY'S STRESS RESPONSE. —BESSEL A. VAN DER KOLK, *THE BODY KEEPS THE SCORE: BRAIN, MIND, AND BODY IN THE HEALING OF TRAUMA*[16]

Understanding how our mind is processing loss and grieving can help us better deal with our grief journey, and transition from loss and sadness to growth and purpose. To do this, it helps to understand the different parts of the brain and how they work to handle stress, drive our reactions, and shape our remembered experiences. Although the brain is extremely complex, we can see it as a triune model with three distinct processing centers.

---

15 Bessel A. van der Kolk, *The Body Keeps the Score: Brain, Mind, and Body in the Healing of Trauma* (New York: Penguin Books, 2014).

16 Ibid.

First, we have the neocortex and frontal lobes. This is the part that makes us uniquely human. This processing center is responsible for our thinking, predicting, and deciding. The neocortex is our logic center, where we process all the different input from the world around us as well as our bodies. From them, we create a story about what we are experiencing in the now, relating the current sensations to our stored experiences, and projecting what this might mean onto our future. We use this part of our brain to think about what we want to do next, and justify our past actions and decisions.

Aristotle referred to this part of our thinking as the *logos*. This is the part responsible for that voice in your head. It's where our conscious thoughts occur.

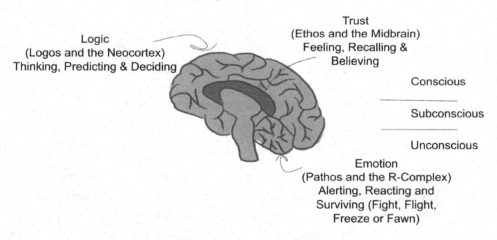

One would think that this part of our brain (the largest part as well as the most evolved and conscious control center) would be in charge of all our actions and decisions so they would be driven by logical thought, but this is often not the case—especially when we are experiencing strong emotions like grief or fear or sadness. *Logos,* this logical part of the brain, can be short-circuited and go offline completely. It can be compromised, which leads to poor decision-making. It can race with random recalls of the past or wild predictions of the future. When struck with grief, other parts of the brain get fired up, getting the blood flow, and essentially steal our logic and conscious thoughts.

Many widowers experience brain fog. While in this state, they make decisions they regret, and do things they normally would not do. When this occurs, the *logos* has been compromised and two other key parts of the brain have taken over.

Aristotle called the midbrain *ethos*. It's the center for trust. Many animals have a midbrain like ours, but ours is more developed to help drive and promote positive social interactions, a key strength to our evolutionary survival and resilience.

The middle brain is where feeling, recalling, and believing resides. This part of the brain contains several glands, releasing key hormones to different stimuli, each of which control our thoughts, reactions, and bodily responses. This includes the pituitary gland, which releases melatonin, the hormone responsible for our circadian rhythm and sleep. It also includes the hypothalamus and posterior pituitary gland, responsible for the release of oxytocin, our feel-good, love hormone, as well as the adrenal gland, responsible to release cortisol for our stress reactions.

The midbrain is your subconscious, providing you with your "spidey" senses about the people and situations around you. It is what helps bond us to our partners, friends, and families, and alerts us about people and situations that may not be good for us.

When a person is grieving, the midbrain may respond with outsized reactions to the environment and reality, releasing too much cortisol (due to trauma and perceived stress), too little melatonin (making sleep more difficult), and not enough oxytocin (inhibiting your ability to find peace). The midbrain still feels a strong attachment to the one you have lost; and out of balance, may no longer be tuned to steer you correctly away from untrustworthy people and dangerous situations anymore.

The final component in our triune model of the brain is the limbic brain, also called the R-complex. This is the most primitive part, and one we share with almost all animals that crawl and walk. This portion of our brains is often referred to as the reptilian (or lizard) brain. The reptilian brain is all about survival, sensing directly what is happening in our environment, and immediately reacting to protect us from danger. It's all about alerting, reacting, and survival, driving our response to fight, flee, freeze, faint, or fawn. When the R-complex is triggered, the body is put into motion. The vagus nerve, running from the R-complex down to the cardiovascular, respiratory, and digestive functions respond, constricting the throat, increasing the breathing and heart rate, and diverting blood flow away from anything other than survival functions.

This part of the brain is unconscious, so we are unaware of the reactions that are happening. All emotion, Aristotle referred to it as *pathos*, the Greek word for suffering. From it we also get the words *pathological* and *empathy*.

When we are in the trauma of grief, this part of the brain can completely take over, overriding all conscious thought. We have all experienced this. Something happens, some random trigger, and before we can even grasp what is happening, a red mist comes over us and we burst into an angry rage, or bolt for the door to flee from an uncomfortable situation, or curl up into a ball on the floor sobbing uncontrollably, or we completely acquiesce with silent resignation, giving up, or we faint, collapsing internally.

In our grief, we should be logical, right? Our neocortex and frontal lobes, the most advanced portion of our brains should be in charge. We should understand that our wife is no longer with us. We shouldn't be accidentally picking up the phone to text or call her about our day. We should be able to control our anxious thoughts from spiraling. We should be discerning about who we let into our lives. We should be sad, but also should be logically moving forwards to find new life and purpose.

However, this is not the case. *Logos* is not dominant, and certainly not in charge in our grief. Instead, because of the intense stress we have just experienced, we are plunged into survival mode. This covers most of our time in the beginning, but then is randomly triggered as our grief journey progresses. When that happens, *pathos* and the primitive R-complex can completely take over. You scream, you run, you hide, you succumb, you collapse, and this directly impacts our middle brain and our neocortex. You can't sleep, you can't discern, you can't find peace.

The good news is that when we understand how our brain is reacting and responding to our loss and stress, we can better react, gain control, and find positive healing and growth-oriented outcomes.

Fostering Healing and Growth with Mary-Frances O'Connor

THE ESSENCE OF TRAUMA IS THAT IT IS OVER-WHELMING, UNBELIEVABLE, AND UNBEARABLE. EACH PATIENT DEMANDS THAT WE SUSPEND OUR SENSE OF WHAT IS NORMAL AND ACCEPT THAT WE ARE DEALING WITH A DUAL REALITY: THE REALITY OF A RELATIVELY SECURE AND PREDICTABLE PRESENT THAT LIVES SIDE BY SIDE WITH A RUINOUS, EVER-PRESENT PAST. —BESSEL A. VAN DER KOLK, *THE BODY KEEPS THE SCORE: BRAIN, MIND, AND BODY IN THE HEALING OF TRAUMA*[17]

YOU ARE DOING A GOOD JOB. YOU'RE DOING BETTER THAN YOU THINK, IN AN IMPOSSIBLE SITUATION. —MARY-FRANCES O'CONNOR

---

17   Ibid.

Mary-Frances O'Connor, PhD, is the author of *The Grieving Brain: The Surprising Science of How We Learn from Love and Loss*. She is a researcher and associate professor at the University of Arizona. Dr. Mary-Frances has been researching grief for over twenty years. In that time, several books have been written about what grief feels like, and that's really valuable, but her work has focused on the *why* and the *how* of grief instead: *Why does it hurt so much? Why does it take so long to understand that they're gone? How does the brain manage to cope with all of that?*

"It's Not All in Your Head!"

Beyond the academics, there's also a deeply personal side to her journey. When she was thirteen, her mother was diagnosed with stage four breast cancer. It was thought that she wouldn't live through the year, but she actually lived another thirteen years. That was a miracle, but she was always waiting for the other shoe to drop. There was a lot of grief in her family as a result.

The interesting side effect of this was that it made Dr. Mary-Frances feel comfortable in talking with people who were grieving. Being able to say, "I don't mind if you cry uncontrollably," enabled her to stick with grief as a topic and really explore it. She was very curious to see if there was a correlation between what people were saying and their biology using MRI scans and blood tests.

She approached the research from a stress perspective first, since she knew it was a key reaction to grief. Science knows a lot about the stress systems of the body and the brain, so Dr. Mary-Frances thought about the join between grief and the stress-related systems likely to be affected.

In time, she began using magnetic resonance imaging (MRI). She looked at brain reactions to the photo of a lost loved one, for example, as compared to just a photo of a stranger. It's not just anyone they're looking at; it's specifically this person with whom they have bonded. She wanted to know how that worked. She saw waves of grief triggered in the scanner, which gave her and her associates a sense of what the brain was really doing. It's not "all in your head!" It's really happening in your brain.

Eventually, she also looked at longer term immune system impact, taking blood tests, and looking to see what stress hormones and different reactions people were having to their loss.

The bottom line is that grief is very complex. Many mental functions are called upon when people see the image of their loved one, and they feel a wave of grief.

First, and to no surprise, memories are activated. Second, our capacity to pay attention is compromised. Most interesting of all, a grieving person would say, "This hurts." We often think of that statement metaphorically, but from what Dr. Mary-Frances saw in the brain imaging scans that might not be just a metaphor.

Science had already mapped out what the sensation of physical pain looked like in the brain. Physical pain often carries with it some sort of suffering. Our brain receives the message that what the person is doing really hurts, so they should pay attention to it, and stop doing it. *She discovered that same pain attention reaction for physical wounds was also present when people were grieving.* So it is no wonder that people describe grief as painful. It is a similar, if not the same, brain reaction.

In her studies, she was specifically using a visual trigger with photographs, but other research has demonstrated that all sorts of stimuli can cause this. Awareness of pain just creeps up on us.

Triggers

Here's an example. Many people experience more grief around the anniversary of a loss, special occasion, or holiday. There's plenty of reminders of loss during these times. The brain has all these expectations of how the world is supposed to be working. So as people are walking around in the world, their brain is actually noticing that something is absent. Someone is missing. This can be very isolating for a widower, for example, because other people aren't noticing that their wife is absent, but the widower is very painfully aware of it.

Why? It can be very subtle. Dr. Mary-Frances relates that her birthday is in October, and she often has particular feelings in October: she'll realize that the sun is at a particular angle in October. And so on, but she's not consciously thinking about her birthday. Somehow, simply the sun being at that angle works on her subconscious right.

Some triggers are obvious, like that wedding picture or song, but many of the triggers that we experience are not that obvious. They reflect our brain's network of things associated with our loved one. These subtle cues bring that person to mind or can even just bring the emotions back in a way that seems unexplainable.

Dr. Mary-Frances describes grief as the natural response to loss. The truth is that people have very little control over what their instantaneous reaction will be. Sometimes, it is just anger. At other times, it is just yearning. Over time a grieving person begins to get more skilled in what they do with their emotions.

A person feeling loneliness associated with grief may learn that this is not a time they should go for a walk by themselves, which might be helpful in other instances. This is a time when they need to reach out and phone someone they know like their sister, so they can talk. In making that call, many positive feelings are introduced into the brain: *I know she's there for me.*

I know she really understands what I'm experiencing. I feel close to her. This changes the emotions and they start to be multi-faceted because of the way the person responded to what was happening.

The intensity and frequency of these waves of grief tends to be reduced over time. That is a natural process, as our brain moves from denial to understanding, and says to itself, "Ah, yes, this really did happen. This is really true. I'm going to get through this moment." Time helps a person become familiar with what is happening and how they feel.

The grief doesn't go away, but it transforms as the person understands what it means. As a person experiences it, they develop some skills around what to do next, and how to express that.

In her research, Dr. Mary-Frances found two types of stressors: loss stressors and restoration stressors.

Loss stressors are the ones most often thought about: the yearning, difficulty concentrating, and all the emotional reactions associated with having experienced death and loss. There's also a different kind of stressor, which is focused on restoring life. It asks these questions: "Given this is true (that my loved one has died), how am I going to restore a meaningful life? What kind of activities can I do now that still feel meaningful?" (Initially, there can be a real sense that nothing is important.) These restoration stressors all relate to what the grieving person is doing now, and what they need to do in the future.

Restoration stressors include things like: "My wife always paid the bills, and now I suddenly have to figure it out," to "We were going to retire together, and we had all these plans, but now I have to figure out what that is going to look like on my own." Stress related to the present and future come into play here, as the partner left behind figures out how to honor the memory of their loved one who's no longer there, while still finding new meaning and purpose in carrying on.

When we think of grief, most people think of the loss stressors, but may not realize how much the restoration stressors affect them too. Many feel frustrated over their progress on the restoration side. Given all the factors already mentioned, it's no surprise that grieving is a form of learning, the one in which a person figures out the following questions: "What does this mean? What do I do when I feel these things?"

A Slow Learning

You can think of the grief journey best as learning. You can't really rush learning. It takes time. Anyone that has ever learned calculus did a lot of arithmetic and multiplication long before they got there, so a certain amount of patience is required to work through this process, as well as kindness for ourselves. The brain is working as hard as it can so people need to give themselves grace. The brain is doing its best to reconcile a broken attachment, and make new neural connections. It doesn't happen overnight.

For those widowers who feel stalled, there's a helpful analogy in learning. Sometimes when we've been grieving for a while, there's something we're avoiding. Now, we might be avoiding a particular person, we might be avoiding a situation, or we might be avoiding some feelings that just seem too painful. Often, when we're stalled, it's because we're stuck in avoidance, which prevents us from learning new things.

Avoiding means we can't learn. If we are avoiding, we're not having the new experiences our brain needs and can incorporate. Here's a simple example: your wife has died, and the two of you used to go out to dinner with friends every Friday night. Since then, you've thought, *There's just no way I can do those dinners again. It just reminds me of her too much. And they're going to feel awkward, and I'm going to feel awkward.*

However, with a little bit of support by telling your friends, "Look, I'm going to try this, but I may bolt after fifteen minutes," you start afresh. That first time you go out to dinner may not go very well. You are probably going to think about her a lot, and you are probably going to feel really sad, and there will be some very awkward moments. But if you do it again, it still may have some sadness and yearning, but you may also have some new experiences. *I never had the lobster bisque before and that was actually pretty tasty. And this friend mentioned a book they're reading. I've never heard of it. Maybe I'll check that out.*

This produces a slow upward spiral. People will still experience grief, but they are now having other emotions and new experiences too. If they just avoid those situations, they're never going to have those present moment life experiences where they feel proud of themselves for having gone out, or even feel loved. Those who are stalled need to figure out what they're avoiding, even if it isn't easy (because you're probably avoiding it for a reason). This is where finding someone to help support you in addressing your avoidance is important. Find some courage and give it a try, and then, try more than once. A growth mindset is definitely the way out of that stall.

When her mother passed away from cancer, Dr. Mary-Frances's father was a widower. Over time, he started adopting other widowers in her little hometown. He'd host dinners and have them over. This is actually one way he coped—by recognizing the weight other people were carrying, seeing that others were not adapting as well as he did, and choosing to serve and help them. He learned that in helping others, he was helping himself too.

He recognized the universal aspect of grief. He was not alone in it. All these other guys had it too. *In that moment of connection, the feeling of isolation was broken.*

Many men are very stoic through the grieving process, and that's an avoidance mechanism, which is ironic. Research shows that when men are trying to be the rock, people (the very ones they are trying to support) don't see their expression of grief and falsely assume that it's not affecting them, which is not at all the case, or that they shouldn't share their grief with them. Stoicism ends up pushing them further and further away from the people they love. Instead they should find ways to express their feelings, even if it's just, "Boy, I'm feeling a lot today. I don't really want to break down right now, but I want you to know that there's a lot going on inside me." Saying that might be enough.

This is especially notable with a widower's children. If they don't see their dad as caring, but going off to work like nothing ever happened, they don't get what they need. They need to see that caring and emotion. Fathers need to be a role model for expressing emotions. Everyone is experiencing wave upon wave of grief. And they're going to recede. Seeing someone else go through that—seeing someone else break down in tears—and then telling a funny story about when Mom did something ten minutes later teaches them that strong emotions come in waves, but don't stay forever. This teaches that this same experience they are seeing in their dad is probably true for them too, and that it's okay to go into their feelings because they will come out the other side. If a person shares openly and allows themselves to be vulnerable, it encourages others to do the same.

Two Separate Streams

The most surprising thing Dr. Mary-Frances found in her research was that the brain has two separate (and conflicting) streams of information, which helps explain some of the behaviors that occur during the grief journey. On the one hand, people have the memory and reality of the loss: they were either at the bedside or got the phone call or attended the funeral. You know this person has died, as there are memory systems in your brain that are holding that reality.

But what's interesting is that *when you fall in love with your partner, your neurobiology is changed* in the bonding. This includes a deep-seated belief that they will always be there for you and you will always be there for them. This means that someone doesn't have to be in your presence for you to know that they are out there for you still. This is very useful. After all, how could a person go to work every day, otherwise, if they didn't know that their mate would return afterward?

The problem with grief lies in this conundrum. Your attachment has you believe that the person is still out there somewhere for you, but your memory has you believe that they have died. Your brain doesn't know how to reconcile these two streams, these conflicting points of view. This is why you may find yourself picking up the phone to call them and tell them something before remembering they've passed away. You may feel like they're going to walk through the door again. This is natural. There's nothing wrong with you. You're not crazy. Your brain is just trying to figure out how to make these two different, really important, pieces of information fit together.

It takes a lot of courage to grow after loss. In fact, growth warrior is the perfect name for the grieving person. Remember that you are doing a good job. You're doing better than you think in an impossible situation. Give yourself grace and believe that. All the effort is worth it, and it's working. It takes longer than we think it should, but it is working.

Regaining Your Health through Acceptance and Surrender with Dr. Kirsten Carter

TRAUMA VICTIMS CANNOT RECOVER UNTIL THEY BECOME FAMILIAR WITH AND BEFRIEND THE SENSATIONS IN THEIR BODIES. BEING FRIGHTENED MEANS THAT YOU LIVE IN A BODY THAT IS ALWAYS ON GUARD. ANGRY PEOPLE LIVE IN ANGRY BODIES…IN ORDER TO CHANGE, PEOPLE NEED TO BECOME AWARE OF THEIR SENSATIONS AND THE WAY THAT THEIR BODIES INTERACT WITH THE WORLD AROUND THEM. PHYSICAL SELF-AWARENESS IS THE FIRST STEP IN RELEASING THE TYRANNY OF THE PAST. —BESSEL A. VAN DER KOLK, *THE BODY KEEPS THE SCORE: BRAIN, MIND, AND BODY IN THE HEALING OF TRAUMA*[18]

---

18   Ibid.

IN EACH MOMENT, WE REALLY DO HAVE CONTROL OVER HOW WE THINK AND FEEL, AND WE DO THIS THROUGH ACCEPTANCE AND SURRENDER. IN ORDER TO GAIN CONTROL, YOU ACTUALLY HAVE TO SURRENDER. —DR. KIRSTEN CARTER

Dr. Kirsten Carter is an internal medicine physician and co-founder of Grace Medical Home, and shares about the impact of stress on the bereaved.

How Stress Works

There are many levels to stress. Emotional stress can manifest physically as our thoughts affect our emotions and then our behaviors. The body, mind, and spirit are tightly woven together, and we often underestimate the impact of stress on these strands—individually and as a whole.

When we feel threatened, cortisol (the stress hormone) becomes elevated. Cortisol affects our ability to sleep, compromises our immune system, and affects how our GI tract works. It even affects epigenetics in regard to how our DNA gets transcribed. So long and short term, there are massive effects.

This stress response is triggered by emotions like loss, fear, and anxiety, so when our mind and body perceive these emotional responses, our body responds. It does not differentiate between stress based on emotions and stress due to an actual physical threat or challenge.

A person could be thinking about their loss or feel very angry, and both emotions get translated very similarly. That means the body might have a similar response to being chased by a real lion as it does when angry or afraid. That's because your epinephrine (adrenaline), blood pressure, and heart rate all increase. Some feel facial flushing or dry mouth. When people speak and get emotional, they often choke up and need water.

Our sympathetic nervous system is large and in charge during times of stress and perceived danger. It activates the fight-and-flight response, speeding up the heart and respiratory rates to deliver more blood and oxygen to those parts of your body to get you out of danger. The parasympathetic nervous system is a network of nerves responsible for running processes like digestion, your "rest and digest" or "feed and breed" activities, and also relaxes your body after periods of stress or danger.

When your sympathetic nervous system is activated, the GI tract changes, so the body is no longer absorbing nutrients. The body prioritizes everything that's important for survival, and your digestion is not important at the moment.

So those functions slow down. The stomach actually ends up getting its blood flow shunted away, and as a result, some people get GI distress, such as diarrhea or cramping. Over sustained periods of stress, people can become malnourished because the body is putting that function on hold.

Usually, the sympathetic response reverses quickly where someone walks themselves through the feelings. It lasts minutes and hours, but it's not a day-long event. After the loss of a spouse, the stress can be prolonged. The day events accumulate, and that's where we really start getting into much bigger problems.

Chronic sleep deprivation is huge. It really takes a massive toll on the body too because it's during sleep that the brain and body reset. Without sleep, this recovery doesn't occur. Throughout caring for a loved one and then the trauma of the loss, a widower is probably already sleep-deprived. Now, there's this empty space, without a way to fill it, and that empty space can be a problem. The inability to fall and stay asleep is usually a thinking challenge. You have to quiet your mind and get out of the anxiety/fear cycle. You have to quell the cortisol and boost the melatonin. In the beginning, a sleep aid, like melatonin or even Benadryl can help. Daily exercise can be a phenomenal treatment for insomnia long term. It uses up the hormones and exhausts the body so it de-stresses the mind.

The stress sustained through loss puts you on alert. Your instincts make you awake so you can be aware and ready to respond to any threat. Cortisol can go up and then cascade to change all the other hormones, including suppressing melatonin (the sleep hormone), boosting norepinephrine (your heart rate and blood pressure hormone), depressing dopamine (your reward hormone), suppressing GABA (gamma-amino-butyric acid, an anti-seizure and anti-anxiety hormone), and several others. It's as if your snow globe gets all shaken up. The little flakes haven't settled down, so you can't see the little village.

P.A.W.S.

PAWS is a technique to keep stress from becoming acute. PA stands for Present Awareness: getting your mind and body connected and into the present. Into the now. Since our emotional responses actually come from what we're thinking, consciously and often unconsciously, we have to bring our attention back into the present.

So just pause, and come back to being present and mindful. Think about where you are. Feel your feet on the floor. Recognize how you are positioned: *I'm sitting in this chair*. Get grounded in the present and in your body.

Breathing exercises help too. Take three slow breaths in and three out, and try to make the exhale longer than the inhale, breathing in through the nose, and breathing out long (twice as long). A standard box breath. (If you google this, you'll find many breathing helps online.)

If that doesn't work, move. Moving muscles quells runaway thoughts and gets the mind-body connection into the now. Walking for five minutes can transform your thoughts and feelings and alter that physiologic response. Our thoughts often get ahead of us, so our body needs to reset. Exercise reconnects mind and body, and uses those stress hormones, so walk them out.

The WS in PAWS is Willing to Surrender. Take thoughts of loss: sadness, anxiety, and fear—the trifecta of loss—and give them all to God. Acceptance and surrender are the keys to all our answers.

Settling Down (and Protecting) Your Village

To cope with, and mitigate, this stress, self-care is key—from the beginning of the day to the end of the day. Begin each morning with journaling. Writing is an amazing outlet for grief. This is an opportunity to start teasing out what you're thinking and feeling, and maybe even discover what's triggering you. The loss of your wife can bring other unresolved and unaddressed hurts to the surface. Many traumatic experiences can rise up: your parents' divorce, an alcoholic or abusive parent, bullying, and earlier losses. Journaling can help you recognize and identify these so you can deal with them individually.

Journaling also gives you the opportunity in the "now" to think about and resolve these hurts. Our body keeps the score, and we have to address past hurts and release them. We have this brain dump, and writing about what you have in there helps you process it. Denial and avoidance is never going to work. Journaling releases the rest of your day from any unresolved emotional stress taxing your body.

Exercise is next: walk, bike, run, swim, yoga, lift, do Pilates, pump iron. It doesn't matter. Just do it. Exercising with someone else helps you stay motivated. Since others really want to help in times of loss, ask them to walk with you instead of bringing a meal. Aside from the exercise, just having someone there, in silence, helps. Other times, it's an opportunity for expression. This gives you an opportunity to not just help your body, but also emotionally process your loss. Walking keeps that emotional response in check, while you're also emotionally connecting. Isolation is where the devil finds you. Isolation is an ugly place to be.

Diet is another focal point. You must start caring about (and perhaps changing) how you eat. If you're not eating, you need to be eating, and if you're eating too much, you need to cut down. Additionally, what you're eating matters. The quality and quantity of the food you eat affects your psyche. There's a 100% gut-to-brain connection. *What you eat changes how you think and feel.*

Science is now calling the gut the second brain. The gut biome is connected directly to the brain via the vagus nerve, a communication superhighway. The gut biome can affect your moods and your emotions. In fact, there's more bacterial DNA than human DNA in our body. What you eat can either reinforce good bacteria that keeps you healthy, or foster a bloom of bad bacteria that prompts inflammation and negative moods. When you're feeling bad and not caring about yourself well or you just need that quick reward, you grab a burger, fries, and a soda. The effect of emotional eating can be the catalyst of (or a contributor to) an overall downward spiral.

Complex carbohydrates are not nourishing, and worse with high cortisol levels. You now just changed your blood glucose levels exponentially too. This can trigger a greater insulin release, which pushes you further downward, promoting inflammation and affecting how we think and feel. People often talk about the brain fog they get after certain meals. It's a real event. A good example is the after-dinner Thanksgiving nap. Everyone thinks it's the tryptophan in the turkey that makes everybody sleepy, but it usually has more to do with what they ate *with* the turkey: the mashed potatoes and desserts, and the amount they ate, not just the tryptophan. Even though emotional eating makes you feel better in the moment, it causes many problems overall.

Another challenge is self-medicating. Emotional distress can begin this process. Whether you're irritable or restless, discontented or whatever, there's all kinds of avenues for relief, including alcohol, marijuana, other drugs, pornography, or even watching too much television. It can be anything that we use to cover up our pain. Alcohol, because it's socially acceptable, often gets abused the most. The issue with it and the others though is that it does not address the real issues, just its symptoms. What we're thinking and feeling at our core is still in there, and all of it will reassert itself when the buzz wears off.

Additionally, alcohol is a toxin. Our body must process any toxins, which causes inflammation. It also raises blood sugars, is an immuno-suppressant, and a depressant. The toxins suppress most of our cortical thinking, so it impairs decision-making. A hangover is the body trying to get rid of the poison. Suffice it to say, the impacts of alcohol and other substances are far-reaching.

The point is that suppressing emotions and grief creates a dragon and locks it in a closet. Self-medicating just feeds that beast, so it gets bigger and bigger and worse and worse. It will never simply go away. It's going to stay, and it's going to break out of the closet at the most inappropriate and absolute worst times in your life. The truth is that any emotional problem we're trying to escape from is really there, and not getting any smaller or going away by itself. It needs attention and care.

Changing poor habits to positive ones changes all this. For instance, gratitude is actually an overriding neuronal pathway. Remember, the neural pathways of the brain can be changed. The brain of an anxious or depressed person actually jumps from an anxious and sad pattern to a healthy one on an MRI when they leverage gratitude, even if it's as light a statement as, "I'm grateful that I'm sitting here." Gratitude is more potent than benzodiazepines in changing anxiety and grief.

There is always something to be grateful for. Always. That means this tool for recovery is *always* available. In fact, a great treatment for insomnia is making a gratitude list before bed. It's amazing how that actually changes and improves neuronal pathways.

Dr. Kirsten believes in God. She believes He is a divine Creator, and has a plan for everyone. She thinks faith is key, and that surrender to His will and acceptance of His will is the answer to all of our problems. Life is hard. And everyone will experience loss. It's a fact of life. If you haven't yet, you will.

So our perspective matters. Trusting God has given Dr. Kirsten a more eternal perspective which helps her rise above what she thinks and feels. When she feels stressed out or anxious, she takes it to God and allows the light of the Holy Spirit to come down upon her in that moment. With His aid, she always thinks and feels differently. When people consider the impact of a problem in the light of eternity, it helps to reduce its impact, but also helps to identify and sort it out. God never leaves us alone in all of this. From the beginning, He always planned to partner with us. This process helps Dr. Kirsten deal with the important things and let the rest go in a healthy way. *Interestingly, from a scientific standpoint, research shows that faith actually helps.*

How Faith Helps

Let's dive a little into our DNA and something called the telomere. Our DNA is a little crosshatch x and the telomeres are the tips, almost like the end caps of a shoelace, the nubs.

Many cancers and diseases come when those telomeres get either snipped off or frayed. Think of what happens when the end cap of your shoelace gets damaged. You can no longer thread the lace through the little eyelet as a result. When our telomeres get damaged, this can precipitate disease. The key to good health and longevity is to either keep your telomeres strong or lengthen them.

There are severe environmental stressors that can impact your telomeres, and break and fray the nubs. For example, smoking has this detrimental impact. When we look at emotional stressors, grief has a strong impact too—almost equivalent to smoking.

As scientists look at worldwide health studies, they have found what they call "blue zones"—areas of the world that have the highest number of people living the longest years, and living the healthiest lives. The lowest morbidity and mortality rates are in these zones. When studying them, they try to see what they do right (that secret sauce, if you will). One of the factors present in populations that lived longer and healthier was a very strong faith of some kind: Christian, Hindu, Buddhist, and so on.

Other studies leveraging polymerase chain analysis (PCR) of white blood cells in people's bodies found that faith was the number one prognostic factor that kept people's telomeres long and strong. How? Think about how faith can help to slow and transcend the emotional impact of your loss and sadness. If you are able to rest in your faith to surrender and accept your circumstances, your emotions are regulated so you are not often in fight-or-flight mode and not traumatizing your DNA.

Dr. Kirsten believes in God, but every person must choose their own path. The takeaway is that faith helps. It not only makes people think and feel differently, it changes our DNA to make us healthier and stronger. Faith *is* the secret weapon. The Bible says that "the joy of the Lord is your strength" (Neh.

8:10). Joy is a choice. People get to choose how they think, and that brings this discussion back to gratitude. Faith is our strength. Our superpower. So when a person is in these places of decision about emotions, they can choose to walk in the light of the Holy Spirit, or Higher Power. When a person does that, everything, even big loss, looks and feels differently—everything, even down to their DNA. The lens of faith is that powerful.

Loss can cause incredible stress: a cascade of short- and long-term emotional reactions and their resultant bodily impacts, including sleep deprivation, GI issues, weight loss (or gain), immuno-compromise, and disease. Your body keeps score. Since faith affects the brain positively, it can get you out of that stress mode and into a much more relaxed one. It can help you to sleep more. It can also help prevent disease and the long-term impacts of grief because it helps keep the telomeres in the DNA intact.

So even though yesterday might not feel good, you can change how you feel in the next moment and the future. It doesn't feel like it, but each person has control over the way they think and feel. Surrendering in faith is how they gain that control.

A Deeper Dive into the Growth through Grief Framework

AND THE GOD OF ALL GRACE, WHO CALLED YOU TO HIS ETERNAL GLORY IN CHRIST, AFTER YOU HAVE SUFFERED A LITTLE WHILE, WILL HIMSELF RESTORE YOU AND MAKE YOU STRONG, FIRM AND STEADFAST. (1 PETER 5:10)

THOSE WHO ENJOY A LONG COURSE OF UNINTERRUPTED PROSPERITY IN THIS WORLD WITHOUT ANY SUFFERING HAVE GREAT CAUSE TO FEAR THAT

THEY ARE NOT IN GOD'S FAVOR, BUT INSTEAD ARE
DEEP IN HIS INDIGNATION AND DISPLEASURE. FOR
IT WOULD SEEM THAT HE NEVER SENDS THEM THE
SUFFERING THAT COMES TO THOSE HE LOVES. ON
THE OTHER HAND, THOSE WHO ARE IN THE MIDST
OF TRIBULATION HAVE GOOD REASON FOR INWARD
COMFORT AND SPIRITUAL CONSOLATION AMID
THEIR GRIEF. —SIR THOMAS MORE

Now, to help you grow as you move through your grief journey. We are going to take a deeper dive into each element of the GRIEF model, to become healthier, more peaceful, and one day, even more joyful:

- Grace - It is important to overcome self-blame and regret in order to create enough space to begin the healing process.
- Reflection - Looking back, you can identify the hurts that trigger your grief and begin the healing process.
- Intention - With determination and prayer, you can pivot from the past to the future, setting your mind and establishing goals for healing and growth.
- Elevation - Taking action to improve your mind, body, and spirit, creating a new and improved you.
- Faith - This allows us to transcend loss and reach an enlightened state through surrender. It assures us protection from future challenges and loss and sustains progress.

These five pillars are the key to healing, and we need each one to deal with the results of the grief and trauma with which everyone who experiences loss must deal. Let's explore more....

Chapter 3

GRACE

CAST ALL YOUR ANXIETY ON HIM BECAUSE HE CARES FOR YOU. (1 PETER 5:7)

THE LORD BLESS YOU AND KEEP YOU; THE LORD MAKE HIS FACE SHINE ON YOU AND BE GRACIOUS TO YOU; THE LORD TURN HIS FACE TOWARD YOU AND GIVE YOU PEACE. (NUMBERS 6:24–26, THE AARONIC BLESSING)

THEREFORE DO NOT WORRY ABOUT TOMORROW, FOR TOMORROW WILL WORRY ABOUT ITSELF. EACH DAY HAS ENOUGH TROUBLE OF ITS OWN. (MATTHEW 6:34)

A s they gathered as brothers at their favorite restaurant over drinks and dinner, each one shared what they were struggling with since the last time they met a few  time they met a few weeks before. There was a common theme. Tom had just returned from a trip visiting his girls at school in California and was feeling guilty about the physical distance between him and his daughters. Why wasn't he out there, nearer to them, or visiting them more often?

Joey opened up too. He was wondering if he had done enough in the fight to beat the cancer. John felt similarly. He and his wife had overlooked the cancer signals, only leaving weeks for the fight instead of possible years. Steve was lamenting how he had underappreciated the healthy times, thinking they would last forever. They all wished they could go back and enjoy time together more now. They should have taken more time off just to be with their families.

Each also felt guilty that they were still here, when their mate was the one truly worthy of life. In each case, the one they lost was the one friends cherished, the community needed, and the kids relied upon every day. Not them.

They beat themselves up like heavyweight champions. Did they do enough? How could they have wasted so much precious time? How could they have fretted over all that little stuff? Had they really been good fathers? Why her and not them? They shared countless doubts, regrets, and guilt.

As Tom listened, it became clear what their mealtime prayer should be: Grace for Grace. He prayed, "Lord, thank You for bringing my brothers here together again tonight—to share, listen, lift, and heal. Throughout this journey You have chosen for us, there have been many times we believed we had come up short. That we didn't do enough. That we weren't the best husband, father, friend, and leader that we could have been through the process. That it should have been us and not our beautiful brides who were taken too soon. Tonight, I pray that You would relieve this heavy burden with Your grace. May we learn to have more grace for ourselves, and stop beating ourselves up over what we could not control. This was Your will. May we accept it the best we can. I thank You, God, for Your divine grace. I thank You that we don't have to be perfect, as You place Your grace upon us—Your love, favor, and forgiveness even though we don't deserve it. Thank You for Your grace. Amen."

The Greek and Hebrew biblical term *charis* refers to "goodwill, loving-kindness, favor, in particular to God's merciful grace."[1] That night—and on many other occasions—they needed to be reminded of God's grace for them. They also needed to give grace to themselves, especially over their circumstances and how they struggled to cope. The truth was that none of them was on some sort of healing schedule. Instead, each had setbacks and challenges along the way, and their transitions to growth might take longer with some than others. It was not going as any of them had planned. They each needed to have grace for those around them—those that didn't know what they were going through, those that were not able to relate, and those that couldn't advise them as they needed.

Most importantly, they needed to access God's divine grace. Divine grace is understood by Christians to be a spontaneous gift from God to people. Generous and totally unexpected and undeserved, grace is "the free and unmerited favour of God as manifested in the salvation of sinners and the bestowing of blessings."[2] It takes the form of love, pardon, and a share in the divine life of God. The Roman Catholic Church holds that "by grace alone, in faith in Christ's saving work, and not because of any merit on our part, we are accepted by God and receive the Holy Spirit, who renews our hearts while equipping and calling us to good works."[3]

---

1 Daniel C. Arichea, "Charis (Name)," Wikipedia (Wikimedia Foundation, September 19, 2022), https://en.wikipedia.org/wiki/Charis_(name).

2 "Divine Grace," Wikipedia (Wikimedia Foundation, February 20, 2023), https://en.wikipedia.org/wiki/Divine_grace.

3 Cardinal Edward Cassidy, "Catholic Culture Library: The Meaning of the Joint Declaration on Justification," Library: The Meaning of the Joint Declaration on Justification | Catholic Culture, accessed March 24, 2023, https://www.catholicculture.org/culture/library/view.cfm?recnum=1334.

Grace

I don't deserve your kindness,
when I couldn't make it better
When I couldn't answer a child's,
"Why Daddy, Why?"

I haven't earned "I'm sorry,"
when I am the one
who is sorry we couldn't do more
When I am the fighter that lost the fight

I am not worthy of the blessings,
when I curse the life I've been cast
When I wish it was me and not her

I pray for grace.

Surprise, Surprise: The Amygdala Hijack

LONG AFTER THE ACTUAL EVENT HAS PASSED, THE BRAIN MAY KEEP SENDING SIGNALS TO THE BODY TO ESCAPE A THREAT THAT NO LONGER EXISTS. — BESSEL A. VAN DER KOLK, *THE BODY KEEPS THE SCORE: BRAIN, MIND, AND BODY IN THE HEALING OF TRAUMA*[4]

NO MATTER HOW MUCH INSIGHT AND UNDER-STANDING WE DEVELOP, THE RATIONAL BRAIN IS BASICALLY IMPOTENT TO TALK THE EMOTIONAL BRAIN OUT OF ITS OWN REALITY. —BESSEL A. VAN DER KOLK, *THE BODY KEEPS THE SCORE: BRAIN, MIND, AND BODY IN THE HEALING OF TRAUMA*[5]

DO NOT BE ANXIOUS ABOUT ANYTHING, BUT IN EVERY SITUATION, BY PRAYER AND PETITION, WITH THANKSGIVING, PRESENT YOUR REQUESTS TO GOD. AND THE PEACE OF GOD, WHICH TRANSCENDS ALL UNDERSTANDING, WILL GUARD YOUR HEARTS AND YOUR MINDS IN CHRIST JESUS. (PHILIPPIANS 4:6–7)

One sunrise on Christmas morning before the kids woke up, Tom jumped in his car to wish his late wife a Merry Christmas by dropping off a poinsettia

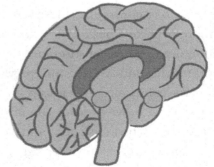

---

4   Bessel A. van der Kolk, *The Body Keeps the Score: Brain, Mind, and Body in the Healing of Trauma* (New York: Penguin Books, 2014).

5   Ibid.

at her gravesite. This was the fifth Christmas since her passing, and with the kids home from college, it had been a very busy time. Tom really needed to spend some private time in reflection, love, and memory with her, and had a lovely sunrise visit.

As he pulled his car back into the garage, "Landslide" by Stevie Nicks, a favorite song, began to play. Its poignant lyrics about change and the insecurity that went along with it triggered him completely, and left him crying hysterically for the next fifteen minutes. He felt frozen in sorrow, and emotionally ambushed by sadness, loneliness, fear, and grief—all at the same time.

This was an amygdala hijack, common in grief. When you have an immediate, overwhelming, and outsized reaction to a stimulus that shouldn't have caused such an extreme reaction, you've been hijacked by your amygdala.

The amygdala consists of a pair of small almond-shaped regions deep within your midbrain, responsible for helping you experience and regulate emotions and encode experiences, especially regarding your most emotional memories. Emotional regulation and memories, no wonder.

When hijacked, as Tom was by the song, your rational neocortex, the most advanced part of the brain, is overridden. Conscious control is surrendered, as the limbic system, the more primitive part, is now in control. This quick emotional reaction to whatever stimulus you encounter takes place so fast that logic and reason cannot prevail.

As mentioned previously, the limbic system is designed to react in order to keep you alive, and not think twice. The amygdala senses an issue, and without asking the neocortex for permission or advice, triggers an immediate fight, flight, or freeze response. This can translate into tearful or angry outbursts, running away, or hiding alone and within. Sometimes all three.

When we are grieving, a seemingly innocent stimulus like a song, a smell, a sight, a touch can cause a recall of painful emotions, resulting in an outsized reaction. Often, you are just going along with life, and suddenly you've been ambushed.

You know you've been hijacked when you experience:

- A powerful emotional reaction
- With sudden onset
- And a post-episodic realization that the reaction was outsized.

Some amygdala hijacks that Tom has experienced included:

- Uncontrollable sobbing at unexpected times like at the grocery store as memories of his wife's favorite food came to mind.
- Tears at work on finding that email she had sent to wish him a great day and good luck before that big presentation.
- Collapsing into a fetal position on his bed after hearing their wedding song.
- Feeling unable to breathe and as though there were an empty hole in his chest where his heart used to be after finding a special picture and the memory it held.

These reactions can often be tied to an amygdala hijack, and almost every widower Tom knew had experienced these reactions too—sometimes all of them in a single day.

You might also begin to see a pattern of angry outbursts over issues you would have easily overlooked prior to your loss. An example is the day Tom's friend, Craig, pulled him aside, and said, "Hey, I know that guy drove by your house a little bit too fast, but did you need to chase after him, cursing as he sped away? What's going on?"

When the emotions are in charge, other parts are hijacked too—compromising not just the mind, but the body and spirit too, releasing hormones and preparing you for trouble, even nonexistent trouble. Once triggered and the hijack cycle begins, it tends to repeat itself. This can lead to high blood pressure, weight gain, and a whole host of stress-related maladies.

This repeated manifestation brings on DREAD:

- Depression – becoming severely despondent and dejected with life.
- Resentment – angry feelings about being dealt a bad hand, particularly manifesting in a passive-aggression or bitterness.
- Explosion – outbursts and meltdowns at an extreme level.
- Anxiety – chronic and extreme feelings of worry or unease.
- Disease – Mental anguish, withdrawal, and dealing with continual amygdala hijacking can cause a myriad of diseases in the body proper.

How to Help? The Four Ts

When overwhelmed with emotional outbursts (and certainly DREAD), what can you do? No one can control the situations they experience or prevent the hijacks, but they can learn to control their responses. The key is to achieve peace. Easier said than done, but the four Ts helped Tom.

Transition

It is hard to do anything when imprisoned by the hijack. The first thing a person must learn to do is escape the grip of the limbic system. You need an escape mechanism, an eject button. A way to transition from this subconscious reaction to conscious thought. Thankfully, you've got options—lots of them.

- Breathing: Dr. Kirsten already mentioned this, and there are all kinds of methods to it, but breathing in a measured way forces your brain to slow down and recognize that you are *not in danger*. You suddenly become more aware of your surroundings as Helen mentioned: You are sitting in a chair, remember? Focusing on slow breathing is calming, and allows the brain to dial itself down. Tom uses a simple breathing technique: two deep breaths in through his nose, holding it for a moment or two, and then one long breath out through the mouth. (Thank you, Dr. Andrew Huberman.) Many therapists and yogis recommend a more advanced "box" breathing:

Step 1: Breathe in counting to four slowly. Feel the air enter your lungs.

Step 2: Hold your breath for four seconds. (Avoid inhaling or exhaling.)

Step 3: Slowly exhale through your mouth for four seconds.

Step 4: Repeat steps one through three until you feel centered.

• Movement: Physical movement can be used to derail an emotional hijack. Tom raises his hands in prayer and then over his head in victory, imagining a godly triumph over the primitive brain. Some do pushups. Tom also walks, runs, and exercises. Additionally, any bilateral movement has the effect of re-centering the brain. This discovery brought about many methods to help people, including drawing with both hands at the same time, alternately tapping one arm and then the other, the butterfly hug, and much more. This is the concept behind EMDR which is done with a counselor. A person moves their eyes horizontally side to side while speaking to a therapist, simulating the body moving forward. This has been especially helpful for those with PTSD. Your body can be used to control the mind through positive, intentional, forward movement.

- Smiling and laughing: These two aren't easy to do when you are being hijacked and crying or angry, but if you can force either of them, the result is immediate and good. You will be amazed at how quickly those big emotions dissipate.

Breathing techniques, movement, and laughter can provide the space you need to begin afresh, and have the capacity to think again.

Think

Once you've wrested control from the amygdala and the emotional and physical impact is lessened, you can finally think about the situation. So now that the neocortex is back in the driver's seat, what do you think about?

In his book *Man's Search for Meaning*, Holocaust survivor Viktor E. Frankl quoted Dutch philosopher Baruch Spinoza: "Emotion, which is suffering, ceases to be suffering as soon as we form a clear and precise picture of it."[6] So what is the "clear and precise picture" of your suffering that you need to form in order for your suffering to cease?

Your brain remembers the past, encodes the present, and represents future outcomes using the shorthand of storytelling, so to understand your suffering clearly when in the throes of a hijack, you need a story. You need to change the narrative. What story do you tell yourself about the situation?

On that Christmas morning when Tom was crying in his car, he came up with two. Perhaps one will resonate with your own.

6   Viktor E. Frankl, Harold S. Kushner, and William J. Winslade, *Man's Search for Meaning* (Boston, MA: Beacon Press, 2006).

- The first story: When times were good, Tom had not appreciated how good they had it. Two beautiful daughters ripping into their Christmas gifts. Judy had stayed up late to wrap them perfectly. Their laughter and screams of joy about that perfect gift that Mom had so thoughtfully selected. Christmas breakfast of homemade French toast and challah bread. It was a big picture stuffed with all kinds of little things Judy did.
- The second story: How was he ever going to find anything like that again? After five Christmases, he hadn't found anything close to that. He haven't been alone all that time, but the girls justifiably did not want another woman (or other children) in their family. Could he ever have a "normal" life again?

Tom had strong regrets and feared being lonely in the future. Not uncommon. He recognized these narratives, writing them down so they were tangible and he could examine them. Now he had a clearer and more concise picture of his challenges. He didn't know how to address the issues yet, but he had achieved awareness.

Thanksgiving

Once a person can see their storylines of loss, guilt, regret, loneliness, or whatever, what happens next? The Bible says, "Do not be anxious about anything, but in every situation, by prayer and petition, *with thanksgiving*, present your requests to God" (Phil. 4:6, author's emphasis).

Once you allow yourself to process the stories you have told yourself and have committed them to paper so they are crystal clear, it is time to pray over them. First, you pray about what torments you from the past, and then turn your anxiety over the future. Interestingly, this Scripture adds another important element. We don't just pray. We pray with thanksgiving.

Tom began by asking God for forgiveness and entrusting his future to Him, thanking Him. He prayed, "Dear Lord, please forgive me for not appreciating all of what I had that You had given me in my life: my beautiful bride, Judy, and my daughters in all our past Christmases—the peace, the love, the joy, the family time. I looked at it as though I deserved it and took it all for granted. Lord, thank You for this Christmas with my daughters. Thank You that we are all healthy and home. Please provide me direction to be able to help my daughters. Help me be more joyful at Christmastime, despite not having Mom here. Please help settle my inner sadness and loneliness. Provide me with the partnership, love, and caring I need in a way that can support my daughters too. May we become a new family with new experiences."

Rather than wallow in his loss and the story Tom told himself, he now prays with thanksgiving to God for what he does have. This simple conversation submitted to God reframed life and reprogrammed the story—and eventually, his response to it. Choosing to be thankful has a positive and powerful impact on a person's thinking, cutting off the downward spiral associated with grief. Prayer calms the soul, connecting a person with God.

Prayer changes things.

Transcend

This is the end product of trusting God in prayer. Let's look at the result of the choice to pray and thank God as outlined in that part of Philippians.

> DO NOT BE ANXIOUS ABOUT ANYTHING, BUT IN EVERY SITUATION, BY PRAYER AND PETITION, WITH THANKSGIVING, PRESENT YOUR REQUESTS TO GOD.

AND THE PEACE OF GOD, WHICH TRANSCENDS
ALL UNDERSTANDING, WILL GUARD YOUR HEARTS
AND YOUR MINDS IN CHRIST JESUS. (PHILIPPIANS
4:6–7)

Prayer brings peace. Prayer is an act of surrender to God. When we give Him our burdens, burdens of any kind at all, He covers us with His peace like a warm blanket on a chilly morning. His peace guards our hearts and minds, so they are no longer exposed and vulnerable. Along with His peace comes His comfort, and His grace, and His mercy, and His love. These assuage our pain and soften the harsh edges of the past realities that assail us daily. Little by little, this process relieves suffering. This daily connection with God also builds strong walls on the solid foundation of His love, which can never be taken away from us. God is called the Master of the Universe, and His love is the fabric from which He created it. Now, that's strong!

The word *transcend* in this case means to exist above and independent of material experience or the universe. If we live only tied to all the earthly things under the sun, we will continue to experience grief. Everything on earth eventually falls away, dies, and crumbles. The more we try to find solid footing based on this fragile existence, the more we fall backwards. Just when we think we have it all, another loss comes our way that hits us hard and that we just don't understand.

Tom lost three close relationships within a short amount of time—his mentor, his father, his wife. The three people that guided him most were gone, leaving him adrift. Just when he thought he came to terms with one death, the next one left him worse off than before.

In order to alleviate his grief, he needed to transcend his earthly life: from just the love of his mentor, his father, and his wife (friend, family, and partner) to begin to include the love of God, and to put that first. Tom broke this down into the acronym SOUL. The four elements that form the SOUL are Surrender, Obedience, Understanding, and Love.

- Surrender: Tom realized that he was not in control, so he gave it up to the Lord, knowing that he was in the good hands of a Higher Power.
- Obedience: Tom asked God to order his life according to God's will, and guide him into exactly what He wanted Tom to do and become.
- Understanding: Tom sought God's understanding and wisdom about what God's will for him even was. Tom knew he needed God to help him to do whatever He had in mind, so some understanding of it helped him embrace it.
- Love: Tom embraced God's love above all else, not relying only on the love of his daughters, family, or friends, which would eventually meet the same fate as everything else on earth. Instead, Tom chose to also rely on God's love which made all his other bonds stronger and allowed him to bask in God's everlasting peace.

This poem was inspired by Tom's grief over the successive losses of the three most important people in his life, and Philippians 4:6–7 and the Four Ts the Lord gave Tom to help him confront and transcend his grief.

Peace Transcendent

Flowers wither, Trees fall,
Idols rust, Sanctuaries crumble—
Fading to dust.

Friends, family, loves—
Each sadly succumbs.

Touch lost. Hopes die.
Dreams fade with each final breath.

Rinse and repeat: Sadness floods, dread.
Overcoming one loss, only to experience another.
I seek shelter from the storm.

Surrender to Your control.
Obedience for Your will.
Understanding of the purpose You have for me.
Love for You above all else and all others.

Transcending beyond time, a space appears.
Beyond understanding, Peace.

Piling On: How to Deal with Compound Grief with Helen Keeling-Neal

MINDFULNESS NOT ONLY MAKES IT POSSIBLE TO SURVEY OUR INTERNAL LANDSCAPE WITH COMPASSION AND CURIOSITY BUT CAN ALSO ACTIVELY STEER US IN THE RIGHT DIRECTION FOR SELF-CARE. —BESSEL A. VAN DER KOLK, *THE BODY KEEPS THE SCORE: BRAIN, MIND, AND BODY IN THE HEALING OF TRAUMA*[7]

YOUR PATH IS YOUR PATH. YOUR JOURNEY THROUGH GRIEF IS YOURS. DON'T LET ANYBODY TELL YOU DIFFERENTLY. YOU CAN DO THIS GRIEF JOURNEY IN THE WAY THAT IS RIGHT FOR YOU.... FEEL WHAT NEEDS TO BE FELT, LEARN AND GROW FROM THE EXPERIENCE ON YOUR WAY TO HEALING. —HELEN KEELING-NEAL

Multiple Stressors Add Up

Compound grief is the layering one on top of another of hurts, losses, and negative experiences when the original underlying grief has not yet been released or processed. There's been no chance to get current, and now the person is faced with additional hurt and trauma on top of the original grief. For example, you may have recently lost a parent, and then a few months or a year or two later, you lose your spouse. Or in more recent context, we have that loss and original grief added to the general health insecurity of COVID-19 along with financial uncertainty and insecurity.

---

7   Bessel A. van der Kolk, *The Body Keeps the Score: Brain, Mind, and Body in the Healing of Trauma* (New York: Penguin Books, 2014), 285.

It may be a loss related to loved ones, but can also relate to other hurt, losses, and risks, from which a person no longer has a sense of safety and well-being.

Now that there is a layered series of losses, the compound grief sets a foundation so that just being around someone who's not well can be a trigger, activating the amygdala, which will then send out a 9-1-1 to the mind and body. When that emergency signal goes out, the prefrontal cortex, the frontal lobes, go offline. This means that your logical thought, prediction, and reasoning can all be compromised. Once again, the limbic system that holds all the emotions takes over, so instead of a thinking response, it's an emotional response, and a flight, flight, freeze, or fawn response is enacted by the brain.

Some people go into a hyper state, experiencing very, very big overt feelings. This can be a panic attack, in which they suddenly tense and get really angry and lash out at someone. Others have a hypo effect, pulling their feelings inside. They feel numb, shut down, and are not motivated. They freeze. In different situations (and sometimes from the same trigger), they experience more than one of these responses. It can be in a sort of an arc, reaching from reaction to reaction and type to type.

After the loss of her husband, Helen went into fight mode. About a year after David's death, they came home and someone was burglarizing their house. This had a traumatic impact on the whole family. Three months later, Helen woke to hear a car alarm going off at five in the morning. What did she do? She ran down the street to catch the burglar, brandishing only her phone in her hand as a weapon. She wasn't exactly sure what she would have done with the phone, but as she put it: "Somebody was going down—and it wasn't her." She was a mother of two in her forties, so this was not a rational response. Her emotional, reptilian brain was in charge, and clearly those frontal lobes were not.

The primitive takes over. People need to give themselves grace about that. People are smart, but the truth is that even though we know about these signs and their mental health impacts, it still takes over.

Grace and understanding is super-important. Helen didn't want to react that way. It was a subconscious response. The prefrontal lobes shut down, and the *logos* was immediately offline while the reptilian *pathos* took over. So an activated limbic system colors everything: every decision, every thought, even the process would be different if the frontal cortex was engaged as opposed to when being triggered.

As Helen ran down the road, she knew she was going to "get someone." Her irrational thinking was: *I'm gonna get these MFers, and somebody's gonna pay for trying to rob me. Nobody is gonna burglarize me and my family again.* Looking back, she knows that was a compound grief response—not only to the loss of her husband, but also of not having her protector around anymore, not having her guy in the house, the one who would have handled anything like that.

Through a Glass Darkly

People live their lives looking through a filter of emotions. This clouded lens skews decision-making. These darkly colored thoughts rarely help people when they are emotionally impacted by grief and loss. They might think that if they yell at someone, it's going to get them the response they want for a need to be met, but it doesn't work that way. It really doesn't.

This is why people must bring the frontal cortex back online. The noticing, thinking, rational brain needs to be in charge. If this is online, the limbic system slows, the brainstem is soothed, the amygdala calms, and the alarm system turns off. It's okay; it's not a crisis. There's no emergency. Then, a person can think it through.

It's a process, but a person can learn how to do that. One technique Helen sometimes uses is to have her client create a character to represent what their amygdala looks like.

One guy, a veteran suffering from wartime trauma, decided it was going to be somebody sitting in a tank with an exploding cartoonlike head. This head represented what it looked like when his amygdala fired. He practiced seeing this guy in the tank, this cartoon character with his head exploding, whenever he got those intense feelings. Over time they developed a technique for him to recognize the firing and bring his frontal cortex back online soon after. To do this, they used another cartoon character and sequence. They created a neocortex character too. This new guy would come in with an envelope in his hand and say to the tank commander, "Sir, yes, sir. False alarm, sir," and hand the guy in the tank an envelope that said, "Sir, okay to stand down, sir. It's a false alarm, sir."

Through this process, he could get his neocortex, the thinking part of his brain, back online. He'd be able to look at the situation and instead of having an outsized emotional reaction, he'd be able to use the cartoon characters to address the alarm properly, so that the loud noise was not perceived as a gunshot with all the reactionary (and very real) emotions that would normally follow that.

A good example of this can be found in the Pixar movie, *Inside Out*. The movie is about all the emotions in the brain of a little girl. Each emotion is a different colored character. Joy, who represented happiness, was yellow; Anger was red, and Sadness was blue. The whole premise of the movie is that the Joy character thinks there's no place for Anger and Sadness, so the Anger character, this little red guy, just gets more and more angry, and the Sad one, more and more depressed. Helen uses the little red angry guy for her own amygdala character, and Joy for her neocortex. She brings in this very soothing sort of calm, sparkly, pale blue light that wraps itself around the red guy, and it says it's okay. The whole idea is to use these characters and representations to consciously notice that you're in a reaction, so you can bring the emotional back to the logical, in order to transcend the reactionary feelings.

Again, breathing raises the alpha waves. When a patient is triggered, breathing is the best way to quickly address that. When that song comes on, and triggers those feelings, and you know you are going to burst into tears, a breathing sequence will bring the emotions back down, so you can start thinking through and processing that reaction, depending on where you are and what you want at the time.

The truth is that if that song comes on, and you're in a place where you can let those tears fly, cry. If you're in a place where you can add sound to it (even more expression), do so. Some countries have paid mourners to wail as you walk through the streets when someone dies, and in other countries, you can wail aloud yourself. People don't wail in Western culture. Instead, Western culture teaches people to repress all that. People have to keep all their reactions contained and small and listen as other repressed people squeak out the usual empty phrases, like: "Oh, well, they're in a better place. They had a good life, don't you think?" To be honest, no! Fuck that! That's how people really feel, but that's not how it works in Western culture. Everybody is forced to shut down. However, it is much healthier to express emotions.

At one point, Helen worked with a couple of kids whose mother left to go somewhere and didn't come back because she was murdered. These kids were left by themselves. By the time they saw Helen, they didn't want anything to do with anybody. In that session, one of the kids literally sat on the floor and wailed. We're taught to be calm, but this boy needed to show his emotions. Helen just sat at a distance because it was their first session. The boy didn't even want to be there, so Helen sat a couple feet away, thinking, *Yep, that sounds exactly right. You should be wailing.*

It's especially important for men to hear this because men tend to repress their feelings too much, so even though they are talking about ways to get control of feelings and emotions, they need to recognize that there are times when they need to just let it go. And that's all right. In fact, it's healthy.

In truth, Western culture does a disservice to both genders: men are taught that they are not allowed to be sad, but they are allowed to get angry, and women are taught that they're not allowed to get angry, but are allowed to be sad. This is why it's so wonderful to have support groups. Those who don't have that support should be encouraged to get it. There is nothing better than a man embracing that sadness and letting it out and

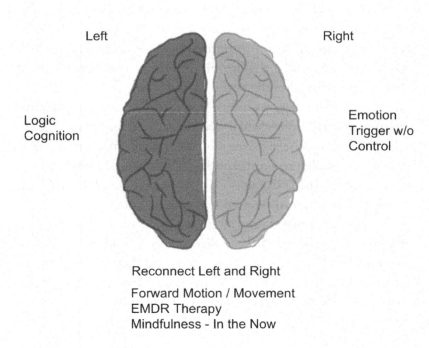

Trauma causes a "split"

Left   Right

Logic
Cognition

Emotion
Trigger w/o
Control

Reconnect Left and Right

Forward Motion / Movement
EMDR Therapy
Mindfulness - In the Now

sharing it with another who has had a similar experience. To be able to be that vulnerable is really being a man. It's healthy in other ways too.

The Greatest Example

Being able to express your emotions is the greatest role model you can be for your child. It's the greatest example of being a man or a human being.

Helen had discussed how Tom had initially dealt with his sadness by being stoic. He chose to not show his emotions in an effort to be a "rock" for his kids, employees, and everyone around him. This really backfired, building a wall around him. His kids didn't think they could go to him, and questioned how much he even cared. It wasn't until he began writing and interviewing folks about grief that Tom's daughters saw that he was really grieving. He was going through intensely deep, sad feelings but not showing it.

There's a beauty in being able to express yourself and make sure that the full range of your feelings are not just hidden or pushed down. This is important because those feelings will come back up in ways that people don't expect, sometimes even larger, and most certainly at the "wrong" times. On top of that, stuffing can have serious health implications, causing gastrointestinal issues, cardiovascular decline, and even a heart attack.

If a client can't seem to overcome amygdala hijack over a period of time, Helen recommends Eye Movement Desensitization Reprocessing (EMDR). It's a protocol that's used for trauma healing, but can also be used for anxiety, grief, or loss. When offered by a trained therapist, it's a wonderful technique. You may see it on some of the police shows nowadays. There's a light bar, and someone is looking at it, and they're just tracking it with their eyes, back and forth. Prince Harry talked about using EMDR and tapping in an interview as well.

When we experience a trauma, like what we have experienced through death and loss, it is believed that there is a split, or a disconnect, between the left hemisphere, more responsible for our logic and cognition, and our right hemisphere, more responsible for our creativity and emotions. In the traumatized brain, the hemispheres may disassociate for "protection": separating our emotions and feelings about the trauma in the right hemisphere and our logic and cognition of it, our rationalization of it, in the left hemisphere.

In the trauma brain, triggers, such as an image, a song, a smell, or a sound, can cause the right hemisphere to activate, recalling the memories and emotions as if the event were actually reoccurring with little to no control and rationalization around the recall from the right hemisphere because of the disconnect. In order to heal the traumatized brain and gather the uncontrolled or negative recalls, you have to reconnect the hemispheres, so that emotion and logical processing and control are hand-in-hand.

In trauma, we store intense memories and feelings from the loss. We store the feelings as a belief, and worse, as a negative belief or a cognitive belief or distorted belief. So, one negative belief might be, *I'm always going to be alone* or *Everybody dies.* These negative thoughts can create negative reactions, and act as triggers to spur often strong amygdala reactions, emotional outbursts, and responses.

To help heal, we access the bilateral brain, activating both hemispheres. In REM sleep, our eyes go back and forth. EMDR works similar to REM sleep in that it's bilateral, and just like in REM sleep, our brain is processing inputs we received during the day, making sense of them and creating a memory, balancing the logic and emotion. During EMDR therapy, we access both hemispheres, making sure they are activated together, *while recalling the negative belief.* To process and replace this belief, we create a positive belief to think about in its place.

We access, process, and rationalize the feelings in connection with that negative belief, and then install a positive belief in its place.

EMDR

Helen had a particularly awful visual memory of her husband as he died in hospice at the very end. This suffering image of him stuck with her for a long time. When she would think of him, instead of seeing their relationship and having good thoughts, that's the memory that she had. It was not just uncomfortable; it was traumatic and triggering.

She had to clear that image, and chose to do it with EMDR. She and her therapist used EMDR to stimulate and reconnect both hemispheres around this memory to clear that negative visual and its associated thoughts, and replace the traumatic image with a positive visualization and statement. To implement bilateral activations to affect the reprogramming, you can use taps, or they use little vibrating buzzers they call tappers, or you can use a light bar. It's a highly recommended therapy for help with this kind of thing.

Your path is your path. And your journey through grief is yours. Don't let anybody tell you differently. You should do this grief journey in the way that is right for you.

You may be a goal setter who decides where they want to be two weeks from today, two months from today, and a year from today. You think you're going to be through with these feelings at this point, and off you'll go. For most, the grief journey doesn't work like that. It's nonlinear. If you rush the process, skip steps, and don't do the work of healing, it's gonna pop up when you least expect it.

And when it pops up, people tend to want to suppress the reaction. Don't push it back down. Feel what needs to be felt; learn and grow from the experience on your way to healing.

Widowers' Survival Guide for Special Occasions and Holidays

I WAITED PATIENTLY FOR THE LORD; HE TURNED TO ME AND HEARD MY CRY. HE LIFTED ME OUT OF THE SLIMY PIT, OUT OF THE MUD AND MIRE; HE SET MY FEET ON A ROCK AND GAVE ME A FIRM PLACE TO STAND. (PSALM 40:1–2)

Special events and holidays can be extremely difficult to cope with when you have lost someone you love. For many, where there used to be anticipation and joy, these special days are landmines of piercing grief and sadness.

There are personal days like your wife's birthday, your anniversary, your birthday, your kid's birthdays. Then there are the shared holidays, like Christmas, Easter, Thanksgiving, and Valentine's Day, not to mention Mother's and Father's Day. And then there's school events that involved Mom. These already had heightened expectations before the loss. Now, a widower may experience extreme anxiety before each one. Some hunker down just to survive them.

Why is this so difficult? First, there were so many things a wife used to prepare for each of these celebrations: the presents, wrapping, baskets, cakes, favorite meals, and traditions. Then, there is the absence, like an echo in a vast canyon. As each of these occasions ticked off after Judy's passing, Tom learned a lot about experiencing this void as he tried to create new celebration traditions, and definitely made mistakes in the process.

The good news is that, finally, after four and a half years, he might have finally gotten *one* of these special occasions right.

Seven Techniques to Reclaim Special Times

1) Don't be afraid to express your grief.

As mentioned earlier, Tom prided himself on being together, showing his kids how to cope with their issues by being strong, a rock so they knew that everything was okay and would be okay.

In truth, Tom was as sad as the rest of the family that Judy wasn't going to be with them to prepare her wonderful Christmas Eve celebration dinner, the feast of the seven fishes in Italian tradition (not bad for a German girl). They were all sad that she wasn't there to wrap the gifts last minute until three a.m. that night (a habit that drove Tom crazy at the time, but was dearly missed now) or there to watch the girls tear into the gifts, always making sure that Tom had something special to open too.

But there he was, holiday after holiday, not expressing his own grief, holding it in. This wasn't good for him, as he was often losing it in private. So his girls thought he didn't care, and that he wasn't feeling the same sadness they were experiencing. Having a family hug and cry from the beginning would have helped everyone. His girls would have known how he was feeling Judy's absence too. So remember, your friends and family want you, the authentic you—happy, sad, grieving—doesn't matter.

Don't be afraid to express yourself in sadness and in grief. If you are sad and need to cry, do it. In fact, grab your loved ones and have a shared moment of grief together—to get it out in love and support.

2) Don't feel forced to celebrate.

Special days often come with special gatherings and expectations to attend parties and gatherings. You may not be feeling much like celebrating. That's OK. Give yourself some grace and don't be afraid to admit that you aren't up for the occasion. Your friends and family will understand as you set boundaries about what you are ready for as well as what you are not.

Tom had a great group of friends with whom they spent most special occasions, and they loved to gather for shared meals ahead of most special days. These friends could be very persistent about their invitations, and there were times he was glad they were getting him out of a holiday rut, and out and about. Sometimes Tom needed that. However, there were other holidays when he really didn't want to participate. He'd recall the absence of Judy the last time they hung out, and on these occasions, saying no was not only OK, but what he needed.

Give yourself grace and set the boundaries you need.

3) Address the absence; don't ignore it.

One long Thanksgiving weekend, Tom was in California visiting his girls at college instead of flying them all the way home to Florida. They were having an amazing trip with some wonderful hikes and good time together. He ordered a feast from a local farm-to-table place so they could enjoy the meal at his daughters' townhouse.

The day started off with tension over a picture and the power being off at the townhouse from high winds, and spiraled down from there. Yes, some was from normal issues, but in truth, they all were feeling Judy's absence, and *no one* would discuss it. Tom took a run into the mountains, the girls sulked around the house, and even though they were together in the paradise that is Malibu, they had one of their worst Thanksgivings ever. They couldn't get through the meal and the day quickly enough.

The next day, they took a road trip to Laguna Beach and had an amazing family day. Looking at the week, which was stellar the day before Thanksgiving and even better the day after, Tom realized their mistake: *They didn't address the absence proactively.* They all felt her absence, but thought that if they didn't talk about it (didn't mention the fact that she wasn't there with them anymore) perhaps somehow it might not be true. And so, they let petty issues get away from them, marring what could have been a wonderful day of thanks.

Instead, they should have mentioned how they wished Mom was there. How she would have loved having a break from slaving in the kitchen, and how she would be dealing much better with the power being out than they were. They could have shared their favorite dishes that she made, or favorite memories from past Thanksgivings—like their Macy's Day parade trip and having Rosie's Mexican on the East Side instead of a turkey dinner.

Ignoring Judy's absence was a sure way to place it front and center, so it should have been addressed if not embraced. One of the best ways to do this is to share the happy times and memories as part of the celebration, taking time to remember what they did to make the occasion special in the past and bring those memories forward to today.

4) Carry on with old traditions.

Every Christmas breakfast, Judy made a family favorite—Challah French Toast. She would grab special bread from a local bakery, and despite being exhausted from wrapping gifts into the wee of the morning, after the stockings were ransacked, as Tom helped the kids with their gifts, Judy served this welcome comfort food as the exclamation point to their holiday celebration.

For several Christmases since, Tom has made sure the girls had a similar experience, picking up the same bread from the same place, and either making it for the family or making it as a group effort in memory of Judy. If you went away somewhere special, went out for a special meal, celebrated a specific way, be sure to carry on with the old traditions as they can provide comfort in the familiar.

5) Create new traditions.

Along with celebrating the old traditions, it is important to establish some new ones moving forward. This past Christmas, Tom desperately needed to create a new tradition, instead of just carrying on with the old. At a friend's suggestion, he made custom ornaments using an online resource for each of the girls—each with special pictures of them with Mom. As a new tradition, the girls opened each as a gift and then placed the ornaments on the tree.

The new tradition could be something big, like a special trip to get away to a new traditional location for the holiday, or something small and personal, like going to a particular restaurant, or a gift of honor and remembrance like the ornaments.

6) Reach out for help if you need it.

Being alone in your grief may be needed from time to time, but human beings are social creatures who often need conversation and a hug for healing. Instead of suffering alone leading up to and preparing for a special day or struggling to get through the day with your own plans, you likely have friends, family, and a partner who would be more than happy to help.

Asking for help definitely didn't come easy for Tom. Saddled with the "three Ss": smart, strong, and successful, Tom could handle and fix everything on his own, it's true. But he didn't have to do things that way. A better thing to do was to discuss how he was feeling and share his anxiety with his friends and family, who might be feeling the same. Of course, ultimately, you can rely on God for help and support, surrendering your anxiety, pain, and sadness.

Tom had just celebrated his daughter's commencement at Pepperdine University, and they were blessed enough to take a congratulations trip to Hawaii. The trip was going really well, but looming on the calendar was Mother's Day, an occasion that particularly highlighted their loss. He had been planning the days with his girls up until this point, trying to fill each day with enough adventure balanced with downtime to make each day new and special. For Mother's Day though, he needed help to make it through the day, so he turned the day's agenda over to the girls. That turned out to be a great idea. They spoke to the concierge for advice, and planned out an incredible adventure for them all—from the crack of dawn into the evening. This made sure they were doing exactly what they wanted, were busy, and felt in control on this special day. And what a day they planned—a dozen or so stops and hikes as they made their way from the south end of Kauai to the north full of waterfalls, vistas, swimming holes, and cliff diving—and along the way they embraced Mom as being with them—shepherding them along to the next highlight and telling stories. Instead of another rough special occasion, both girls exclaimed that this had been the best day of their lives!

7) Give back to heal yourself.

There is nothing better to aid in your own healing than giving to others. There are many special occasions like Thanksgiving and Christmas when volunteer and charity organizations need a hand. What a better reminder of your own blessings than serving those without a home and regular meals, or volunteering as a steward for a Turkey Trot or Valentine's Day running event.

This same perspective can be instilled in your children, so look for volunteer and charity events that you can participate in as a family, making this perhaps a new tradition too.

Celebrate Again?

Every holiday and special occasion,
we feel the absence
Like a birthday with cake, but no candles
Like Christmas with Santa, but no gifts
Like Easter with bunnies, but no eggs

To plan and make every one special,
You were the one that
made every celebration bright

And even though I try,
there is always that deficit,
That absent elephant-in-the-room
No one acknowledges,
but sadness and tension reveals
Anxiously waiting for you to join the party,
toast a glass and open the gifts
Tell the girls how much you love them
and how proud you are

Every special event, I pray for the emptiness
to be filled, the sadness lifted
And the normal, as much as it ever can be,
to return.

Mother's Day Sparkle

From a single cell to more than
all the stars in heaven,
Grown within, nurtured,
Warm ocean suspended,
synchronized heartbeat, voice echoes,

GROWTH THROUGH GRIEF

Delivered to this life at the risk of your own,
You teach all they will ever need to know
How to hug tightly and feel safe,
To wipe away tears with a tender kiss.

How to tell right from wrong,
To pick yourself up
when the world knocks you down,
To work for what you want,
and treasure what you already have.
How to serve others before you do for yourself,
To be humble before a Higher Power,
To live with purpose, faith, and peace,

How to love well, and be loved better,
To be the best person,
sparkle in your eye, meant to be.

Dealing with Guilt and Regret with Helen Keeling-Neal

RESENTMENT IS THE FEELING OF FRUSTRATION, JUDGMENT, ANGER, "BETTER THAN," AND/OR HIDDEN ENVY RELATED TO PERCEIVED UNFAIRNESS OR INJUSTICE. IT'S AN EMOTION THAT WE OFTEN EXPERIENCE WHEN WE FAIL TO SET BOUNDARIES OR ASK FOR WHAT WE NEED, OR WHEN EXPECTATIONS LET US DOWN BECAUSE THEY WERE BASED ON THINGS WE CAN'T CONTROL, LIKE WHAT OTHER PEOPLE THINK, WHAT THEY FEEL, OR HOW THEY'RE GOING TO REACT. —BRENÉ BROWN, *ATLAS OF THE HEART: MAPPING MEANINGFUL CONNECTION AND THE LANGUAGE OF HUMAN EXPERIENCE*[8]

SHARING IN SAFE SPACES WITH SAFE PEOPLE IN TRUTH. THAT'S THE WAY TO RELEASE YOUR GUILT, REGRET, SADNESS AND GRIEF. —HELEN KEELING-NEAL

Most that have lost their mate at the end of a long illness have struggled through the disease process and there were times that were less than ideal. They were dealing with a lot and that put a strain on the relationship. Many widowers regret words that were left unsaid or angry words that were exchanged, things they did or said that they wish they had not. Regret is often based on guilt you racked up over time, a retrospective of looking back and wishing things had been different.

Unfortunately, when you lose someone there are ample opportunities for regret. There's the regret that you didn't spend enough quality time and do certain activities together, maybe

---

8   Brené Brown, "A Quote from Atlas of the Heart," Goodreads (Goodreads), accessed March 24, 2023, https://www.goodreads.com/quotes/11091846-resentment-is-the-feeling-of-frustration-judgment-anger-better-than.

not taking that trip you promised, or the regret in harsh words, like calling them an idiot for not putting the hose away, or something really minor. There's the regret of an emotion, like regretting feeling angry. There's the regret of doing something bad and now feeling incredibly guilty about it. There's the regret of perhaps not doing enough to help them through.

The trouble is that people don't have a way to make it right with them anymore as they did when they were alive. The best way to counteract regret now is to lean into it with loving acceptance. There isn't a do-over opportunity to say what you wanted to say. There isn't an apology that can be made, but there can be emotional process work, in which one can "own the regret."

Everyone has regrets about something in relationships, usually things that aren't really a big deal like being irritable toward them because of a habit they had, like doing things last minute or often being late. Today these things wouldn't even register in the same way as they did in that relationship.

Compound grief is a player in this. Regret is another layer. You are already grieving the loss of someone you love, and on top of it you are also grieving these other issues: lost time, not taking advantage of time, wishing you had been more patient or cheerful, or any number of things. This eats away at you, and gnaws at you today.

EMDR can be a really great way to work with a therapist on the regret, releasing that negative belief and association and replacing it with a positive thought. Regret is stored in a statement like one of these: "I didn't do the right thing." Or "I should have done better," or "I wasn't good enough for her." Using EMDR as a technique to release those negative beliefs can be very helpful. It allows the negative stories stored in our memory to be recalled and reprogrammed, replacing the negative *would have, could haves* in the story with "I did the best I could," and "I did enough in love." This can bring great relief.

Relying on Grace, and Self-Forgiveness

Grace and forgiveness for yourself is also huge here. People need to accept and understand that they didn't know what the timeframe was and were in survival mode a lot of the time. On top of that, your relationship as a couple was also in survival mode. *That was very, very difficult.* Therefore self-forgiveness is important and brings a compassionate lens to the fact that, if you did have to do this over again, you would do it differently. The trouble is that we don't know what we don't know—until we know.

Another common regret after a long illness is resentment. Through the process, couples begin to resent each other. Deep down, they really loved each other, and they were together through it all, but it wasn't all good. On some level, the one that is dying resents the fact that the other will go on living. There's also tension over the fact that they can no longer do many of the things they used to enjoy. A dying person goes through all the stages of grief as well, so they're handling a lot emotionally and physically.

And vice versa. When someone's dying, they're not the same person they were before. That's hard to deal with day to day. Many have harsh thoughts and feelings at the time, that they later regret having. In truth, those feelings were partly due to you trying to adapt to what was going on. None of this is instant.

Basically, *you lost your person before you lost your person*. And she, in a way, lost her person too. Before she left. Illness separates and changes everything. The Brené Brown quote at the beginning of this section said that resentment isn't anger; it's envy. Just as the dying partner envied the other's ability to continue and be healthy, the one left envied others who had a partner that could do normal things. It's complex, but *all* of those feelings are very normal, and absolutely appropriate, leaving you afterward with this sense of sadness and regret.

This is a time to rely on grace once again. Grace is not just a spiritual term. Grace also means giving someone (*including one's self*) the space to be human, to err, to make mistakes, but still know that they're a good person and did their best in a bad situation.

The truth is that this is an ugly process. You are all doing your best. One is trying to hang onto their loved ones and everything they stood for as long as they can, but their time is running out. The other is trying to hold it all together and provide the best care and it's just not often a graceful time. Many suffer from PTSD as a result.

In every possible way, being with someone that is dying is impactful, but coming out of that, you have to claim that grace again, and find room in your heart to say, "Yes, I wasn't perfect, but I'm human." Until you start to give yourself grace, you really haven't created that healing space yet.

Helen went through an incident that plagued her after she lost David. David had been in rehab for drug treatment. After he came out of rehab, they went to the hospital because he was having trouble breathing. At this time his cancer was undiagnosed. They didn't know that liver cancer was present. They'd been at the gastroenterologist a week before, and that doctor just dismissed him and said he needed to do a scope.

Helen didn't know David was suffering from severe liver failure right then and there. So they admitted David and were trying to prescribe him pain medications. Helen was saying, "Wait a minute. He just got out of rehab! He's an addict. No, you can't do this. Didn't you hear me? He's an addict!" Finally, the doctor looked at her, and he said, "This is not the time for that." Helen didn't know that David was dying. He was dying right there. He was in the last stage of liver failure. And they didn't know. It has taken Helen years to stop being upset with herself for being upset with David and that doctor.

Helen remained angry for a long time, and eventually gave herself grace. However, her experience is not at all unique. No one has a perfect relationship with their spouse. Every couple has things they dislike about each other and many have long-standing problems. That's just the way it is. Then, after someone passes, you are expected to remember only the good stuff, even putting them up on a pedestal of some kind.

However, that can be very difficult. It was for Helen. She had been angry with David because he had abused his body with drugs and alcohol (which contributed to his death), and then the anger changed and she was angry that he was gone. Now she had to deal with everything by herself: raising children, finances, etc. But underneath the anger was just a desperate sadness about the loss.

We all have issues in relationships—that's normal. That's the human condition. That's the partnering condition. Another part of compound grief is dealing with the issues that were in the relationship, even maybe before they were ill. And now there's the loss of that person too.

Being able to share how you really feel afterward is difficult, but also important.

Three years after her husband died, Helen's eldest daughter (now nine) was having a really hard time. Angry and upset, she burst into tears, crying, "I'm so angry at Daddy for dying." She paused for a moment and then said, "And I feel so terrible about myself—for being angry at him for dying."

This little nine-year-old was experiencing that kind of conflict. Everyone does at times, but especially those in this situation. Helen still experiences this every once in a while in a moment when she feels overwhelmed with the fact that she has to deal with everything with both her kids all the time—everything all the time by herself. And is also very sad to be doing it that way. That dichotomy of feeling is really hard, and we can feel both at once.

It's really important that people talk about the really difficult things. You have to learn to talk about how angry you are at them or how resentful you are. It could be over something that happened during care or something that was never resolved in the relationship to the satisfaction of both parties.

It might be something like being inordinately angry over having to change a person's diaper a second time because they just had another accident. You might have yelled at them over something unimportant or been grouchy and out of temper. You could also have regret over the fact that you had not spent more time with them doing their favorite thing, or that you had not worked as hard as you could have to solve your relational problems over the years. And now they're gone and you can't. All of this is extremely overwhelming and stressful, and people often feel terrible about a variety of factors.

It's really best to talk realistically about these issues. You don't have to glorify relationships as though the ones you lost were these perfect, angelic people. No one is like that. Everyone struggles. That's reality. People need to be able to talk about all of it: the dark things that were said or done as well as the good things. And they need to be able to talk to somebody in safety.

Everyone needs someone who cares for them, no matter what. Everyone needs people who will just sit with them in their sorrow and that darkness and say, "That makes sense. I understand," and most of all, "You are not a bad person because of all of this."

That person can be a therapist or a fellow widower who understands what you are going through. It could also be a dear friend, male or female, with whom you are comfortable.

The point is that you have an outlet in talking about these challenges and getting them out there. Getting your thoughts out of your head gives you a better perspective and allows you to examine them more practically.

This is important as it gives you an outside perspective rather than the internal, reactionary one driven by your limbic system. It may take sharing something very sad or distressing more than once to be able to process it, and that's OK. In fact, that's normal.

Verbalizing regret and guilt puts it into the logical part of your brain, so you can gain that outside perspective and process why you feel as you do. So give yourself time.

The very first time Helen told that story about her daughter was extremely emotional for her. It was the first time, but now she can share that without the same effect. Other techniques that help include journaling, using writing as a way to express and put your grief and regret out there. Art or music help in a similar way.

A Spiritual Connection

A spiritual connection (with God or a Higher Power) is powerful, and that power comes in part from forgiveness, letting go of the negative experiences throughout life. Journaling those experiences and looking at your pain is part of the forgiveness process. Doing this brings tremendous freedom.

Here's an example of the process: Tom took a solitary walk in the woods at a retreat and went through his journaled list, forgiving each offense aloud. He said, "God, please forgive me for the resentment that I have felt for my late wife, and for not being as gracious and forgiving as I should have been through the difficult journey we were in." Tom was grateful for the acres and acres of space around him and for the connection he felt with God and the natural world at the time. Just putting it out there helped him clear his soul.

GROWTH THROUGH GRIEF

Forgiveness is key to strong mental health—and not just toward others, but also toward your own self. Many times, a person is unaware of all the stuff they've been holding onto, so this is very healing. Taking time for solitude is a great way to calm yourself as you deal with grief and regret, as is honestly sharing in safe spaces with safe people. That's the way to release your guilt, regret, sadness, and grief. You want to live realistically regarding the memory of a loved one. Life wasn't perfect when they were alive and it isn't perfect now. You want to be respectful *and* truthful. There's a balance for the healing process to proceed best.

Chapter 4

REFLECTION

IF YOUR MIND CARRIES A HEAVY BURDEN OF THE PAST, YOU WILL EXPERIENCE MORE OF THE SAME. THE PAST PERPETUATES ITSELF THROUGH LACK OF PRESENCE. THE QUALITY OF YOUR CONSCIOUSNESS AT THIS MOMENT IS WHAT SHAPES THE FUTURE.
—ECKHART TOLLE, *THE POWER OF NOW: A GUIDE TO SPIRITUAL ENLIGHTENMENT*[1]

FALL DOWN SEVEN TIMES, STAND EIGHT.
—JAPANESE PROVERB

SUFFERING HAS BEEN STRONGER THAN ALL OTHER TEACHING, AND HAS TAUGHT ME TO UNDERSTAND WHAT YOUR HEART USED TO BE. I HAVE BEEN BENT AND BROKEN, BUT—I HOPE—INTO A BETTER SHAPE.
—CHARLES DICKENS[2]

---

1   Eckhart Tolle, "A Quote from the Power of Now," Goodreads (Goodreads), accessed March 27, 2023, https://www.goodreads.com/quotes/648017-if-your-mind-carries-a-heavy-burden-of-past-you.

2   Charles Dickens, "A Quote from Great Expectations," Goodreads

WE ARE GOD'S MASTERPIECE. HE HAS CREATED US ANEW IN CHRIST JESUS, SO WE CAN DO THE GOOD THINGS HE PLANNED FOR US LONG AGO. (EPHESIANS 2:10 NLT)

Kintsugi, A Golden Joinery - Finding the Beauty and Strength in Your Breaks and Imperfections

One by one and soon after Judy's passing, the ceramic hearts fell from the walls of Tom's home. Each precious piece, so lovingly collected during their many adventures, shattered—not unlike the broken hearts she'd left behind. Broken and in pieces.

(Goodreads), accessed March 27, 2023, https://www.goodreads.com/quotes/141511-suffering-has-been-stronger-than-all-other-teaching-and-has.

When Japanese fifteenth-century shogun Ashikaga Yoshimasa broke his favorite Chinese tea bowl, he sent the pieces back to China for repair. When the fixed tea bowl was returned, the repairs were made, but with ugly metal staples. He wasn't happy, and turned to his own Japanese craftsmen for a better aesthetic. They went to work, using lacquer mixed with powdered gold, expertly rejoining the broken pieces and sealing the cracks. In the process, the practice of *kintsugi* was said to have been created. Each of the cracks and imperfections mended with gold were transformed, from eyesore to precious art.[3]

With golden joinery, the cracks, instead of being hidden and disguised, were actually highlighted to show respect for the object's shattered history, and showcase the beauty of a broken thing made whole.

Like Yoshimasa's broken tea bowl, my family's ceramic hearts were shattered with the loss of Judy, and we desperately needed something akin to *kintsugi* to put the pieces back together again. Grieving, sadness, and tears and time passed, but still the shards lay scattered and shattered.

Tom started his repair working on his mind and body (and they helped), he eventually realized that if he wanted the breaks in his heart to be filled and true healing from his grief, he needed more. No matter how hard he worked out in the gym, how many miles he clocked in spin class, or how many growth podcasts he listened to, he just could not put the pieces back together again on his own.

He needed the help of something more. He needed his faith. He didn't just want to join his pieces with staples. They required delicate assembly and artful golden joinery. He didn't

---

3   "Kintsugi," Wikipedia (Wikimedia Foundation, March 24, 2023), https://en.wikipedia.org/wiki/Kintsugi.

want to hide his deep scars. He needed Someone who knew how to highlight them beautifully.

Jesus did not reach His full glory until he had been broken on the cross. The many scars on His hands, feet, head, and body were not hidden, but visible and highlighted, worn beautifully as a symbol for His suffering for our sin.

No matter how broken you are, God can heal you. Jesus will not hide your pain in a closet. He will use them both to showcase your renewed strength and unique beauty. Through you, He will show how the broken and scarred can be restored and renewed—more useful and valuable than ever before.

Tom's friend and preacher Chris Wassmann says it well: "The broken vessel cannot hold anything, but if you allow God to heal the brokenness you can not only hold what is poured into you, the water of the Holy Spirit, but overflow the love, joy, and peace to others as well." Broken, joined with gold, and stronger, and even more beautiful than before. May you become a *kintsugi* vessel holding the sparkling water of the Holy Spirit and overflowing into the world around you.

Kintsugi

Fallen to the ground,
Irreplaceable heart pieces, shattered
Twenty years, sweat and tears, splattered

Can I ever be complete again?

Your mercy light shined
Through the heart-used-to-be empty space

Understanding what was
Lifting what is
Visions of what could be again, better

Broken pieces found, gathering sweep
Hand caress compassion
Chipped edge, finger cut, sharp

Patient, perseverance heals
Grace, loving mends

Fused with gold, seams
Artful broken highlights, imperfections embraced
Empty space beauty filled

Becomes whole, strong and renewed.

Kintsugi: Beauty through Healing with Chris Wassmann

I THINK THAT'S WHAT WE'RE CALLED TO IN THIS LIFE: TO FIND PEOPLE AND CONNECT TO THEM. TO FIND THIS COMMON THREAD OF BROKENNESS, AND TALK ABOUT THE WAYS TO LEVERAGE THEM FOR GROWTH. —CHRIS WASSMANN

HE HEALS THE BROKENHEARTED AND BINDS UP THEIR WOUNDS. (PSALM 147:3)

Chris Wassmann, cofounder of Istoria Ministry Group, spent many years serving in high-impact roles for several of the fastest growing churches in the nation, along with serving

as a VP of Sales and Marketing in online travel. He is also a retired United States Marine who served in Desert Storm and earned multiple service awards during that time. Chris has had the opportunity to learn and lead at every level. He has a Master of Arts in Pastoral Counseling from Liberty University and is presently working on life coach certification.

As you just read, *kintsugi* is the Japanese art of golden joinery. Japanese culture respects, even venerates, the elderly and the idea of legacy much more than Western culture. Americans are quick to dispose of things when they are old or broken. It's all about recycling, and we often put the elderly out to pasture when they're no longer useful to society. Japanese culture is very different.

The Value of Brokenness

Japanese culture values even the broken, and so *kintsugi* emphasizes the cracks. Japanese potters intentionally showcase their repairs by mixing resin filled with pure gold when they rejoin the pieces, so the end result is beautiful: a piece of pottery that was clearly broken but is now rejoined. It's more valuable because of the gold that's in it and the uniqueness of its breaks. It's also stronger than before. It tells a story, not of perfection, but of the *life* of the pottery.

This analogy shows that there's beauty and value in brokenness, so rather than hiding flaws, those breaks should be honored. People can honor their flaws as part of their story, and use them to connect with other people and be real. Something that's broken will never be the same. You want to make sure the pot can still hold the tea (and function), but it is no longer as it was before the break. Hiding imperfections and breaks doesn't work. Instead, embrace them. Even emphasize them.

Week after week, people go to church and go through the same routine: "Hey, man, good to see you. How's everything going? I'm doing great, everything's great. Let's get the kids together." All that is on a very surface level. American culture tells us that people should display those perfect highlights and live perfect lives. That's just not realistic.

However, when you highlight brokenness, you can say: "Man, this is what I've had to overcome, but let me tell you what it's done for me…." That connects people and helps faith grow within relationship instead. It's not superficial, but highlights a person's growth. It's just countercultural.

Those healed breaks are what makes us beautiful, not those rare and fleeting moments of perfection. But American society does not encourage sharing deep wounds and pain, so these areas are often left unattended and un-mended. People actually need some help from their friends and church brethren to repair these breaks. When people break, they're reluctant to talk about it because they don't want to appear weak. Trained to keep a perfect mask on, they don't see what's really beautiful in their breaks, especially those repaired with God's golden joinery.

To make matters worse, many people are uncomfortable when they're around somebody that's been through something difficult. Since they don't know what to do and say, they withdraw instead of embracing them. American culture sets people up poorly for grief and brokenness. It should be okay to talk out loud about grief and loss. People should know that good will come from trial (there's always good!), but they don't.

A good and powerful God is working through this process, so there's freedom, huge freedom, in being able to just be real with people. Maintaining that false front is exhausting. Conversely, when people see the real you, it's almost infectious. They immediately begin to share what they've been dealing with as well.

The one is the catalyst for the other to open up. Everyone needs some kind of healing. Some people have a hard time opening up or have never had the opportunity to do so, but sharing the bad, and seeing the good that can come from it, is healthy.

It's all about sharing the hurts and sharing the healing, and the beauty in both. As difficult as that can be, it is vitally important that this is done. Otherwise, you live two lives: one in which everything is just fine all the time and one in which pain and exhaustion reign supreme.

The first step is to remove the distractions and get to a place where you can find all you need in God. In His strength, healing and victory follow. So, it begins with finding this path of seeing. First, a person must identify their pain. Sometimes a person doesn't realize just how much they're hurt until they take stock of it. This requires time to look back and take inventory. That is when people can see that those hurts are leaving a mark along the way.

Since we often don't deal with hurt at the time, they get repressed. It's like an overstuffed suitcase. At some point, the zippers on that bag are going to break. People look at the lies that stem from these bursts: when they told themselves that they're insignificant or didn't do a good enough job on whatever it was. So much guilt and shame. Either they've been let down by others, by circumstance, or themselves because they did not respond to something well. This process continues until you're in a place where you can reconcile your faith with God and what He says about those things.

Going Back

This requires time and self-reflection. People need to dig deep, past their recent loss. This is an opportunity from God to live authentically. It's going back, and then going back some more, and going back even further.

Many therapists take you back a long way, and this is important. It's true that your loss is the immediate hurt, but it is definitely compounded by any unresolved issues from your past. If you don't address the root hurts and issues, you will find yourself wondering why you're not healing the way you thought you would from your grief. Most cannot properly clarify their loss and grow through it without dealing with their foundational hurts.

It can be easy to look back and think: *My dad was tough on me. That's no big deal. Being in the service toughened me up and made me strong.* However, you have to finally acknowledge the lies that come from those experiences. People build up unforgiveness over certain circumstances, so that later when they deal with a big loss, those hurts compound the loss with devastating effect.

The loss of a spouse is the perfect platform for pouring out all the hurt from the past. All those negative life experiences and thoughts join together to make you question yourself. Until you have the opportunity to sit down, reflect on the past hurts, and come to some sort of resolution over them, it will be a tough, tough battle to carry that stuff along, and deal with something as tremendous as the loss of your wife.

The lies we tell ourselves are deep-seated, at a subconscious level, and rooted in our unresolved hurts. If not dealt with, they turn into resentment and become destructive, causing you to respond in unexpected ways. You get angry in the car when someone cuts you off or explode at the ticket counter because of a delayed flight. Or perhaps, you run away from responsibility and friends. All of these fight-and-flight behaviors are a byproduct of the unresolved hurts and lies.

With loss, new lies compound the old lies and spring to the surface. The familiar thought of: *I'm inadequate because I couldn't take care of my spouse's disease,* adds itself to your parents' failed marriage, business failure, that too-tough dad, that non-attentive mom, that tough childhood situation. These unresolved hurts create even more negative thoughts and doubts: *Unlovable, not smart enough, not good enough, not successful enough.* These negative thoughts automatically come to mind to create current angst and future anxiety.

Forgiveness is the key. People tend to be a bit tentative about forgiveness. Some of that comes from a misunderstanding about what forgiveness is and what it's not. Forgiveness isn't condoning. It doesn't mean that what you experienced was right and that the other person didn't wrong you and has a get-out-of-jail-free card to do it again.

Forgiveness isn't reconciliation. It doesn't mean lowering an important boundary to prevent the hurt from reoccurring or putting yourself back in a bad situation.

Forgiveness is taking the hurt and handing it off to a Higher Power, handing it off to the Lord where it belongs. He's the One to whom every offender is accountable. He is the One that can handle them best.

Unforgiveness imprisons the one that holds onto it, consuming them from the inside out. Forgiveness sets you free—free to move on and grow. When you forgive yourself and others for their transgressions, it gets you out of jail.

You'd be surprised how many people need to hand things off to God. Until you sit down to take inventory, you are often unaware of the size of your list. Many also discover that their list has shaken their belief system: *How could God let this happen to me?* Even though they're living in a fallen and broken world, people often forget about man's free will and blame God for the past hurts inflicted on them by others. As a result, many need to go through a forgiveness process with God Himself—sometimes first, before the rest of the forgiveness journey can occur. This is quite common actually.

The good news is that God is ready, willing, and able to help. It's not God that is responsible for the sins of others, so it doesn't make sense to be angry with Him. He helps people identify the sources of their pain and then walks through it with them.

It's through this process and daily communication with God that we *transcend* as we learned a few chapters ago when looking at Philippians 4:6–7. It seems laughable to "not be anxious about anything" in this busy, anxious culture, especially for a widower whose entire world has been turned upside down. That phrase is really difficult to swallow, but if you do what it says, it becomes the route that explains how you get to this place of peace. No other way works.

> DO NOT BE ANXIOUS ABOUT ANYTHING, BUT IN EVERYTHING BY PRAYER AND PETITION, WITH THANKSGIVING, PRESENT YOUR REQUEST TO GOD, AND THE PEACE OF GOD, WHICH TRANSCENDS ALL UNDERSTANDING, WILL GUARD YOUR HEARTS AND YOUR MINDS IN CHRIST JESUS. (PHILIPPIANS 4:6–7)

Nothing about losing a spouse makes sense. You could easily drive yourself crazy asking *why*. That could be said about most of the trouble and pain people experience. People go through terrible things, situations you wouldn't wish on your worst enemy. It's heart-wrenching. There's never a good reason anyone can find to answer that *why: Why is this happening? What glory could God possibly get from what's going on in my life right now? This makes no sense. How are my kids going to benefit from what's happening?*

But there is hope that allows you to not look at it as meaningless, but look at your circumstance in the scale of God's glory and eternal vision. His peace can't be obtained from outside Him in talking to your therapist or pastor or another widower. It is only available via a one-on-one relationship with Jesus. People must acknowledge that there is no earthly way to achieve true peace on their own, and come to a place of real brokenness before God. Surrender is the most difficult admission for most people. Chris was in the Marines, and surrender was not in their vocabulary. Nevertheless, faith is all about surrendering to God, and saying, "I cannot do this alone. I need a Savior. I need Jesus to help me."

Even though this is true, we fight it. We don't surrender. We try to fix our problems on our own. Surrender is counterintuitive to everything people think they know. This is especially true of men. Once you decide you don't have to fix or control something, or figure life out on your own, it's a great relief to find that God can help you. You can get help as you process loss and sadness. You don't have to do all this work on your own. You can just hand it over to God and say, "This is Yours. I can't handle it. It's too heavy for me. I need You to carry it for me. I need You to carry me through this fire. I need You to carry me forward, God." And He'll do it.

An unbelievable release occurs at that point of surrender. His peace: that is the transcendence.

Science shows the power of faith. Scripture speaks about the renewal of the mind, so it's possible to rewire how we think and feel about life using spirituality, faith, forgiveness, and surrender. We are spiritual beings that happen to live in a physical body. Each person has a mind and a will, which is what makes them different from animals.

When we think of health, most think about taking care of their physical body. When you get hurt or feel ill, you go to a medical doctor. No question. The mental health part is newer, but it is becoming more mainstream today to seek a mental health professional if you're struggling with sadness, loss, and depression.

The obvious next step is to move to a place in which we're comfortable talking about ourselves spiritually too, the third element of our three-part self. That's the way it is spelled out in the Bible. That's the way God created man—with this spirit God breathed into him.

People need to nurture their spirit. It can't be nurtured in an hour on a Sunday by checking the box and going to church. Nurturing your spirit is a process in which you recognize your needs as a spiritual being, and then, try to meet those needs. Chris recommends meeting these needs through a relationship with God.

However, today's culture tells you to do the very opposite. It's all about doing whatever makes you happy. *Where you spend your time is who you are.* Someone might say, "I'm Christian and this is what I believe in." However, if you looked at their checkbook and their calendar, you would question that immediately.

So it's a good idea to see how much time you are spending on your spirit life every day. If it turns out that it is, on average, minutes a day versus hours, that's why you haven't found peace yet. The answer is right there. If you take spiritual inventory, you can then make a conscious effort to find balance. Add Bible study and devotional time. Listen to Christian music. Fellowship with other Christians and work on building strong and honest relationships.

If you want to heal and become a beautiful *kintsugi* bowl, you've got to work on the breaks, so they are joined in a more special, golden way. Additionally, spend time taking care of yourself physically as well as mentally: work out, read, listen to podcasts, on top of time reading the Word of God. Balancing these three is an important aspect toward complete healing.

Reflection: An Honest Self-Assessment

> BUT THERE WAS NO NEED TO BE ASHAMED OF TEARS, FOR TEARS BORE WITNESS THAT A MAN HAD THE GREATEST OF COURAGE, THE COURAGE TO SUFFER. —VIKTOR E. FRANKL, *MAN'S SEARCH FOR MEANING*[4]

> IT TAKES ENORMOUS TRUST AND COURAGE TO ALLOW YOURSELF TO REMEMBER. —BESSEL A. VAN DER KOLK, *THE BODY KEEPS THE SCORE: BRAIN, MIND, AND BODY IN THE HEALING OF TRAUMA*[5]

> YOU ARE AWARENESS, DISGUISED AS A PERSON. —ECKHART TOLLE, *THE POWER OF NOW: A GUIDE TO SPIRITUAL ENLIGHTENMENT*[6]

Once you have worked on reducing triggers and reactions, it's time to consider your bigger challenges. To help with this, you can conduct an honest self-assessment of your struggles, and where you are today. You can rate these three growth improvement areas (mind, body, and spirit) on a scale of 1-10 where 1 represents the item as a non-issue for you, and 10 means it is one of the worst issues for you.

---

4   Viktor Frankl, "A Quote from Man's Search for Meaning," Goodreads (Goodreads), accessed March 29, 2023, https://www.goodreads.com/quotes/67974-but-there-was-no-need-to-be-ashamed-of-tears.

5   Bessel A. van der Kolk, *The Body Keeps the Score: Brain, Mind, and Body in the Healing of Trauma* (New York: Penguin Books, 2014).

6   Eckhart Tolle, "A Quote from the Power of Now," Goodreads (Goodreads), accessed March 29, 2023, https://www.goodreads.com/quotes/924230-you-are-awareness-disguised-as-a-person.

Body Assessment

#	Body Challenges	No Issue	Challenge	Serious Challenge
1	Drinking alcohol	1 2 3	4 5 6 7	8 9 10
2	Drug use	1 2 3	4 5 6 7	8 9 10
3	Eating healthy (timing, ca-loric intake, diet mix)	1 2 3	4 5 6 7	8 9 10
4	Drinking healthy (water and tea vs. soft drinks and coffee)	1 2 3	4 5 6 7	8 9 10
5	Sleeping well	1 2 3	4 5 6 7	8 9 10
6	Taking dietary sup-plements (vitamins, probiotics, etc.)	1 2 3	4 5 6 7	8 9 10

7	Regular anaerobic exercise (daily weight lifting, yoga, etc.)	1 2 3	4 5 6 7	8 9 10
8	Regular aerobic exercise (daily walking, running, biking, spinning, etc.)	1 2 3	4 5 6 7	8 9 10
9	Frequent / chronic illnesses	1 2 3	4 5 6 7	8 9 10
10	Reliance on prescription medicines	1 2 3	4 5 6 7	8 9 10
11	Weight / body mass	1 2 3	4 5 6 7	8 9 10

Total Body Score:

Mind Assessment

#	Mind Challenges	No Issue	Challenge	Serious Challenge
1	Depression / Hopelessness	1 2 3	4 5 6 7	8 9 10
2	Anxiety	1 2 3	4 5 6 7	8 9 10
3	Anger / Outbursts	1 2 3	4 5 6 7	8 9 10
4	Self-esteem	1 2 3	4 5 6 7	8 9 10
5	Work and career (Are they supportive of your journey and aligned to the new you?)	1 2 3	4 5 6 7	8 9 10
6	Family relationships	1 2 3	4 5 6 7	8 9 10
7	Friends	1 2 3	4 5 6 7	8 9 10

8	Partner re-lationships (dating and commit-ment)	1 2 3	4 5 6 7	8 9 10
9	Growth mindset (including podcasts and books)	1 2 3	4 5 6 7	8 9 10
10	Fun and play	1 2 3	4 5 6 7	8 9 10
11	Meditation	1 2 3	4 5 6 7	8 9 10

Total Mind Score:

Spirit Assessment

#	Spirit Challenges	No Issue	Challenge	Serious Challenge
1	Grace for yourself	1 2 3	4 5 6 7	8 9 10
2	Forgiveness of your sins	1 2 3	4 5 6 7	8 9 10
3	Forgiveness toward your loved one who passed	1 2 3	4 5 6 7	8 9 10
4	Forgiveness of others who have hurt you	1 2 3	4 5 6 7	8 9 10
5	Regular prayer and conversations with God	1 2 3	4 5 6 7	8 9 10
6	Belief that God has a new plan for you	1 2 3	4 5 6 7	8 9 10

7	Regularly reading the Word / Bible	1 2 3	4 5 6 7	8 9 10
8	Participating in regular Bible studies with spiritual peers	1 2 3	4 5 6 7	8 9 10
9	Having a spiritual mentor	1 2 3	4 5 6 7	8 9 10
10	Regularly attending church	1 2 3	4 5 6 7	8 9 10
11	Regularly serving others in some way / charity	1 2 3	4 5 6 7	8 9 10

Total Spirit Score:

Your Total Score:

You are unique, so your score is not a judgment and should not be used for comparison. It's here to provide you with personal guidance as to where you may want to prioritize your efforts. Take note of where you scored highest in each section, and then, where you still might have challenges to overcome and work to do. You can use this assessment over time (like every three to six months) to track your progress and reassess priorities. It can help you see your progress over time, and discern where you need to do more work.

Ditch the Mask: Letting Your Authentic Self Shine with Jon Thurman

THE GREATEST SOURCES OF OUR SUFFERING ARE THE LIES WE TELL OURSELVES. —BESSEL A. VAN DER KOLK, *THE BODY KEEPS THE SCORE: BRAIN, MIND, AND BODY IN THE HEALING OF TRAUMA*[7]

"MY GRACE IS SUFFICIENT FOR YOU, FOR MY POWER IS MADE PERFECT IN WEAKNESS." THEREFORE I WILL BOAST ALL THE MORE GLADLY ABOUT MY WEAKNESSES, SO THAT CHRIST'S POWER MAY REST ON ME. (2 CORINTHIANS 12:9)

---

7   Bessel A. van der Kolk, *The Body Keeps the Score: Brain, Mind, and Body in the Healing of Trauma* (New York: Penguin Books, 2014),11.

IF YOU LIVE LIFE BEHIND A MASK, ONLY THE MASK
IS GETTING THE LOVE. —JON THURMAN

Jon Thurman is a business performance expert, currently serving as executive vice president and a board member
of Insurance Office of America (IOA). As a life coach, he
and his organization help business leaders grow as transformative leaders in their community, integrating their faith and
their work in the marketplace. Jon calls this his "Ministry of
Availability."

What Is a Mask?

It is anything that people might put on metaphorically that
prevents them (and others) from seeing (and being) their authentic self. The key word here is *authentic*. Everyone has masks.

It's important to note that the fact that someone uses a
shield to feel safe and protected doesn't suggest they're *not* an
authentic person. They may be doing the best they can now.
It simply says that life came at them hard, hitting them with
challenges through hurt and loss, which caused them to forge
that shield in the first place. The downside is that even though
we made the masks for protection, they also block the world
from seeing who we really are.

Because of each person's inherent drive to survive, each person will naturally protect themselves to the degree in which
they have experienced pain in their life—to the degree that
they've lost something that once captivated their hearts. That
protective mask is supposed to keep them safe from another loss
of that depth. Grief hits at the very heart and soul of who we
are, piercing through whatever protections we thought we had.
The normal mask (the brain's go-to in this situation) is quickly
replaced. In fact, the speed of that process is remarkable.

Since the purpose of a mask is protection, we naturally accept it as a way to guard ourselves from the potential pain of what might be around the corner. We want to shield ourselves from that. Grief takes a person to a place in which the old masks come off, old troubles resurface, and a new protection must be immediately implemented. The work of a moment, people put on the new mask for a little while, so they feel safe, but *then they leave it on for far too long.*

Beneath these new masks, hearts can atrophy over time. The grieving person can cease to feel the love of others that may be reaching out to them—numb to their actual intent, or even no longer having any desire for that interaction. They don't let love through the mask. They can't. Some masks don't allow for very much input. Survival depends on it. Nothing can be allowed to penetrate them right now.

Albert Schweitzer wrote, "The tragedy in a man's life is what dies inside of him while he lives."[8]

This loss of genuine feeling is a byproduct of the mask, and its subsequent numbness can keep us from feeling again. This is a situation in which individual worlds get smaller and smaller and smaller. The person checks out of their life, and no longer lives in the vitality they once did. Life as it's meant to be lived eludes their grasp. If their participation in life is not restored, their loss will invade every corner, even coloring and altering their identity.

People begin to believe that the mask represents who they really are. With that, they find themselves living in this kind of never-ending identity crisis: they've put forth a false self, when in reality, they're not living in their true, inner self. They're struggling between the two and often afraid of both.

---

8   Albert Schweitzer, "A Quote by Albert Schweitzer," Goodreads (Goodreads), accessed March 29, 2023, https://www.goodreads.com/ quotes/448782-the-tragedy-in-a-man-s-life-is-what-dies-inside.

A widower has an added issue: a true and natural identity crisis as they must figure out who they are—now alone—after being closely entwined with another for a long time. That doesn't happen overnight either. So there's the masks that are developed as a person grows and there's this new one. A widower has this deep sorrow hidden within them while they do their best to juggle life and be everything for everyone on the outside. Many, like Tom, choose the stoic route. You've got this persona and this mask that you're portraying out there to your friends, to your family, to associates, to the world, and then you've got your real self, but there's an incongruity between them. That's where depression and sadness strike. Until you've got that worked out, you can't find true joy and happiness. You're never living up to the expectations of the mask, and the mask isn't revealing your true self. Therein lies most of the strife that they experience. Additionally, if their experience covered years through the sickness, and then hospice, there are all kinds of factors around the disease and the loss when they were just trying to keep it all together. It is exhausting to keep the mask on and maintain that façade. Sometimes they walked in that room and put on that happy or strong mask because they felt like they had to do that, but over time, it's just too much.

Jon has not experienced the loss of his spouse. However, he has dealt with an estranged relationship with his father. Unfortunately for them, his dad was a dead man walking. Sounds harsh, but that was the reality of their life: his dad got knocked to the mat as life dealt him a strong left hook. Jon was required to put on a false self in order to be safe from the person his father had become. He could no longer live life as his true self because he needed to protect his heart.

He was not alone. Over the years, Jon learned that many men spend their life's energy on who they're *not*, living in fear of being found out. It's like running in a race with no finish line. Just exhausting. So is wearing a mask; it's exhausting.

There is no finish line to the false front. You're not living out of your true self and your true identity, and this leaves you empty and spent at the end of the day.

There are as many masks as there are people, in fact.

The Ministry of Availability

This understanding brought Jon to form his "Ministry of Availability," which has been going on for twenty-three years or so, and helps folks navigate life from looking out their front window to peeking around the corner. It's effected by removing the masks and becoming available.

If you keep that mask on too long, it gets so comfortable you forget it's there. One of the solutions to this dilemma is having a true friend, someone who will be real with you, someone who will speak life into you. An accountability partner is huge in helping you navigate your life.

The simplest and most expeditious way to lose that mask is to invite people into your story. An interesting phenomenon about human nature is that as you invite people into your story (and almost irrespective of your story), they will see something of themselves in it. And when that happens, you've made an emotional connection that transcends the mask level.

Inviting others in requires vulnerability. You have to be vulnerable in order to allow people to see you as you are. Ultimately, people find that there's real power in transparency. As you come out from behind the mask, you begin to see the way we've all been designed to be. This is the person we desire to be. This is who we long to be.

The power of the transparency frees you, and truth be told, can be used to be an agent of healing in the lives of other people too.

It's interesting that the most amazing stories that we get sucked into are those of superheroes, but for us to relate to them, they have to have a weakness, so even though they have superpowers, they are not "super" in every way. *No one connects with a flawless superhero.* People connect with the flaws in those superheroes, the humanity in them. So the better, more authentic, story exposes those vulnerabilities which endears people to them. It's the same for everyone.

A person's honest story will endear them to others, while the masks imprison them. Presenting our authentic self allows for real connection. In fact, authenticity is a foreign language in our world, but one that people are desperate to speak—and hear. *The best way to help someone be authentic is to be real yourself.*

> BUT HE SAID TO ME, "MY GRACE IS SUFFICIENT FOR YOU, FOR MY POWER IS MADE PERFECT IN WEAKNESS." THEREFORE I WILL BOAST ALL THE MORE GLADLY ABOUT MY WEAKNESSES, SO THAT CHRIST'S POWER MAY REST ON ME. (2 CORINTHIANS 12:9)

In this letter, Paul is talking about this thorn in his flesh, and begs the Lord three times to take it away. The Lord clearly says no. He's not going to remove it. Instead, God says, "My grace is sufficient for you." He will help you find His strength in your weakness.

For the longest time Jon had read that passage and thought, *I'm clinging to that. Why am I still struggling with some of this?* And that's when he realized that he'd read the verse and stopped without connecting it to the second part, the "therefore": Paul boasting all the more of his weakness, so as to rest in God's strength rather than his own.

So the principle behind it is this: *If you want to unleash the Higher Power, you have to embrace your own weakness.* His strength will be revealed through this process.

Practicing *Kintsugi*

This means leading with transparency by showing your hurts, weaknesses, and breaks. Literally practicing *kintsugi*. You have to invite people into your real self; this neutralizes the lie. Transparency makes people endearing and loveable, and that's what makes us strong.

A great quote from the annals of the armed services goes like this: "The irony of surrender is that it ends in victory, not defeat." When people surrender to their own vulnerability and express real needs, hurts, and wants, that's the point of their greatest strength. That's where they find a victory—not a defeat. The mask tries to convince you to stay behind it, covered up and hidden, but if you choose to remove it, you're not going to be defeated. Living authentically and fully is the path of victory and beauty.

So being well known is absolutely essential to living an authentic life. People tend to listen to the lies that they tell themselves, the ones that have been written on their heart, such as: *You're not good enough. You don't matter. You're unlovable. You should stay away from people. You will always be alone. You will never have another strong relationship.*

The truth is that everyone needs a refrigerator friend. This is the guy that will come to your house, doesn't knock, walks in, goes to the refrigerator, gets food, doesn't ask, sits down, and says, "Hey, man, how are you doing?" Jon enjoyed the blessing of having a refrigerator friend for nineteen years. They spent over 7,000 hours together.

This is a person with whom one can be truly comfortable, a place to be not well known, but *known well*. There's no safer place to be than to be fully known. There's no need to run. There are no secrets. Instead, we get to plumb the depths of our transparency and *simply rest and be.*

It is challenging to find folks like that, but as a person is vulnerable and speaks with a measure of authenticity inviting people into their story, they will accelerate this process within a relationship. Moving beyond superficial conversations into more substantial areas is of a healing nature to both parties. By plumbing the depths of transparency, you are weaving the fabric of life together and getting stronger together. That's the key.

Honest Sharing

A widower needs honest sharing with someone else that has gone through a similar life experience. That really helps them. The truth is that many men desire the same connection. Someone has to take the initiative, so you must lean in and engage.

Discover the revelation of God's will each and every day, by faithfully engaging the day. Approach someone you see each morning at the coffee shop with an open seat, and introduce yourself. If you see someone, reach out and see what happens. You never know. You just never know.

When Jon looks back at his refrigerator friend, he can clearly see what that intimacy of friendship brought him. It was this circular pattern of a desire to be pursued, a desire to be understood, a desire to be fully known, and a desire to not be judged. *Because you don't judge me, you love me, and because you love me, you pursue me, and then you just understand me and allow me to be me and fully known.* That's a beautiful picture of friendship.

But someone has to take the initiative. It's just what is required. Take the initiative to get together. The next step is dealing with the mask. To get the process going, you've got to take that mask off first. If you want to be fully known, and you want to fully know the other person, you have to be vulnerable. It's difficult, but worth it.

So here's a statement to think about. It's simply this: *If you live life behind a mask, only the mask is getting love.* Many people only know love at the mask level, and by extension, they only know how to give love at the mask level. If you're not willing to take off that mask, you only know a shallow love. It doesn't go deep. It doesn't really touch the true you.

Sometimes generations of people experience this. They have only been loved at the surface because that's what their parents did too. The generations cascade in a generational impact of surface love.

And so, you can kind of plant the flag, and set the course, and be the guy to take the mask off, lean in, and change that.

The truth is that God made people relational. He designed people to be in an authentic relationship with Him and one another. He calls on us to love others, but a person can't give what they don't have. When people take off their masks, they are freed to receive love from others in an authentic way, and given the opportunity to extend that love to others.

This requires action on each person's part as they allow themselves to be transparent and loved—below the surface. It can be a challenge to engage in conversation. To get things going, take a risk. Instead of asking someone how they are, ask them how they *really* are. See if that helps you get below the surface sooner. You could also begin by sharing how you really are. Either way, once you begin, it's amazing how quickly you can get there—if you just remove your mask.

Chapter 5

INTENTION

The Meaning of Life: Purpose from Our Pain? with Tom Pisello

BEING TRAUMATIZED IS NOT JUST AN ISSUE OF BEING STUCK IN THE PAST; IT IS JUST AS MUCH A PROBLEM OF NOT BEING FULLY ALIVE IN THE PRESENT. —BESSEL A. VAN DER KOLK, *THE BODY KEEPS THE SCORE: BRAIN, MIND, AND BODY IN THE HEALING OF TRAUMA*[1]

LIFE IS NEVER MADE UNBEARABLE BY CIRCUMSTANCES, BUT ONLY BY LACK OF MEANING AND PURPOSE. —VICTOR FRANKL, *MAN'S SEARCH FOR MEANING*[2]

CALL TO ME AND I WILL ANSWER YOU AND TELL YOU GREAT AND UNSEARCHABLE THINGS YOU DO NOT KNOW. (JEREMIAH 33:3)

---

1   Bessel A. van der Kolk, *The Body Keeps the Score: Brain, Mind, and Body in the Healing of Trauma* (New York: Penguin Books, 2014).

2   Viktor Frankl, "A Quote by Viktor E. Frankl," Goodreads (Goodreads), accessed March 29, 2023, https://www.goodreads.com/quotes/62900-life-is-never-made-unbearable-by-circumstances-but-only-by.

For it is God who works in you to will and to act in order to fulfill his good purpose. (Philippians 2:13)

Ripping up a spin class as he did most evenings, striving to top the leaderboard and prove to himself that he could still be a bad-ass at almost sixty, Tom didn't think he would ever end a class in tears. But that's what happened.

Maybe it was all the hearts festooning the room to celebrate their Valentine's Day ride? Perhaps it was Whitney Houston singing "I Have Nothing" from the movie *The Bodyguard*. And then there was simple remembrance. He hadn't sent a text to his brotherhood all day, knowing that Valentine's Day was a huge triggering tradition. What the heck could he say to make them feel any better, when he wasn't in a great place himself?

After the class, he shared his tear-filled spin experience, and everyone chimed in. John wrote, "I have a tough time during these festivities. Too many memories. The food, the music, everything: just a killer!" He confessed to his own cry-fest with his dinner date, a wonderful woman whose own husband had passed away two years ago. She understood.

Chris recounted this: "For my first year, most special days were difficult, and I cried quietly in bed many nights. I would remember the good times and fun times and feel better. I also would usually plan something with my family that was a fun memory." Chris leveraged his faith on this day to make it through.

Steve had lost his wife only a month before this. He was away and surrounded with special friends out West, and replied with only two words: "Bad day."

Joey responded by saying how emotional the day had been, and expressed his gratitude in being surrounded with the love of family and friends, but also recounted that "nothing replaces the hole in my heart." Joey "celebrated" Valentine's Day by attending his first grief counseling group, which was certainly not how he thought he would be celebrating it, even a year ago.

Joey went to the group, but was really unsure about sharing his story with strangers. So was another man there—sorrow-filled and not open to sharing. In time, as others shared, so did Joey.

After the session, that quiet gentleman thanked Joey for telling his story. Joey's heartfelt words made the man feel like he was not alone. Joey realized that by sharing his grief and love, he was able to help others, even if it was just this one person, so he was able to turn this ultra-sad first Valentine's Day without his beloved from a time of deep sadness into one of reverberation and healing. By being open, transparent, and vulnerable, he had helped another man understand that he was not alone. A purposeful shared experience, transcending loneliness.

A few days later, the widowers' brotherhood gathered. After their Valentine's experiences, they were thankful to gather. Holding hands, Tom prayed, "Lord, thank You for bringing us together tonight. Admittedly, it has been a rough time for this group and our families. We thank You for the strength to make it through, and the lessons You would like us to take away from our sorrows, struggles, and experiences this past week. And, Lord, as we grow in our grief, I also want to thank You for all the many ways You help us, like bringing this quote from Viktor Frankl to my attention: 'Those who have a "why" to live, can bear almost any "how."[3] We were sure of our *why* in the past. We were loving husbands to our wives and joined together as parents to our beautiful children, but no longer. Our loss of identity and meaning is as big as the hole in our hearts, so we look to You, Lord, to guide us to our new *why*. We will not forget where we have been, but use our grieving experiences as a new foundation and source of strength, knowing that in finding our new *why*, our new purpose and our new identity will be renewed. We pray that You would reveal the new purpose You have for our lives, and deliver the perseverance needed to accomplish what You have planned. Amen."

Finding Purpose from Your Pain

Why has this tragedy befallen me?
The center of my universe, around revolved
My identity, defining life, gone.

I search for meaning in this life without you.
What is to come from my missing you?

My grief becomes a garden from which to grow,

My misery becomes my mission,
My affliction becomes my assignment,
My pain becomes my purpose.

---

3   Viktor Frankl, "A Quote from Man's Search for Meaning," Goodreads (Goodreads), accessed March 30, 2023, https://www.goodreads.com/quotes/315385-those-who-have-a-why-to-live-can-bear-with.

Busyness and Refining Your Priorities

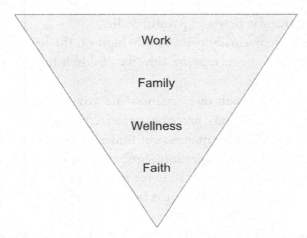

We live in an anxious world, and are rewarded by being as busy as we can be. When was the last time you sat still in silence, without texting or listening to a podcast, or checking your social media? If you are in public, just look around you. Try to find someone who's not on a device or running to their next appointment. Doesn't anyone just sit and think, ponder and reflect?

In our loss and trauma, the last thing we need is a world that prioritizes busyness, but that is just what we have. It is easy to fall into this trap. Busyness is a great medication. It is easy to forget the emptiness and sadness when you are busy, so you dive into work, bury yourself in that project, and don't think about your wife no longer being there. However, when you do eventually take a breather, the hurt and pain is just as severe as before, if not worse.

A widower is prone to trying to find relief in work, shoving everything else aside, thinking work will protect them from accepting how much their world has changed. There's the mistaken belief that work will keep them warm through this dramatic loneliness. The "busyness norm" prioritizes life like this: Work, Family, Wellness, and then Faith.

Focusing on work helps avoid the quiet time needed to actually face the new and painful reality.

Next, they usually place family high on the list, caring for those around them, making sure the children have what they need to carry on.

Meanwhile, their own wellness and any semblance of self-care which was already probably neglected through the disease process and subsequent loss, continues to remain neglected. They put off doctor appointments, deprioritize exercise and nutrition, and don't make time for much needed therapy.

Angry at God, faith is at the bottom of that list. They don't want to face the church community or anyone that might ask the "how are you doing" question. They don't want to sit there alone, when their partner would normally be right by their side. It doesn't help that church is couples coordinated either. They also don't want to be alone with God, as they're hung up on *why* this happened as opposed to moving forward and seeking His will for the future.

To change this, they need to flip the pyramid. Faith should be first as they forgive and surrender, seeking a new, bigger

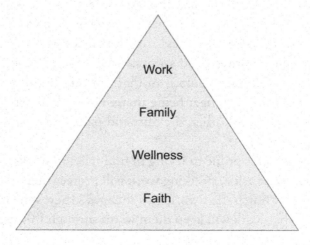

purpose in His story for them. This is closely followed by self-care. No one can take care of others if they are not first caring for themselves. They need to put on their own oxygen mask before putting a mask on those that need them.

With a strong foundation of faith and wellness, they can tend family needs. Lastly, comes work. For Tom, set in his workaholic ways and busyness, this did not come easy.

Busyness

In my busyness, I run away:
Making noise, so I can't hear His voice—pain,
Making waves so I never achieve inner peace—chaos,
Making haste so I don't have to face my reflection—raw,
Creating distance—not worthy, not enough.

When all along
Slow my heart,
Quell my breath,
Quiet my mind,
All I needed to do—silence to
Hear His voice,
Capture His peace,
Bathe in His Love

Embracing a Growth Mindset

WHEN WE ARE NO LONGER ABLE TO CHANGE A SITUATION, WE ARE CHALLENGED TO CHANGE OURSELVES. —VIKTOR E. FRANKL, *MAN'S SEARCH FOR THE MEANING OF LIFE*[4]

We want to heal and grow from the grief experience, transcending from deep sorrow to what is next. But how?

To do this personally, Tom began seeking out and consuming podcasts and material about a growth mindset. What is a growth mindset? Tom recommends *Mindset: The New Psychology of Success* by Carol S. Dweck of Stanford University for inspiration.[5]

Dweck describes her efforts thus: "My work bridges developmental psychology, social psychology, and personality psychology, and examines the self-conceptions (or mindsets) people use to structure the self and guide their behavior. My research looks at the origins of these mindsets, their role in motivation and self-regulation, and their impact on achievement and interpersonal processes."[6]

This research-driven guide helps people understand how their conscious and unconscious thoughts affect them and drive success in every aspect of their lives.

Dweck explores two primary mindsets: one which is fixed and one which is growing. The fixed model believes knowledge is static and limited by inheritance and other factors. Those with this approach seek validation, wanting to prove themselves

---

4   Viktor Frankl, "A Quote from Man's Search for Meaning," Goodreads (Goodreads), accessed March 29, 2023, https://www.goodreads.com/quotes/52939-when-we-are-no-longer-able-to-change-a-situation.

5   Carol S. Dweck, *Mindset: The New Psychology of Success* (New York: Random House, 2016).

6   "Carol Dweck," Department of Psychology, accessed March 29, 2023, https://psychology.stanford.edu/people/carol-dweck.

correct over and over instead of learning from their mistakes and growing from their experiences. The fixed mindset enthusiast looks for peers and friends that boost their current belief system and self-esteem versus those that would challenge them to grow.

A more successful model that Dweck presents is the growth mindset: a belief that your mind, body, and spirit can be developed and improved incrementally over time. According to this view, we are plastic, moldable, and shapeable versus inflexible like steel. With today's emphasis on measuring achievement and success, a growth mindset focuses on improving and optimizing the pursuit, not the outcome. Of particular importance, according to Dweck, is the fact that those who implement a growth mindset "seem to have a special talent for converting life's setbacks into future successes."

Losing a partner is an enormous setback. What better mindset could a person adopt? One centered on growth has the power to convert this terrible calamity into one that we can leverage for future success, and for good. This is why having a growth mindset, you grasp the challenges placed before you, knowing a positive outcome can still happen in your life. The pain of your experiences can actually strengthen your mind, body, and spirit instead of breaking you. Tom needed to change his perspective from asking, "Why me?" to "What's next?"

When you adopt a growth mindset, you realize that your mind, body, and spirit all need to be strengthened, and that any (and all of these) may have been weakened in the process of your loss. So now even though there will be struggles and setbacks on your path to address the grief, you push forward anyway. That will look differently for everyone. For Tom, it meant maintaining an exercise program, prioritizing the development of his mind over work, and slowly shifting that balance. He sought the inspiration and help of others to gain perspective and guide the healing and growth process. This took the form of listening to podcasts and finding a mentor. And finally, a person with a growth mindset also seeks to help others in their healing process, so they take the journey in community instead of alone.

Rewrite

Who are we?
The stories we tell ourselves,

The love we fondly remember,
The pain we hold onto, but should forget,
The anxiety of what comes next

Me, a hero anew
Fighting old demons, with loving purpose forward
Reveal, complications, climax,
Happily ever after

Changing my living truth,
Evolving my narrative,
Rewriting my story:
Growth actualized

Intent: What Are You Seeking in You 2.0?

WITH DETERMINATION AND PRAYER, YOU NOW NEED TO SET YOUR MIND AND ACTIONS ON HEALING YOUR WOUNDS AND GROWING FROM THE EXPERIENCE. —TOM PISELLO

From the assessment you just completed, you can create a short list of areas you want to address. Select three to five of them to begin addressing with intention. This means you will take regular and diligent action to improve your score in those areas. Take each of the challenges on your short list, and decide how to implement improvements. To do this, you need to establish a value code—the principles you will use in order to make sure your intentions are good, and that will help you accomplish your improvement goals. Your value code guides your intentions, actions, and conduct.

Intention is about establishing your goals for a better future. Version 2.0 is the new you, the one you are becoming as a result of your loss and grief. To assure that Version 2.0 is a better you, take the time to create this code, a foundation of rules and directives to live by. Whenever you consider a change in priority or relationship, you can use these principles to help guide decisions so they are congruent with how you see yourself in the future—the You 2.0.

Tom's personal value code could be summarized as transparency, growth, and love, as well as the following:

Mind

- Live in a growth mindset.
- Learn something new each day—reading, podcasts.
- Drive creativity every day—piano, poetry, and writing.

Body

- Respect the vessel that you have been provided.
- Maintain complete sobriety—lucid and vivid at all times.
- Exercise every day, twice most—to begin and end each workday.
- Continually improve and optimize your diet, supplements, and exercise program.
- Rest better and get the right amount of sleep to support proper recovery.

Intent

- Live in transparency and truth.
- Enjoy the journey and process (instead of focusing on the destination).
- Put in the work every day.
- Prioritize life over work.

Relationships

- Lead with compassion and understanding.
- Seek mentorship in all dimensions to learn from others and be accountable.
- Love with honesty and intent.
- Seek to give more than you receive.

Spirit

- Be grateful—give thanks for every day, activity, and all your blessings.
- Read/listen to the Bible every day to learn from the Word.

- Pray every day—ask for help, pose questions, have real conversation with God.
- Dream big to serve others.

To help guide your intentions and form a foundation of improvement, fill out your own Personal Value Code for each of the following: Mind, Body, Intent, Relationships, and Spirit.

Dealing with Loneliness after Loss with Helen Keeling-Neal

When WE Becomes Just ME

> I THINK THE CURE TO LONELINESS LIES IN TAKING
> ACTION TO BE AROUND OTHERS. TO GET BEYOND
> THE 'I DON'T HAVE IT IN ME.' YOU WANT TO FEED
> THE INTERACTION; DON'T FEED THE LONELINESS.
> —HELEN KEELING-NEAL

When you've lost a loved one the energy changes in your house. That warmth of a presence is just gone. It's like being in an emotional vacuum. The person you were accustomed to being with and who you were used to feeling in your home, is now gone. It has an echoing sense of loneliness to it. You wonder, *All right, what am I going to do now?*

Loneliness is formally defined as being dejected by the awareness of being alone, solitary, desolate.

Helen defines it as a move from *we* to *me*. What could be sadder? You've been navigating through life with a *we* in every situation: What are *we* having for dinner? What are *we* going to watch on television today? What are *we* going to do for the holidays? What color are *we* going to paint the house? Everything was done as *we*.

Now it's simply a *me*. Now, you don't have your brunch person, your adventure-outside-of-the-house person, your take-care-of-the-house-and-kids person, the one that did everything with you. Instead, you are doing it all by yourself, both physically and emotionally.

Loss is a large fracture. You want your primary attachment figure, your spouse or partner, to help you navigate through these painful feelings. The paradox is that the person that would normally help you navigate through the difficulties and painful feelings is the one who's gone. It's quite profound. It really is.

Three Types of Loneliness and Attachment Styles

Brené Brown talks about three types of loneliness: emotional, relational, and collective. When you lose a spouse, you're losing all three. You're losing the person that you can talk with about your feelings that provides you with emotional support to be the real you. Relationally, you just went from a joint parenting couple to being a sole parent and a single friend. Collectively, your social standing and status have changed. You are single in a society which holds couples in greater esteem.

How well you deal with all of that depends to some degree on your attachment style. Attachment refers to the relationship you developed as an infant with your initial caregivers and onward, including parents, babysitters, or anyone close that provided care, establishing the foundation for your future relationships.

If your caregiver was there for you, and met your emotional and physical needs consistently, you have a Secure Attachment style. Because of this, you grow up with a healthy self-esteem and you're able to connect with people in a resilient way. You're able to navigate through conflict and deal with life's trauma better.

However, there are other attachment styles in which you may not have had your needs met or had them met consistently. This can manifest as an Anxious Attachment style, in which you are nervous about those around you. Anxious Attachment's hallmark is insecurity. You are insecure with others, often clinging tightly and finding it hard to trust that somebody's going to be there and meet your needs. Those with Anxious Attachment styles crave closeness and affection. They need constant reassurance via touch and affirmations to help them feel comfortable in the fact that the attachment is real and can be trusted. Their boundaries are often fuzzy or non-existent, as they fawn, rolling over to gain the affection and love they feel they might not deserve, or that they need to earn.

The Avoidant Attachment is usually the result of neglect. Instead of craving intimacy like the Anxious Attachment style, avoidants try to avoid emotional connection with others. They're loners who'd rather not rely on others—or have others rely on them. They often withdraw from clingy relationships, and like to cope with difficult situations on their own. They can appear dismissive of other people's feelings.

And then there's Disorganized Attachment that comes from trauma. If you've grown up in a lot of trauma and extreme neglect, you're going to have Disorganized Attachment from a center of fear because there was no secure base. Disorganized Attachment adults feel they don't deserve love or closeness in a relationship; they are not deserving of love. Those with Disorganized Attachment have a low self-esteem, can seem more emotionally dysregulated, and fear emotional intimacy and abandonment. Their romantic relationships are inconsistent or non-existent due to their extreme trust issues (stemming from the early trauma and abuse).

Commonly, people have all four attachment styles to different degrees, and they play a part as to how we connect in our relationships. When you lose someone, you may have a reaction that's based on these attachment styles.[7]

This fractured attachment after losing a spouse often looks like the Anxious Attachment style. They may go out and find a relationship and get very involved in that relationship as a way to regain that attachment, but that doesn't always work out

---

7   Kia Miakka Natisse et al., "What's Your Attachment Style? Take This Quiz to Find Out," NPR (NPR, February 15, 2022), https://www.npr.org/2022/02/09/1079587715/whats-your-attachment-style-quiz.

in a way that helps with loneliness. Others with an Avoidant Attachment go the other way. They don't need a relationship. They're fine by themselves. Helen was on Helen Island, autonomous and independent. But that was just a cover for her fear. She didn't want to lose another person again. So attachment styles play out pretty significantly with loneliness.

Helen initially missed the warmth of David's presence most. She missed having someone to laugh with. They had all these stupid funny things they did. Impressions they shared. The silly dances, like the bear dance, and all these little intimate things that they had developed during their years of connection. It was like living in an echo chamber.

She focused on her kids, which is not always the healthiest thing to do. That can turn you into a helicopter parent. If you direct your loneliness into them, you can become overinvolved in their lives.

For a period of time, she was over-involved in their feelings and what they were going through. She eventually got some help with that and was able to back off a bit, which was good. However, when you have young children in particular, it's not easy to leave them after that kind of loss, and go out and socialize. She certainly wasn't going to easily or quickly bring someone home to the house. She felt it was unsafe, so spent a lot of time being single.

Holidays and special occasions amplified her loneliness. Those times can ratchet up the loneliness. However, we need to acknowledge that those times are difficult for a lot of people, even if you're not feeling lonely because of loss in general. And then there were those that lost family members and spouses through COVID-19. That accentuated loneliness to a level that was way beyond the norm. People weren't able to be around others at all. Loneliness leads to depression. We are designed as human beings to need human contact; even the introverts do.

Statistics show that many widowers get into serious relationships within the first year, and unfortunately, the failure rates for those relationships are extremely high. Why? You're not the person you need to be yet in your grief journey. Until you are the healed person on the other side, you're not ready to develop a serious relationship. You don't understand that this fractured attachment style has taken over.

Additionally, your own home can be triggering. The house is 100% a reminder of who's not there. Some people can't even bear to be at home or sleep in their own bed after a loss. They have to sleep on the couch. Or they can't handle being in certain parts of the house or outside because it's just so incredibly painful and lonely for them.

Time helps, but finding a support group and maintaining a connection there is so important. It helps to be able to share your experiences with people who've been through the same thing and understand. That helps alleviate the loneliness. You want to feed the interaction; don't feed the loneliness.

Your Children in Grief: How to Best Help Them Heal and Grow with Helen Keeling-Neal

BRING IN RESOURCES AS SOON AS POSSIBLE. DON'T
WAIT TO DO IT. AND GIVE YOUR KIDS GRACE.
—HELEN KEELING-NEAL

Everything changes when a spouse loses a partner and everything changes when a child loses a parent. There is great difficulty in being able to cope with one's own grief and loss, as well as supporting and helping a child navigate theirs.

Helen feels life intensely and has a history of complex trauma, which meant that when she experienced grief she was unable to contain her very big feelings. They just came right out. There was no stopping them at times.

Her children were four and six. When she took them to therapy, the therapist told Helen she needed to regulate her grief more with her youngest. She was not helping them, and that's what can happen. A child watches their parent crying a lot. Then they see that parent nosedive into depression and shut down. Anger can come out sideways. Helen was very upset that her daughter felt a lack of security.

The reverse also has bad effects. In fact, both have the same impact. Either way, the message to your child is to *not have feelings*. With one, there is not enough room for the child's feelings. The child has to be the one that tries to regulate the family, when they really are struggling to regulate themselves emotionally. There's only space for the big feelings of the parent.

Meanwhile, stoics allow no room for their grief. There's no room for their sadness. There's no room for their anger. There's no language for their feelings. There's no permission to let feelings up and out. It's back to business as usual, as if nothing has happened. It's a game in which they all pretend as if everything is OK.

The good news is that as hard as it is to look back and see your failures, as parents in the face of this loss, your children had safe houses and safe people and a safe support system, and safe attachments where they could go and process their feelings. So, in that sense, their needs were cared for. It may not have been directly the way you would choose today, but they did have people around them that could help them emote.

An extended support system is key to children and grief. The grieving parent needs help—friends and family—who can step in, especially in the times when the parent cannot.

And that parent has to give themselves grace to know that there are other people that can help. You do not have to do it alone. Every party has their own feelings, and they are deep, and each one needs help. Allow others to help make sure your children are cared for.

If the children are young, whether it's four to six or ten to twelve or teenagers, professionals see increased rates of depression, anxiety, and a tendency to turn towards drugs, alcohol, or sexual relationships as a way to fulfill that need and be comforted if they do not get support. *Having a way to grieve age-appropriately is really important.*

Consistency

Children are very vulnerable when they're young, and you have to be careful about who you trust to watch them and help them heal, even as you're depending on friends and extended family members, or perhaps a new third party for their care. Children can be very vulnerable after the loss. Because they can be prey for predators, you must be careful about trusting just anyone.

What they need most is consistency. They need the boundaries that were in place before the loss to continue consistently afterward. This is very difficult because the parent is so exhausted.

Keeping consistent boundaries, especially if you're struggling with your own feelings, is very difficult. A parent will inappropriately tend to say, "No, go ahead, have dessert, use the iPad, stay on the video game." The earlier boundaries flee because the parent is exhausted. Having to set and maintain boundaries alone (which requires attention and follow-through) falls to the side. You see it and feel bad for your children.

Children are designed to run against these fences (the boundaries) developmentally as they age, peaking in adolescence. Think of having fences around a child. The child's job is to run up against the fence, and that fence is what helps them feel safe, even though we think children should not be running against fences. Running against fences is part of their development.

If the fences are too porous, and they break through the fence, a child will start to feel unsafe on the inside. If the fence is too strong and it pushes back and walls them in, the child will start to feel angry and resentful. So we want safe, appropriate fences—boundaries that are as consistent as possible.

It's enlightening to think of it that way. It's not a matter of discipline. It's really about safety.

A Whole New Bunch of Triggers

Your children will also be triggered in life because of their grief. Tom's older daughter took the younger one to a mother/daughter event at their school, but it didn't take them long to realize that, even though they had each other, Mom wasn't there. Just seeing all the other girls with their mothers made them leave the event in tears.

Similar emotions are going to come up at other events like graduations and weddings. It's going to come up when there's a child born. Children need to be able to honor their grief, and as awful and as hard as it is, you can't protect them from that. And in a sense, you don't want to because it is important that those feelings come up and out.

Helen can't even say "Doughnuts with Dads" (one of the many father/daughter events that are common) without feeling mad because kids become marginalized in those kinds of situations. These events are supposed to be such a lovely thing, but their loss is accentuated in an event focused on a parent when that parent is not there.

So the bottom line is: don't over protect them through their grief journey. Even though a dad may want to protect and *fix* the issue, the children's sadness and tears are a vital part of their healing process. Let them experience all that.

Helen's youngest had never had tantrums before, but started having them at age four. Her daughter was so angry and so upset, so Helen taught her kids to punch a pillow. One night when a local ice cream place didn't have her favorite blueberry flavor, she lost it. She'd never lost it over something like that before. She felt a strong lack of control in not being able to get her favorite. She felt it at a deep unconscious level in connection with her loss of control in losing her dad and that intense grief and loss. A lot of feelings needed to come up and out of her. So a parent's job is to teach them how to express these feelings in a way that's not angry or violent or self-destructive, but appropriate and regulated.

The amygdala hijack isn't just for adults. Teenagers are already wired to fight because they're trying to differentiate, but that anger and that fighting component might be escalated even more as a result of loss. Obviously, Helen's little Sarah was fighting. She would fight with her body. She would flail and Helen would hold her. She knew Helen's rules that she was not allowed to hurt herself or anybody else. And you can't break anything. So what could Helen do? She could hold her while she punched stuff. She'd say, "You can punch this pillow. How would you like to get it out?"

The flight response can be sneaky. It can be the child running away physically, like leaving for a friend's house or running away from home. But it can also be escaping into the phone. It can be escaping into alcohol or substance use. It can be escaping through eating disorders. It can be escaping through hooking up.

Others freeze and curl up into a ball and cry, or sit still in their room for hours on end.

A child can also easily take over or be enrolled by a parent (or volunteer) as the surrogate spouse in the family. They can fawn by trying to be the perfect student, perfect athlete, and overachiever. This is equivalent to the adult expression in busyness and workaholism.

Someone to Talk To

In all cases, getting children into therapy is vital. Teens can be especially resistant to this. This is why setting up therapy immediately, so that it is a family norm, can be so important. You have to let them know firmly, that as a family, you're getting therapy: "We're going to do this. We're going to go to a New Hope for Kids on teen night, and you will meet other teens who are going through the same thing. We're going to have an individual therapist too."

It is key to get some extra help outside of the parent because your children will need space to talk about you. They need to be able to go and unload about how Mom cries all the time, or how Dad doesn't show any feelings, or that they're angry because it doesn't look like he misses her at all.

For those who haven't gotten a therapist yet, you're taking it all on yourself, or you're putting it on friends. Your friends aren't professional therapists, and you don't have the tools that a therapist has. A parent doesn't know exactly how their kids are feeling. Being in a group setting with other kids helps them with that. They have to sort their feelings out.

There's a lot of groups all over the country that can be a resource. Kids can do things like go to camp where they do a lot of art, which can be so helpful and expressive for them. This kind of thing helps immensely in dealing with special occasions later.

The truth is that everything has changed. In that first year, every birthday, every Mother's Day, every Father's Day, every Easter, every Hanukkah, every Christmas, every New Year's, every Valentine's Day, and so on, is grueling. They have to go through each one with a hole in their family and hole in their hearts.

There's a way to create new traditions that can honor the lost parent. Of course, there will be tears and grieving, but if you bring an element of fun into it, it helps. There are many things you can do: Float a balloon away for the little children. Take that family picture and hang it on the tree (to make sure Mom's on the tree)—and the lost Grandma and Grandpa are too. New traditions can be creative. Doing a search online will bring up lots of ideas on how to bring in new traditions, so look around and see what fits your family.

One of Helen's traditions is to take the girls to a favorite restaurant they used to enjoy with their dad. She takes them there every year on the anniversary of David's death, and they have a hamburger and a milkshake. Personally, she's not a big fan of that particular restaurant, but she goes anyway. They get their food, sit by David's favorite tree (Daddy's tree), and hang something on the tree. One year it was a letter, another a card, or some beads, and they hung their tributes on it. That's what they do for that anniversary.

When the first birthday came around for another family, they had a family dinner, and set a place for the lost dad. Then each person shared a story about him—a "remember when" story, which is lovely. There were certainly a lot of tears, especially on that first birthday, but it was loving and healing for the family.

Over time, a "sweetness" comes to these occasions. Imagine a bunch of jars. One is labeled "grief." That jar doesn't get any smaller, which is what people think happens with grief. Instead, the reality of grief is that it stays the same size, but the jar of life around the grief gets bigger. As the life around their grief gets bigger, people get older, and grow up. Their traditions evolve, and they become more reminiscent and sweet. They are able to breathe outside the grief that's still in there.

A year or two later or sooner perhaps, you may begin a new relationship. This can be hard for the kids. The struggle in the new relationship is often because that new person in your life is a reminder that Mom isn't there anymore. It's important to be very aware and mindful of what you're doing. Additionally, that new relationship needs to proceed very slowly.

Future Relationships

If you begin a new relationship quickly, especially when you have young children, you have to remember that those children are going to get very attached. They're going to see that person as filling the hole. They've got someone who's hugging them and cooking for them. All the stuff that Mom used to do is now back in their lives. However, if that relationship doesn't work out, you now have compound grief going on as the child has now lost another relationship.

With older children, there is less attachment and typically greater resentment. This resentment centers around this new person potentially taking their dad away from them, and losing time with him. This new person is becoming a priority, at the same time that the grieving child has a doubled need.

So as you begin relationships and the children become aware, it is important to have conversations with them to check in and see how they're doing about the new changes.

Communication is key.

Before a relationship is attempted, it should be discussed: "You know, one day Dad might be going on a date again. What do you think about that? Would that be weird for you?" Whatever the response, you are readying them for a change. You are dropping suggestions by communicating that you are thinking about this, and want them to think about what that would be like.

Once a relationship begins on any level, these kinds of questions should be asked: "Is there something you want to talk to me about? What do you think about so and so? What is it you like about them? Is there anything that you're not really comfortable with? Let's talk about how we can change that and make that more comfortable."

It's wise to meet outside of the house at first and not in the home, especially if you're in the same home where the spouse has been lost.

It's best to communicate slowly and carefully with every change with your children. You have to lead them down the path and normalize the process. You're dripping that information to them. You're letting them process the changes in pieces. This is true of a new relationship, a new home or apartment, a new school, a new anything. This helps them process it all subconsciously, if not consciously.

Those are just little things. There are some bigger things too. It's best to have rules about some things, such as not going on a family vacation with your new partner in the first two months. It's all about taking things slowly.

Overall, the most important single thing you can do to help a grieving child is to bring in outside resources right away. Don't wait to do it, and don't try to do it all alone. It's that important. There are many common signs that help is needed: a child starts acting out, brings home lower grades, or acts depressed, angry, or anxious. Stay ahead of all that by bringing in resources as quickly as possible to help them in their journey.

Also, be sure to give them grace in their behavior. Maintain your boundaries so they feel safe, but also give them grace. They're hurting. That's why they're behaving in ways they may not have done before. Grief has escalated their behavior.

Chapter 6

ELEVATION

Transcending to Peace, Grief to Growth

LONG AFTER A TRAUMATIC EXPERIENCE IS OVER, IT MAY BE REACTIVATED AT THE SLIGHTEST HINT OF DANGER AND MOBILIZE DISTURBED BRAIN CIRCUITS AND SECRETE MASSIVE AMOUNTS OF STRESS HORMONES. THIS PRECIPITATES UNPLEASANT EMOTIONS, INTENSE PHYSICAL SENSATIONS, AND IMPULSIVE AND AGGRESSIVE ACTIONS. THESE POSTTRAUMATIC REACTIONS FEEL INCOMPREHENSIBLE AND OVERWHELMING. FEELING OUT OF CONTROL, SURVIVORS OF TRAUMA OFTEN BEGIN TO FEAR THAT THEY ARE DAMAGED TO THE CORE AND BEYOND REDEMPTION. —BESSEL A. VAN DER KOLK, *THE BODY KEEPS THE SCORE: BRAIN, MIND, AND BODY IN THE HEALING OF TRAUMA*[1]

When transcending from grief to growth, it is important to understand how each part of your brain reacts to grief to keep you stalled and stuck in a processing loop that makes your grief journey circular.

There is usually a sequence of reactions that repeat as has been related earlier in this book. The point is that grief

---

1   Bessel A. van der Kolk, *The Body Keeps the Score: Brain, Mind, and Body in the Healing of Trauma* (New York: Penguin Books, 2014).

progresses. It goes from reacting to a trigger to feeling and re-living pain and sadness to manifesting negative thoughts.

Once again the Four Ts (Transition, Think, Thank, and Transcend) help a person shift from grief to a growth mindset, ultimately achieving healing along the way.

	Grief	Growth
Emotion (Reacting)	Run away Fight Hide Succumb Collapse	Transition: After triggering, you can get a handle on your reactions through breathing, motion, or other methods.
Trust (Feeling)	Anger Fear Sadness Anxiety Guilt	Think: Reflect on the sources of your reactions and feelings. Thank: Express gratitude for everything in your life that is good.
Logic (Thinking)	Regret over the past A sense of inadequacy Poor boundaries Bad thoughts about the future	Transcend: Leverage your faith, understanding that everything in this world is fleeting and rusting away. There is a longer timeline beyond our mortality and this dimension.

Three Things You Can Do Today to Address Your Sadness

One Small Step toward Healing and Success

> IN ORDER TO CHANGE, PEOPLE NEED TO BECOME MORE AWARE OF THEIR SENSATIONS AND THE WAY THEIR BODIES INTERACT WITH THE WORLD AROUND THEM. PHYSICAL SELF-AWARENESS IS THE FIRST STEP IN RELEASING THE TYRANNY OF THE PAST. — BESSEL A. VAN DER KOLK, *THE BODY KEEPS THE SCORE: BRAIN, MIND, AND BODY IN THE HEALING OF TRAUMA*[2]

> YOU ATTRACT AND MANIFEST WHATEVER CORRESPONDS TO YOUR INNER STATE. —ECKHART TOLLE, *THE POWER OF NOW: A GUIDE TO SPIRITUAL ENLIGHTENMENT*[3]

One widower brother who lost his wife almost two years ago has a new relationship, a growing family, a busy life, and good friends. Nevertheless, you can still see the sadness he carries, a weight of grief. Observational studies have categorized the physiological impact of sadness thus: "Sadness is typically characterized by raised inner eyebrows, lowered corners of the mouth, reduced walking speed, and a slumped posture."[4]

---

2   Bessel A. van der Kolk, *The Body Keeps the Score: Brain, Mind, and Body in the Healing of Trauma* (New York: Penguin Books, 2014).

3   Eckhart Tolle, "Eckhart Tolle Quotes (Author of The Power of Now) (Page 5 of 79)," Goodreads (Goodreads), accessed March 30, 2023, https://www.goodreads.com/author/quotes/4493.Eckhart_Tolle?page=5.

4   Arias JA; et. al.; "The Neuroscience of Sadness: A Multidisciplinary Synthesis and Collaborative Review," Neuroscience and biobehavioral reviews (U.S. National Library of Medicine), accessed March 30, 2023,

You may be noticing these physical indicators in others (or see them in yourself) as you journey through the grieving process.

This brother reached out to Tom recently about how heavy his loss still felt. Since his wife had passed only a short time ago, this was not unexpected. He shared that any reminder—a song, a place they used to walk, any medical facility, and more—was sure to put him into a funk. He wasn't happy with his progress in the healing process, often feeling stuck in a ditch. Most widowers have had this low-down kind of feeling at times in their journey. It can happen right after their loss or even persist for years.

You Can't Crawl Back Into a Made Bed

Many look for distractions to take their mind off their feelings, but this only acts as a temporary patch, as the grief returns and repeats. Tom's friend desired a permanent fix, but expressed how hard it was for him to find a way out and up. He read through the Growth through Grief tools and while he loved the suggestions, he was admittedly overwhelmed by the long list of potential to-dos and improvements to consider. That list had been compiled by Tom over a period of five years as he struggled to reconcile his loss and create Tom 2.0, so this wasn't unexpected. Wanting to help him, Tom wanted to guide his friend on his way to better healing.

So how do you break out of these feelings of sadness, and not be overwhelmed by the multitude of potential improvements and the longer-than-anticipated journey that stretches before you? Considering this, Tom recalled the first couple of things he had done to try and get out of his own funk.

The day after his wife passed away, he had wanted to crawl back into his bed and hide away from the world. Who wouldn't? But he resisted that urge, and did something differently instead.

---

https://pubmed.ncbi.nlm.nih.gov/32001274/.

He took the time to make the bed. He had not done this in years.

And so making his bed gave him intention, and let him do something that he had never done. He felt that doing this honored and appreciated what his wife, Judy, had done for him all those years. And certainly, his newly made bed made it difficult to jump back in and hide.

In a commencement speech at the University of Texas, Retired U.S. Navy Admiral William H. McCraven, author of the book *Make Your Bed: Little Things Can Change Your Life… and Maybe the World*, told the students that one of the most powerful lessons he learned during his time as a Navy SEAL was this: "If you make your bed every morning you will have accomplished the first task of the day. It will give you a small sense of pride, and it will encourage you to do another task and another, and another. By the end of the day, that one task completed will have turned into many tasks completed."[5]

This advice is echoed by several other experts. The folks at verywellmind.com indicate that some of the benefits of making your bed include: a feeling of accomplishment, a sense of calm, better sleep, enhanced organization, and improved focus and relaxation.[6]

Stress Reduction

Clearly, achieving an accomplishment in the face of a loss—no matter how small—is important. Forward momentum filters

---

5   William H. McCraven, "Adm. McCraven Urges Graduates to Find Courage to Change the World," UT News, September 7, 2021, https://news.utexas.edu/2014/05/16/mcraven-urges-graduates-to-find-courage-to-change-the-world/.

6   Sarah Vanbuskirk, "The Mental Health Benefits of Making Your Bed," Verywell Mind (Verywell Mind, January 29, 2021), https://www.verywellmind.com/mental-health-benefits-of-making-your-bed-5093540.

into other areas of your life, relieving stress. It helps to calm the amygdala first thing in the morning. These benefits help a grieving person overcome their triggers and build momentum toward positive improvement. Making the bed was the start for Tom, and his first piece of advice to his buddy. As he thought some more, he added two other "doing different" initiatives.

Lemon Water from Lemons

A fitness trainer friend of Tom's shared one of her secrets to a healthier life, and one she practiced religiously and recommended to all her clients. Before any morning coffee or breakfast, she felt it was essential to get your metabolism going with some lemon water.

So after Tom made his bed, he took step two. He cut up a whole lemon, squeezed out the fresh juice, put the lemon wedges in there too, filled it with water, shook it up, and drank it. In some Asian cultures, the water is heated, which is supposed to amplify the benefits, but since Tom is in a hot climate, he prefers his lemon water at room temperature.

So, what do the experts say about using lemon water first thing each morning? It's a digestive boost. Lemons are acidic, and setting up your stomach first thing in the morning with an acidic environment can help break down any food you might ingest later. As we age, it may be a helpful supplement to declining stomach acid levels. It's also a hydration jumpstart, which is very helpful because most people don't drink enough water each day, so starting off with a big glass gets at least a decent baseline established.

Lemons contain phytonutrients, which protect your body against disease and have powerful antioxidant properties. This prevents oxidation and its resultant cell damage. When we are under stress, it impacts the most fundamental parts, as cells react and become damaged. Oxidation is the culprit (the same mechanism that causes metal to rust), so we are truly rusting away, and the stress of loss and grief are like throwing salt into the rusting process. Lemon water protects.

And then there's the welcome vitamin C. A freshly squeezed whole lemon only has a few calories, but can deliver about a third of your daily vitamin C needs. This boosts any compromised immune system, which widowers often have due to stress and lack of sleep, and prevents cell damage, boosting cell repair capabilities.

Lemons, like many other fruits and vegetables, also provide potassium, which your body needs for proper nerve-muscle communication, blood pressure regulation, and transporting nutrients and waste. A body under the stress of grief can be compromised in all of these areas, so starting off with a potassium boost can help improve your nervous system, muscular capabilities, and cardiovascular health.

Lemons are also weight-loss friendly. Tom tried and after a while, could feel the difference. He is now some sixty pounds lighter, and believes the lemon water helped (at least partly).

One Step Away

Those who work with trauma victims know the importance of forward movement in calming the amygdala and PTSD triggers, while providing positive visual cues of forward momentum to get the mind oriented similarly. This was covered earlier, so suffice it to say that this kind of therapy with a licensed therapist has helped many people. In truth, physically moving your body is part of gaining a sense of equilibrium again.

Tom began reprogramming his brain to a growth mindset by walking to calm the emotional brain, enabling him to be "in" the podcast content with his thinking brain. He was lucky to have Ruby, his dog. Walking the dog everyday got his heart rate up a little and produced some sweat. The podcasts were also important to the process. To get himself moving forward, he was walking briskly and listening through ear buds to the stories of others that had faced struggles and maintained a positive mindset to triumph over them. This was essential.

Walking helps restore a much needed balance. A body under stress is out of balance, and exercise can help to naturally restore this balance, burning off the excess adrenaline likely being produced from your grief and stress, not because your body needs it. Exercise also releases those "feel good" endorphins, which can significantly change your mood long-term.

According to WebMD, "Endorphins can trigger a positive feeling in the body, similar to that of morphine. For example, the feeling that follows a run or workout is often described as 'euphoric.' That feeling, known as a 'runner's high,' can be accompanied by a positive and energizing outlook on life."[7] Regular exercise, like Tom's initial foray into walking, has been proven to reduce stress, ward off anxiety and feelings of depression, boost self-esteem, and improve sleep.

All of these improvements are vital to helping your mind overcome the initial sadness, preventing depression from taking root, as well as establishing and reinforcing a positive growth mindset. And a side benefit, as your body begins to feel better and you peel off a little weight, the initiative becomes self-reinforcing.

Making Changes Stick: Forming Good Habits

Taking these initial first steps was important, but needed to be maintained. This is where forming habits comes into play: turning the action of making the bed, preparing the lemon

---

7   "Exercise and Depression: Endorphins, Reducing Stress, and More," WebMD (WebMD), accessed March 30, 2023, https://www.webmd.com/depression/guide/exercise-depression.

water, and taking that walk into an automatic process, one that Tom would miss if it wasn't part of his day.

It needed to become a habit. James Clear, author of *Atomic Habits*, says that it takes more than two months before a new behavior becomes automatic—sixty-six days to be exact.[8] This counters earlier beliefs that it only took twenty-one days, indicating that habits are harder to form than first believed. You must think about the small steps and put in the work in order to reap the reward of implementing a good habit.

That's a little daunting when you think about it, but James Clear has some great advice we should all take to heart, "At the end of the day, how long it takes to form a particular habit doesn't really matter that much. Whether it takes 50 days or 500 days, you have to put in the work either way. The only way to get to Day 500 is to start with Day 1. So forget about the number and focus on doing the work."[9]

One Small Step Away

One small step away
From the ashes of a life, all I knew
Revolved around you and who I defined to be
Gone with a final, stilted breath.

One small step away—
Overwhelmed afraid, rain down landslide of fear
Desire to crawl inside and hide
Push through for my girls, to light the way forward.

One small step away
From the battle lost towards a greater victory righteous,
To a body restored, a mind renewed
Bathed in the light, faith recaptured

---

8   James Clear, *Atomic Habits: Tiny Changes, Remarkable Results: An Easy and Proven Way to Build Good Habits and Break Bad Ones* (London: Cornerstone press, 2022).

9   Ibid.

GROWTH THROUGH GRIEF

One small step away
Reflects a never forgotten why
Towards a new life, purpose journey begin.

You Live the Way You Eat: Food for Healing with Carly Paige

DOING ONE THING FOR YOURSELF TODAY, THAT'S
BETTER THAN YESTERDAY, THAT'S GOING TO GET
YOU CLOSER TO WHERE YOU WANT TO BE TOMOR-
ROW. —CARLY PAIGE

Carly Paige is a culinary nutrition expert, a chef, founder and president of FitLiving Eats, a private concierge chef company, and the author of the cookbook, *Simply Swapped Every Day*.

Even though Carly has not experienced the grief of losing a spouse, she is no stranger to trauma. As a student, she dealt with debilitating anxiety, so she can relate to some of the symptoms that you may find yourself dealing with in loss.

In her own challenges, she discovered that food really did have the power to heal. She didn't recognize this until she focused on what she was eating and became aware of how it made her body feel.

A Dietary Focus

As you look at different dietary focuses, one of the most important things you can do is to stabilize your blood sugar levels. You can do that with food, so you avoid that big sugar-rush energy high, and the subsequent crash and burn that follows, which can really feed into the feelings of sadness, anxiety, and stress already present in grief.

Most times people think about sugar as a dessert. Cakes, cookies, candy, and ice cream all contain plenty of sugar, but the truth of the matter is that anything high in carbohydrates can contribute to your sugar intake and cause the same high-to-low energy impact. That's because your body processes these carbohydrates into sugar.

When it comes to carbohydrates, some are "bad" and some are "good": simple carbs and complex carbs. Complex carbs, like fruit, come with fiber attached, which means your body can process those carbohydrates in a better way than a simple carb. You want to focus on eating more whole nutrients and dense fiber-rich carbohydrates—the more complex "good" carbs versus the simple, highly processed ones.

When you eat a simple, processed, high-carb food, like say, a bagel, you don't necessarily think of that as eating sugar. But you are. There's no fiber in the bagel, and you're maybe getting thirty grams of carbs that your body is processing as it would sugar. So you're still going to experience that high, and then the crash and burn. You'll ebb and flow in energy throughout the day.

So the "good" complex carbs are fruit, vegetables, whole grains, beans, and legumes. Everyone's a little bit different in the way food affects their body. Some people thrive on a higher carb diet that's done the right way, while others do better on a lower carbohydrate diet with higher protein and higher fat.

This is why you need to pay attention to your own body and how it feels as you're eating these foods. Generally speaking, those are the kinds of complex carbs that you want to incorporate into your diet, which will weed out the more simple carbs.

When you think about simple carbs, think about processed foods. Anything made with white flour comes in here. White flour is extremely processed, so all of the nutrients are stripped from that grain and then the flour is used to make other foods. That flour might go into cookies, bagels, cupcakes, or pizza dough. There's a lot of different ways white flour is used in our food. And then, of course, anything high in cane sugar (or even more natural sugars, like maple syrup, honey, agave) must be used carefully. Natural sugars are better for you, but they are still sugar, and so you want to be mindful of them.

Gut Health

Another healing focus is gut health. There is a lot of new research on the connection between our gut and our brain and its impact on our emotions and mental health. So the gut biome is what we're now calling our second brain. It is responsible for our moods and many of our actions. There is more bacterial DNA in our gut biome than human DNA in our entire bodies. An amazing eighty percent of our immune system lies in our gut, which is pretty crazy when you think about it. It's also the regulator for many important physiological functions.

When people first hear the word *gut*, they think of digestion and bowel movements, but it is so much more than that. The gut biome is the microflora, the balance of good and bad bacteria, in your intestinal tract that has the power to control and change how you feel and function throughout your day.

There's a lot of research coming out now about the connection between the gut and the brain, mental health, and wellness, and just how many hormones are produced in our gut. It's all tied back to, again, that balance of good and bad bacteria. More good bacteria and your mood will be better, and your body will flourish. Too much bad bacteria and you will have health and mental issues. That's how profound the impact of food is.

Therefore, it is important to feed the good bacteria with the right kind of foods, and starve the bad bacteria to keep them at bay. This helps you feel like you're thriving and not just surviving.

When she started, Carly used trial and error, adjusting her diet to see how she felt. It is important to note that everyone is different: some foods that you may perceive as healthy and that your body and gut tolerates may not react the same for someone else. Some who eat broccoli and other cruciferous vegetables may get inflamed and bloated after eating them. You may have an allergy or a sensitivity to certain foods. Others have no reaction like that at all. So listening to your body and the reaction after eating certain foods or experimenting via editing can be a big help. There are also fairly inexpensive gut biome tests. Getting tested can determine precisely which foods fuel the good bacteria and help you avoid viruses and foods that fuel bad bacteria, which may have blossomed in your gut biome.

It's important to note, too, that our gut microbiome is always changing. So when you do gut biome testing, it's important to continue to do them over time, because the flora is always changing, which means the balance you need is always changing as well. What worked for you two years ago might need to be adapted a little bit two years later. If you are someone that really likes to dive into the testing and increase your knowledge in that way, keeping up with it is a really great way to fine-tune your health from the inside out.

Although each of us is unique, there are a couple of general food groups that are typically good for optimal gut health. First, fermented probiotic foods like yogurt, kimchi, sauerkraut, and probiotics can help. Second, miso soup and prebiotic foods like artichokes that are full of fiber can also be of benefit. Finally, get back to the basics, and make sure you are getting a variety of food by "eating the rainbow."

Diversity

The bottom line is that you shouldn't feel like you have to eat something just because you know it's good for you. Just because it's categorized as "good for you" doesn't mean it actually is. You may get brain fog by eating cashews, or bloat from broccoli. Instead, get in tune with your body and how it's reacting to specific foods, so that you can find what works well for you.

It's easy to get stuck in a rut, eating the same foods all the time—especially if it's just you at home. Maybe you're an empty nester, or maybe it was your loved one that passed away that used to do the cooking. Maybe your kids are out of the house, or you never had kids. So it's just you at home. It's really easy to get stuck in the same patterns, eating the same thing over and over. You might also feel pressure to make different kinds of food, but when you are alone, one person can only eat so much. As a result, a bunch of the food goes to waste at the end of the week.

Eating different colors is the key. When you're at the grocery store stocking up on fruit and vegetables, pick foods of different colors to get variety.

Or maybe you're switching up what you get week to week, so instead of focusing on getting variety daily, just focus on getting variety over the weeks moving forward. If you got a handful of fruit this week, maybe get a different fruit the next week, and switch it up that way. If you are going out to eat, try a "build your own bowl" place. That's a great way to find healthier options and get a good variety in your diet.

Back to the Basics

But most importantly, just get back to the basics by buying unprocessed foods, focusing on those whole nutrients. That is going to be the biggest game changer. Carly likes to switch it up with changing the ingredients in her daily smoothie. Smoothies are a great way to get a complete healthy meal on the go. They're easy to digest because the blender has already done some of the work for you. Carly uses handfuls of greens, and then switches up the fruit and proteins, whether with yogurt or a clean protein powder. She likes to switch up healthy fats as well. She always keeps a couple of different nut butters on hand, like almond butter or cashew butter. You can put a little bit of avocado in there too or some cinnamon. This is a great way to switch up your nutrients and an insurance policy to make sure that you're getting a balanced and complete meal.

If you find yourself short on time and energy at the end of the day, you can leverage prepared meal options to fill in the gaps of those times where you're feeling like you're behind. She would not necessarily recommend relying on all prepared food as your store of energy every day, but would definitely keep a handful of nutritious and fresh options on hand to alleviate some of that pressure, and the feeling like you have to make everything from scratch at home in order to be healthy throughout the week.

Changing your diet shifts mindfulness. In fact, the practice of cooking is an active form of meditation. This is good news for those that struggle with traditional forms of meditation. Sitting somewhere for ten to twenty minutes with no stimulation is difficult for many. Sometimes you're not able to fit that into your day, but creating space for cooking produces a delicious meal that does not have to be complicated.

When you have kids at home, it's really important to pass on the cooking habit to them, and connect with them around the table. Many of Carly's best memories were times spent cooking in the kitchen with her mom, and the many nights they spent sitting around the table and talking. It didn't have to be complicated. Their recipes could be simple and semi-home-made, but their connection with each other, and that space outside of the busyness of the day was (and still is) a great way to connect with those that you love—friends or family.

Small Steps

A focus on food and developing good cooking habits can go a long way to overall good health.

The lemon water habit is a good one. You get dehydrated overnight, and that lemon water helps wake up our digestive system. It's even better if it's a little warm. Detoxing naturally from the get-go is a great way to start the day.

Making a small dietary change and positive habit like using lemon water in the morning is a really great way to set your day up for success. Once we get going into our activities throughout the day, it's really hard to divert the other way and then make positive change. Making positive change from the start makes everything else throughout your day feel that much more smooth and fluid.

Some substances need to be used with moderation to maintain good health. You can really get a lot of positive benefits from reducing or eliminating alcohol from your diet. Too much coffee and caffeine also does a number on the body as a whole, and the adrenal system specifically. You are already likely fatigued from chronic stress, so when you reinforce that stress with a significant amount of caffeine, your body's never able to settle. It's not good for you to drink a lot of coffee over the long term. Reducing or cutting out caffeine can be a really great way to realign and reset your baseline in moving forward.

At one point, Carly tried using a healthy fat in her coffee (like medium chain triglyceride [MCT] oil). After blending, it's creamy and frothy and delicious. However, every time Carly used it, she got a really bad headache. Tom, on the other hand, calls it his secret elixir, and finds it very helpful. He uses just a few drops in his tea. What works for one person might not work for the next.

But that aside, MCT oil is essentially a saturated fat. When we think of saturated fat, we often think of unhealthy fat, but MCT is a medium chain triglyceride, which is different from short chain triglycerides (the saturated fat we get from animals and the ones we want to watch and reduce in our diet).

People often think that to promote weight loss, they need to cut out fat from their diet. That's not the case. Fat can actually help you burn fat. Getting a little bit of fat throughout your day is really critical for your overall health and well-being. So it's not surprising that some people experience these positive benefits from putting MCT in multiple cups of tea throughout the day.

Many people that are trying to lose weight are choosing intermittent fasting nowadays. Out of all of the different dietary theories out there, intermittent fasting is one of the better ones. It's not necessarily controlling what you're eating, it's controlling when you're eating and giving yourself boundaries around that. With her clients focused on weight loss, she suggests doing this, and they're really successful. It's more sustainable than trying to follow a specific diet.

Being in Tune with Your Body

Only eating when you're hungry is a great way of being connected with your body. Nourishing it when it needs that nourishment is key. However, grief depresses the appetite. So there may be times where you don't feel like eating, but you probably *should* because you need energy to keep going. Other times, people stress eat in their grief.

Generally speaking, being in tune with your body and listening to it, and eating when you're hungry, stopping when you're full as well as eating more slowly, chewing your food, putting your fork down in between bites: all of this can lead to mindfulness around food and your diet and your habits throughout the day.

The point is that you find a healthy diet that is sustainable and makes you feel good. Keto is essentially a very high fat, very low carb diet with moderate protein. The goal is to get your body into ketosis which forces your body to burn stored fat. Many derive a lot of benefits from it.

Originally created for epilepsy patients, it helped reduce the amount of seizures they were experiencing throughout the day. However, it is very challenging for the average person to get into, and stay in, ketosis. And if you're not in ketosis, then you're essentially just eating too many high fat foods which means you're not getting the benefit of burning fat as fuel, and you're still burning carbohydrates. On top of that, you are also getting a lot of fat, perhaps too much, into your diet. So if you're going to do it, just make sure you're setting yourself up for success. There's different testing strips you can use to gauge if you're really in ketosis.

One friend who tried a ketogenic diet was eating ground beef, spaghetti sauce, and cheese at nearly every meal. Where are the vitamins and minerals and nutrients in that? It worked for him because it got him into ketosis, but that's not necessarily going to be healthy for you long-term, or even short-term for that matter. Focusing not just on the numbers, but the quality of the food, is essential.

Calories

With regard to the whole calorie thing, you need to maintain a balance between paying attention to overall calorie count and being mindful of what those calories consist of. Not every calorie is equal. You're going to feel significantly different if you eat a bagel rather than a scrambled egg. They both have about the same 300 or so calories but completely different nutrients, obviously.

Really paying attention to the quality of those calories and leaning into the more whole, unprocessed, variety of colors and foods is going to help your body feel like it's thriving and not just surviving from one day to the next.

It's also important to not look at supplements as a golden ticket to a healthy diet. They are meant to back up your diet—like an insurance policy. So you can't have a green superfood, drink some lemon water, and pop a vitamin once a day, and then eat fast food for the rest of your meals and think that you're going to be healthy and experience positive benefits.

First and foremost, focusing on a healthy diet, and then pulling in these supplements as reinforcement can be a really great way to elevate your health. Unfortunately, no matter how healthy our diet is these days, the quality of our soil and the way that produce is grown is not the same as it once was. So we're probably not getting all of the nutrients we need in our day anyway. So it is definitely a good thing to reinforce that with a multivitamin.

Carly takes a multivitamin, fish oil, and a probiotic. She uses a superfood green powder called Athletic Greens that she absolutely loves and uses more days than not. She has noticed a big difference in her energy levels when she takes these supplements compared to when she doesn't take them, so she's a big advocate for supplements. You can definitely go overboard with them, but incorporating supplements into your day to support a healthy diet and the habits that you're adopting can be a really great thing.

Gentleness

Being too strict and tough on yourself in regard to food is not a good idea though. It's a good thing to indulge in the foods you like from time to time. If your goal is perfection, that is unachievable. Seeking perfection brings disappointment and sets us up for failure. Allowing yourself moments of indulgence and enjoyment around food is really important. Shifting away from thinking of food as being good or bad is also important. Your focus should be, "What food is going to help me feel my best and nourish me?" Those are the foods you want to use more consistently.

Not looking at an indulgence as a bad thing helps break the cycle of the all-or-nothing dieting mindset so prevalent. If a food isn't going to make you feel your best, you allow for it once in a while. This shifting of your mindset allows for more freedom and sustainability in the changes you're looking to make. When you are already going through grief and trying to grow again, you should not beat yourself up over an indulgence or two. Try to not feel guilty over it. You can give yourself some grace, and not feed that cycle of negative thoughts. It's okay to have that cup of coffee, or that drink, or that ice cream, as long as, overall, you're making progress and improving.

Remember, taking control of your health is an ongoing process. There's really no finish line; there's no end goal. And it's going to change over time. There is no such thing as perfection, and there's always room for improvement. We all have ways that we can improve, no matter where we're at on our journey.

Carly likes to remind people of this anonymous quote: "Doing one thing for yourself today is better than yesterday, and that's going to get you closer to where you want to be tomorrow." We want that quick fix and overnight success, but this is not usually sustainable over time. Going at it more slowly and more patiently, and just doing what you can with where you're at, is the most important thing you can do for sustainable, healthy success.

DAVID + KOOKIE

Becoming 2.0: Growing through the Grieving Process

LOVE ALWAYS PROTECTS, ALWAYS TRUSTS, ALWAYS HOPES, ALWAYS PERSEVERES. (1 CORINTHIANS 13:7)

BE AT PEACE WITH THE STRUGGLE; IT'S A PART OF THE PROCESS.... IF YOU PUSH IT AWAY AND RESIST ADDRESSING THE LOSS AND NAVIGATING THE GRIEF JOURNEY, IT JUST GETS WORSE. —DAVID BROCK

David Brock is a successful sales and marketing consultant, and a widower of two and a half years, having lost his wife Kookie (pronounced Cookie) of thirty-eight years in 2020.

Their Business World

David and Kookie first met at IBM in New York City. David was hired to sell mainframe computers, and came in as this cocky, young recent graduate with a decided California attitude into a New York office. Kookie had been selling computers for a number of years, and was one of IBM's top five salespeople in the world. So, everybody in the office was kind of looking at David, and thinking, *Who the hell is this guy?* He dressed a little bit flashy then, rather than wearing pinstripes which the bankers they sold to anticipated.

After about six months, through luck, David happened to close a really big deal for IBM. You typically went through about an eighteen-month onboarding program and weren't put on quota until after that, so David just fell into a good situation. Kookie took note of this early success, and they started socializing in the group.

At one point, Kookie and a number of the married women in the office said, "Dave, we need to set you up." For a couple of years, they kept trying. They'd say, "You're Californian, so let's find a blonde, blue-eyed woman for you." They kept setting him up and it failed. It failed and failed and failed. Finally Kookie took pity on him.

Their marriage was built around their professional lives. They had no children. Everybody—customers and those in the workplace alike—loved Kookie.

Once a senior manager told her she had to change her business cards. Kookie (as a name) is undistinguished for selling multimillion dollar computers. They wanted her to use her given name, Ann Marie, but she said, "No, everybody knows me as Kookie!" The man replied, "No, no, no, you must change your business card." "Okay," she answered. "I'll take care of it"

A week later, the Chairman of the Board of IBM got a call from Jack Welch, David Rockefeller, and Edmond J. Safra. Each asked the same question: What's happened to Kookie? And just like that she went back to her old business cards. She was almost a force of nature; people just loved her and gravitated towards her.

As she built her career, she was recruited away to another technology organization as a regional vice president of sales. At the time, David was going up the food chain and running parts of the business at IBM. When Kookie was recruited by a competitor, they had to figure out how to keep their relationship intact and communicate while they competed. What was considered out of bounds? What couldn't they talk about? It turned out that they talked about them anyway, but managed not to let that influence how they worked.

She had one account that was also David's responsibility. He told her that she could not tell him anything about it. He was going to have his team compete against her and beat the crap out of her, he told her. She said, "You know I'm the best salesperson in the world, so good luck with that." At one point, she worked for Wang Labs, which was, at the time, one of the fastest growing computer companies around, but it hit a peak and started plummeting soon after.

At the time, David was being recruited away from IBM to be the EVP of sales for a technology company on the West Coast. Kookie was working for a guy named John Chambers, who went on to run Cisco. One day, John said, "Kookie, you gotta lay off 130 salespeople in the region." She was trying to figure out what she wanted to do, and if she and David were moving to the Northwest. John had offered her a job as an RVP there. She went back to John, and said, "John, I have always overachieved my objectives, so I'm not laying off 130. I'm laying off 131, and here's my resignation."

A New Vocation

She had always dreamed of becoming a professional chef, and she took this move as a way to do that, so she completed a three-year program at the Culinary Institute of America and became a professional chef. She then started a catering business.

Kookie was amazing. She moved into managerial roles usually reserved for men and was an inspiration and a mentor. She had high expectations of everybody, but really deeply cared. When she left and became a professional chef, people who worked for her in sales often called for her advice.

Some of them went on to be VPs of big organizations themselves, but they still called Kookie for mentoring and ideas. She listened really well. She cared and was wickedly smart. David has had many conversations with people who worked for her in the past, and they always bring up that deal or a situation where she helped.

Their Last Three Years

Kookie passed away on January 14, 2020. They had just celebrated their thirtieth wedding anniversary on the day she went into the hospital. They had planned on a fancy dinner, but Kookie wasn't doing well, so they ended up in the hospital instead. Over the previous three years, she had struggled with cancer, so they went through that roller coaster experience.

At first, Kookie went through radiation and chemo, and they were reasonably optimistic with the results. So were the doctors. Unfortunately there was a recurrence. And again, the doctors thought they could save her life and have it go into remission. About six months before she passed away, the tune dramatically changed, and they said, they could only try to extend her life.

So the last three years were difficult for them, emotionally and physically. She was always quite an active person, but now she was on oxygen and carrying around an oxygen machine. She was a huge golfer, but no longer had the physical capability to participate, even though everybody was so accommodating, saying they'd put the oxygen machine on the golf cart, and all those sorts of things.

She just didn't have the energy to do that. So, she went from being tremendously outgoing, active, and social to becoming increasingly isolated. Friends visited and came over, but you could tell that that, emotionally, it was devastating.

Being heavy type-A people, Kookie and David approached cancer as though there was no problem they could not solve. It went with their chosen profession. So they spent all sorts of time doing research and talking to different people and saying, through sheer force of willpower, that they could solve this problem. Unfortunately, this was something they couldn't change. It was a real struggle for David from a mindset perspective. He'd been involved in really complex, difficult business situations, and most of the time, had prevailed. But he couldn't do anything about this. Coming to accept this was a challenge, and he's still not sure he dealt with it well today.

As he accepted it, he'd also find himself checking out yet another study and wonder about trying new tests. Over and over again, he did that, and finally Kookie said, "Dave, stop doing that." She was amazing, particularly those last six months, as she managed it in a much better fashion than David felt capable of doing. She had accepted. He continued to fight for healing.

David tended to travel a huge amount, but he stopped, and began doing a lot remotely. Through his clients, he began learning about the goodness of human beings. He didn't publicize what was going on, but usually the sponsor was a CEO or EVP of sales, so he'd explain his situation and they'd set up meetings remotely. They'd often respond with, "Dave, whatever you need." The way people acknowledged his circumstance helped him a lot through the struggle.

And he's still struggling. In the last few months, and particularly the six or seven months that followed, he kept himself busy. He went through the motions but knew he wasn't 100%. He was easily distracted.

Kookie passed away a couple of months before COVID-19 hit, and those changes and the isolation that followed shut down his inclination to travel more, be more engaged in business, and get out and do things for the distraction. All of a sudden, life shut down. He couldn't do those things, not even church. He was alone in his house with no friends or community groups that he could see. Even working out at the gym was no longer an option; it all shut down. When he needed to be engaged and involved with people most, he could not.

Isolation

Digital interaction was not the same. That human touch wasn't there, so he had lost his wife, and then also lost much of the resources needed to recover from it at the same time. When you are grieving, there's a tendency to shut down. But that's probably not the right thing to do.

However, the restrictions of COVID-19 forced him into that. That left him looking for alternative ways to get past and beyond it. Once again, the goodness of people blessed David.

Folks came out of the woodwork. Good friends changed the conversations they had with him. People who had gone through similar situations called and said, "Dave, I just want to let you know I'm here. I'm going through the same thing you are. Anytime you need help, just give me a call." To know that there are people that are thinking about you and praying for you is really special.

Being isolated and a heavy type-A person, David threw himself into activity. Some of it was meaningless activity, but it was activity. They lived in a home in southern California overlooking the water for eighteen years. Kookie had found the place, and made it their home. After she passed away, David felt like a foreigner there.

He sold it immediately, and it sold very quickly. Unfortunately, the day they closed was the day the real estate industry in California shut down because of COVID-19. He had been planning to move to northern California, but was told that he would not be able to see any real estate because a house had to be empty for him to look at it. Dave told them he'd pay the people to go to Starbucks or McDonald's for a half hour so he could see one.

They said it would take him nine months to find a house. David had a friend who had a house he couldn't sell in Lake Tahoe, so David leased it for a year, and spent a year up there, just camping out. The setting difference was good for him. His old house was full of memories everywhere he turned, twenty-four hours a day, so this was a good change. In time, he bought a house in northern California, where he still lives now.

During their relationship, David and Kookie had collected all sorts of things. He still has their collections, but now they're in a different context. He can remember the fun of collecting and doing those things without getting hung up on the emptiness of the old home.

Moving

It's true that psychologists recommend not making big decisions after a trauma because your decision-making abilities might be clouded, and you might make a more emotional rather than logical choice. But for David, this was definitely the right choice. He has no regrets.

In hindsight, it might have been escaping, but it has worked out really well for him.

Everyone is different. This choice depends on each individual and their circumstances. Throughout David's professional career, he'd always traveled a huge amount, and he and Kookie moved often. They started out in New York City with a second home in Pennsylvania, and then moved to the west coast, and then back east again, bouncing around a number of times. Moving was something with which David was really familiar and comfortable, so it seemed the best thing for him.

Now he has a chess board and some other things around him. He and Kookie collected a certain kind of game board, and he has thirty-five of them scattered through this house. She collected kerosene lamps and he's got some of them too. He also has two pictures of really joyous times they had together that he displays, so he has been able to create a comfortable space that still has their collections and reflects Kookie, but is not overwhelming.

Smaller Steps

One thing David did was adopt little habits. Some may seem silly. He had been journaling for a number of years, but changed it in the evening to be a letter instead of a journal entry. Every evening they'd talk together about their day and their business. Even though Kookie moved to being a professional chef, her business mind never stopped. She was the chairwoman of their company, and she'd say, "As the Chairperson of the company, we have to forecast how much money is coming in, and what I could spend this year...." So they always talked about their days, their professions, her clients, some menus that she was doing, what David was working on, and so on. They did this every evening. So now, David has those conversations with her by writing her letters in his journal.

It was also good to get out into the natural world. David couldn't ski because of a previous injury, but hiking and bicycling was a way of refreshing himself. Lake Tahoe was radically different from the masses and masses of people in southern California, even though they had lived in a beautiful area. Lake Tahoe offered lots of fresh air and less people.

He did have some family close by he could visit. He knew a kind lady who'd gone through breast cancer, and had been a coach and a confidant of Kookie's to talk to as she lived close by. He was able to stay connected with her and other people who cared.

As a fairly private person, David's natural inclination was to not talk about his loss and put a wall around it. He's not totally comfortable talking about it yet, but has become more so over time. He and Kookie used to have date nights every Friday. They'd go out to dinner and a movie or just dinner. After she passed, he wanted to continue that tradition, so he went to a movie. He chose the same seats they always sat in, but couldn't pay attention to the movie, because the seat next to him was empty. So he struggled doing some of those things, and finding new routines.

However, he has become much more comfortable being open about it. It took him a while to be able to talk.

One of the interesting things David has discovered was that a person who'd been a manager reporting to Kookie hadn't been aware that she had passed away. A mutual friend shared it with him, and he immediately called David. He was so embarrassed. He said he hadn't known and wished he had, and David could tell he was a little uncomfortable talking about it. This was about two years after Kookie passed away, and he hadn't known, and they had been close. He just didn't know how to approach that. Through that conversation, David actually found that he was more comfortable talking to him, and help-ing him become comfortable, and not embarrassed by it.

So he's more open to discussions, but sometimes still feels discomfort. He'd much rather talk about the future of sales. However, talking is therapeutic, and you can't keep it all bot-tled up inside of you.

David struggled most with unstructured time after losing Kookie. During the week, he lost himself in busyness. Friday and Saturday were more difficult. Those were the days they were together—going to theater, dinners, parties, or just seeing friends. He still struggles to fill his weekends. He tried com-peting in triathlons, but not very well. He'd always been phys-ically active and riding his bike. Swimming was a little bit of a problem though because all the pools were shut down during COVID-19, and he wasn't going to jump in Lake Tahoe in December!

So there were certain aspects of fitness that lapsed and he's trying to rebuild right now. He's not where he used to be, but he's two and a half years older than where he was before as well.

He just started something new with eating because he found he was only making easy things. Since Kookie had been a professional chef, dinners were simple but stunning. So, he took a recipe he knew was one of her favorites, and his goal each week is to create a meal on the weekend using that reci-pe. This way he could both remember her and have exquisite food at the same time. He hasn't managed to replicate the way Kookie mixed flavors quite as well though. She had such sub-tlety and depth in the flavors. So David has literally hundreds of recipes. He's even making dinner for new neighbors using one of her recipes. The recipes are a small part of Kookie and a great way for him to continue to celebrate their relationship.

David has yet to date at all. Kookie made him promise that he would go out, and that if he found somebody to marry again, to do so. He hasn't, partly because of still emerging from

COVID-19, and partly because he's in a new community and slowly getting to know his neighbors. He is doing things again though in the community center there. He's signed up for evening classes as a way to perhaps meet people.

However, he was awkward at dating when he was young, much less now. If you remember his story, it was Kookie that finally put David out of his misery way back when. He's trying to figure out how to go about that. Thinking about dating sites, he's not sure he really wants to sign up for one. How does a person meet people? He's not sure.

He met Kookie through work and friends, and the thought of dating sites, or hanging out at bars again doesn't seem like an option, especially with his track record of miserable failure. Perhaps he'll find someone in a more organic route. He started doing yoga and some tai chi, and also works out at the gym. Friends keep an eye out for him, and hopefully he won't struggle as much as he did in his youth!

In the end, David thinks it's best to be at peace with his struggle. It's part of the process. If he pushes it away and resists addressing his loss and navigating his grief, it just gets worse. Meanwhile, it's amazing how much you discover about yourself and the relationship through conversations with other people, so just be at peace with the grieving process and the journey.

Home Alone: Addressing Ghosts, Sleeplessness, and Potential Moves

THEREFORE DO NOT WORRY ABOUT TOMORROW, FOR TOMORROW WILL WORRY ABOUT ITSELF. EACH DAY HAS ENOUGH TROUBLE OF ITS OWN. (MATTHEW 6:34)

YOU ALSO REALIZE THAT ALL THE THINGS THAT TRULY MATTER, BEAUTY, LOVE, CREATIVITY, JOY, AND INNER PEACE, ARISE FROM BEYOND THE MIND. —ECKHART TOLLE, *THE POWER OF NOW: A GUIDE TO SPIRITUAL ENLIGHTENMENT* [10]

LET THE PAST SLEEP, BUT LET IT SLEEP IN THE SWEET EMBRACE OF CHRIST, AND LET US GO INTO THE INVINCIBLE FUTURE WITH HIM. —OSWALD CHAMBERS, *MY UTMOST FOR HIS HIGHEST*[11]

Many loved ones pass away at home. Each of the widowers in Tom's group viewed this as an incredible gift—to know their wives were comfortable in the home they had created surrounded by family and enveloped in love. However, after a few weeks, every one hit a point in which that became an issue. The ghosts remained, especially when they were home alone.

---

10 Eckhart Tolle, "A Quote by Eckhart Tolle," Goodreads (Goodreads), accessed March 30, 2023, https://www.goodreads.com/quotes/69994-all-the-things-that-truly-matter-beauty-love-creativity-joy.

11 Oswald Chambers, *My Utmost for His Highest: Selections for Every Day* (Grand Rapids, MI: Discovery House Publishers, 1995).

Ghosts in the Machine

For Tom, ghosts were a good description of what remained. Or at least this was the story his fragile mind told him. Three precious ceramic hearts he and Judy collected over the years had fallen off the walls at different times. Over a couple of months following her passing, one by one, they fell. One for each of them who remained behind.

In the rest of the home, lights flickered, alarm systems screamed. Tom struggled with these perceived hauntings, and couldn't bear to enter the room where Judy had passed for months.

Was his home haunted? That was not his core belief, but there were enough oddities to make him uncomfortable in the one place he needed rest: the place that he relied on as his sanctuary from the stress of business and the world. It was not so peaceful anymore. Even though Tom knew God was governing his life, he still felt unsettled.

He had to change his environment, so he waited until after Judy's celebration of life ceremony, and then asked her sister, Jean, to go through her things and donate much of it. They kept a few special dresses, sweaters, and outfits that Jean knew Tom's daughters would wear along with jewelry and keepsakes, and put them into a closet dedicated to Judy's memory. Today, Tom has great peace and absolutely loves the fact that his girls can share in "Mom's Closet" and often sees one of them in one of Judy's sweaters or shirts. He loves that they are wearing a Mom memory proudly.

This process doesn't have to happen swiftly. Other may take much more time. It's important that you don't go overboard, but approach this process logically. Acting too quickly could lead to regret for some of the key items you later realize you should have kept.

It may be better to wait a little longer to decide what you keep and what you donate. The word *decide* comes from the Latin *dēcīdere* which means to cut off. So to decide means to cut off, and although some serious change was in order, Tom wasn't quite ready to cut off everything in regard to Judy's memory and the few items left behind. For Tom, having her items sorted by a third party and storing those they kept in a special closet, slightly removed from his living space, was healing.

Moving? Sometimes Sorting Might Not Be Enough

Joey admitted that he was having significant trouble even being in his home at all. His girls were off at school and despite the amazing memories the home held, seeing the pictures, clothes, and everything left behind just as it was when she passed, caused sadness.

As a result, Joey did everything he could to get away which minimized his time alone at home. He was out and about town as much as possible: at the gym, coffee shop, spin class, dinner with friends. He traveled to see his girls at school, and visited with friends for long weekends in St. Petersburg or Miami. Anywhere but home alone. Every time he returned, it was too much for him to bear.

Some suggested selling his house, but Joey wanted to keep it. They had raised their two girls and shared so many good times in their house. He didn't want to move away from these memories, wanting to stay connected to his late wife and the thirty years they spent building a life together as long as possible. He also knew that over time, this overwhelming sadness would give way to the happy memories and the positive.

Most of all, Joey knew that making big decisions when you are under the stress and anxiety of loss, the victim of an amygdala hijack, wasn't wise. Heck, for many in the initial stages of grief, making any decision was a struggle. So any big decisions should be postponed, and when made, deliberated over extensively, much more than you would have in the past. The key when under the stress and anxiety of loss is to *slow all your decisions* down dramatically. Postponing and delaying gives your brain a chance to calm down. You need to think effectively and make wise choices.

According to the folks at verywellmind.com, it is often recommended to wait six months before making any major, life-altering decisions which can include: buying or selling a home, eliminating memories or possessions of the deceased person, quitting one's job, moving in with family, loaning money out, or even making major investments.[12] Joey knew that making any rash decisions, like selling his home and moving away, would not be wise, so he stayed put.

Sleepless in Sadness

One thing many widower brothers had in common with being in their homes was struggling to sleep. Tom woke every morning at two a.m., coinciding with the time of Judy's passing, and then struggled to get back to sleep. When he began monitoring his sleep, he found he was extremely sleep deprived. His workouts were intense, and his sleep interrupted, but it was recommended that he get nine hours of sleep or more, just to get him into a somewhat optimal level of recovery. He hadn't really needed a monitor to know he was tired, as he yawned way too often during the day, had trouble keeping his eyes open most afternoons, and was more irritable than usual (which was scary on top of his normal crankiness).

---

12   Chris Raymond, "Why You Should Avoid Making Big Decisions after Experiencing a Death," Verywell Mind (Verywell Mind, July 21, 2020), https://www.verywellmind.com/decisions-to-delay-if-youre-grieving-4065127.

Tom wasn't alone. Joey spoke about how little sleep he was getting and how he also woke up several times during the night with his head spinning with thoughts. This was impacting him daily as well.

Some Practical Advice

Sleep deprivation, even over a relatively short period, can result in some serious issues, including obesity, depression, and suppressed immunity. Less than normal sleep over a period of time can wreak havoc on hormone production, suppressing growth hormones and testosterone and increasing the release of additional stress hormones, such as norepinephrine and cortisol.

Already compromised, decision-making can be affected. Sleep deprivation can degrade neocortex function, affecting logical decision-making, judgment, and discernment, and causes the amygdala to boost emotions like fear, anxiety, and irritability. A lack of sleep has also been tied with memory challenges and learning barriers.[13]

Chronic lack of sleep can add up to serious health impacts, with a higher incidence of high blood pressure, diabetes, heart attack, heart failure, or stroke. Add genetics to that and many in Tom's group had reason for concern.

So how do you get better sleep? These are the tips Tom and his group came up with:

- Get to bed earlier: When an early wakeup call for working out, walking the dog, or working looms each morning, sleep is cut short. If you don't get to bed early enough, you don't have a chance to get the sleep needed. Tom's friends make fun of his regular schedule

---

13   Eric Suni and Nilong Nyas, "How Does Lack of Sleep Affect Cognitive Impairment?," Sleep Foundation, February 6, 2023, https://www. sleepfoundation.org/sleep-deprivation/lack-of-sleep-and-cognitive-impairment.

of "early bird" dinners that get him in bed before ten, but they've helped him get better sleep.

- Ditch the caffeine: In his book *Caffeine*, Michael Pollan indicates that more than ninety percent of Americans drink caffeine in coffee, soft drinks, and more. As it's a positive boost to your nervous system, it can help you early in the morning, but drinking caffeine into the afternoon (anything after three) can start impacting sleep.[14] One study indicated that consuming caffeine six hours before bed significantly worsened sleep quality.[15]

- Dim the lights: Artificial ambient light can disturb your circadian rhythms, making us think nighttime is day. Think about that streetlight coming through the blinds or a nightlight that's always on. To maintain deep sleep, your bedroom should be as dark as possible. This means using a motion sensor night light and covering windows, so outside light doesn't disturb you. Blackout shades and drapes help. Some even cover up power indicators to further ensure a dark environment.

- Get off the devices and turn off the TV: Blue light from phones and TV impact your circadian rhythm more strongly than ambient light does, making us think nighttime is day, and affecting the brain's ability to know when it's time to sleep. Aside from the light,

---

14   Terry Gross, "Michael Pollan Explains Caffeine Cravings (and Why You Don't Have to Quit)," NPR (NPR, February 10, 2020), https://www.npr.org/sections/health-shots/2020/02/10/803394030/michael-pollan-explains-caffeine-cravings-and-why-you-dont-have-to-quit.

15   "Sleep and Caffeine," Sleep Education, October 6, 2022, https://sleepeducation.org/sleep-caffeine/#:~:text=Caffeine%20also%20can%20reduce%20the,sleep%20time%20by%201%20hour.

the content from any of those quarters is not going to prepare you for sleep. That requires relaxation.

- Don't eat too late: When your body digests food, the blood flow to the digestive system is maximized, leading to less blood to the brain. Deep sleep needs that blood to flush the brain, and you will not get this important cleansing when you eat dinner late or snack before bedtime. Additionally, drinking a lot before bed will guarantee that you wake in the middle of the night for a bathroom run.

- Exercise to fatigue: The value of exercise is obvious, but timing is also a factor. When Tom worked out earlier in the day or early evening, his body was exhausted and his mind clear and quiet, which made it easier to sleep. However, working out too late in the evening had the opposite effect, keeping him pumped up and unable to get to sleep earlier. Find your balance and timing so you sleep well and deeply.

- Calming your thoughts: Meditation can quiet the stress and anxiety in your heart and head—the factors that can make it hard to fall asleep or wake up partway through the night. Measured breathing helps quiet your mind while meditation can guide your meditative practice and boost its effectiveness.

- White noise: Ambient noise can be an issue, especially in more urban environments: sirens, cars racing by, airplanes overhead, animals outside—all of these can disrupt your sleep. White noise covers these sounds and sets the stage for sleeping. There are many choices out there that you can set for sleeping.

- Keep it cool: In warmer climates, it can be difficult to keep bedrooms cool enough for optimal sleep. In fact, one study indicated that bedroom temperature affected sleep quality more, while other studies indicated that increased body and bedroom temperature can decrease sleep quality and increase wakefulness. A rather cool 70°F (20°C) is reported as the comfortable temperature for the best sleep.[16]

- Boost the melatonin: Melatonin is produced in the brain and responsible for triggering sleep. Darkness prompts the pineal gland to start producing melatonin while light causes that production to stop, so you can think of melatonin as your internal light switch.[17] Stress can suppress melatonin production. You can take supplements to boost melatonin, or use them when you have trouble sleeping. However, there are side effects, so they should not be taken every day.
- Other natural ideas: Besides melatonin, there are many natural sleep aids and supplements:

  ○ Ginkgo biloba: A natural herb with many benefits, it may aid sleep, relaxation, and stress reduction, but the evidence is limited and it should not be taken along with nonsteroidal anti-inflammatory drugs (NSAIDs).[18]

  ○ Glycine: Studies show that taking 3-5 grams of the amino acid glycine can improve sleep quality.[19]

16   Edward C. Harding, Nicholas P. Franks, and William Wisden, "The Temperature Dependence of Sleep," Frontiers in neuroscience (U.S. National Library of Medicine, April 24, 2019), https://www.ncbi.nlm.nih.gov/pmc/articles/PMC6491889/.

17   Eric Suni and Alex Dimitriu, "Melatonin: An Overview," Sleep Foundation, March 10, 2023, https://www.sleepfoundation.org/melatonin#:~:text=Darkness%20prompts%20the%20pineal%20gland.

18   Tran Nguyen and Talal Alzahrani, "Ginkgo Biloba - Statpearls - NCBI Bookshelf," National Library of Medicine (National Center for Biotechnology Information, July 4, 2022), https://www.ncbi.nlm.nih.gov/books/NBK541024/.

19   Nobuhiro Kawai et al., "The Sleep-Promoting and Hypothermic

- ○ Valerian root: Several studies suggest that valerian can help you fall asleep and improve sleep quality, but should not be taken along with other medicines that reduce stress, anxiety, or depression.[20]
- ○ Magnesium: Responsible for over 300 reactions within your body, magnesium can improve relaxation and enhance sleep quality.[21]
- ○ L-theanine: An amino acid, L-theanine found in green, black, and white tea and can improve relaxation and in so doing, impact sleep.[22]
- ○ Lavender: A powerful herb with multiple benefits, oral lavender oil can calm anxiety and agitation. It can be used in many ways, including in a diffuser.[23]

Of course, there are a host of pharmaceutical options as well, including diphenhydramine, alprazolam, and many, many

---

Effects of Glycine Are Mediated by NMDA Receptors in the Suprachiasmatic Nucleus," Neuropsychopharmacology : official publication of the American College of Neuropsychopharmacology (U.S. National Library of Medicine, May 2015), https://www.ncbi.nlm.nih.gov/pmc/articles/PMC4397399/.

20 Jay Summer and Abhinav Singh, "Valerian Root: Sleep Benefits and Side Effects," Sleep Foundation, March 17, 2023, https://www.sleepfoundation.org/sleep-aids/valerian-root#:~:text=After%20analyzing%2060%20research%20studies,in%20a%20deep%20sleep%20stage.

21 "Office of Dietary Supplements - Magnesium," NIH Office of Dietary Supplements (U.S. Department of Health and Human Services), accessed April 2, 2023, https://ods.od.nih.gov/factsheets/Magnesium-HealthProfessional/.

22 Jay Summer, "L-Theanine for Sleep," ed. Anis Rehman, Sleep Foundation, March 3, 2023, https://www.sleepfoundation.org/sleep-aids/l-theanine-for-sleep.

23 Peir Hossein Koulivand, Maryam Khaleghi Ghadiri, and Ali Gorji, "Lavender and the Nervous System," Evidence-based complementary and alternative medicine : eCAM (U.S. National Library of Medicine, 2013), https://www.ncbi.nlm.nih.gov/pmc/articles/PMC3612440/.

others. However, it might be best to stay away from them until you have exhausted the more natural methods first. Unfortunately, many physicians don't even discuss the natural remedies because taking a pill is easier than slowly adjusting herbal dosages and changing a behavior. However, long-term behavioral change is a much better solution. Pharmaceutical options should *only* be used short-term to get through a here-and-now issue until you can find a natural and healthier one. There's no such thing as a free lunch. Each and every drug doctors offer has profound negative side effects to consider, and some are also addictive, making the risk outweigh the reward.

Alcohol is another common remedy. Initially its effect is to dull your senses and quiet your thoughts, possibly even help you get to sleep quicker, but it affects your sleep quality—in particular that deep sleep we need to recover. Additionally, it's a depressant, so it's a no-brainer that taking a depressant when you already feel depressed is not going to help in the long run.

"Alcohol may seem to be helping you to sleep, as it helps induce sleep, but overall it is more disruptive to sleep, particularly in the second half of the night," says researcher Irshaad Ebrahim. He is the medical director at The London Sleep Centre in the U.K. "Alcohol also suppresses breathing and can precipitate sleep apnea,"[24] (pauses in breathing that happen throughout the night). The more a person drinks before bed, the stronger the disruption. One to two standard drinks seem to have minimal effects on sleep, Ebrahim says.[25]

---

24   Denise Mann and Laura J. Martin, "Alcohol and a Good Night's Sleep Don't Mix," CBS News (CBS Interactive, January 23, 2013), https://www.cbsnews.com/boston/news/alcohol-and-a-good-nights-sleep-dont-mix/.

25   Ibid.

GROWTH THROUGH GRIEF

Sweet Dreams

Sleep, take me away
Into my dreamland

Beauty first met
Radiance shines
Broken, gone
Scars, healed

Clear my mind
Cleanse my sadness
Enrich my soul
Raise my spirit high.

Vision Journaling: Your New Story from the Future

MINDFULNESS NOT ONLY MAKES IT POSSIBLE TO SURVEY OUR INTERNAL LANDSCAPE WITH COMPASSION AND CURIOSITY BUT CAN ALSO ACTIVELY STEER US IN THE RIGHT DIRECTION FOR SELF-CARE. —BESSEL A. VAN DER KOLK, *THE BODY KEEPS THE SCORE: BRAIN, MIND, AND BODY IN THE HEALING OF TRAUMA*[26]

PEOPLE OFTEN SAY THAT MOTIVATION DOESN'T LAST. WELL, NEITHER DOES BATHING—THAT'S WHY WE RECOMMEND IT DAILY. —ZIG ZIGLAR[27]

PLEASURE IS ALWAYS DERIVED FROM SOMETHING OUTSIDE YOU, WHEREAS JOY ARISES FROM WITHIN. —ECKHART TOLLE, *THE POWER OF NOW: A GUIDE TO SPIRITUAL ENLIGHTENMENT*[28]

To help cement the growth you need, picture what the future will look like if you were able to solve the challenges you identified. What would the opposite of each challenge holding you back look like? How would you feel and act? What benefits would this have on your life?

---

26   Bessel A. van der Kolk, *The Body Keeps the Score: Brain, Mind, and Body in the Healing of Trauma* (New York: Penguin Books, 2014),285.

27   Zig Ziglar, "A Quote by Zig Ziglar," Goodreads (Goodreads), accessed April 2, 2023, https://www.goodreads.com/quotes/784099-people-often-say-motivation-doesn-t-last-neither-does-bathing-that-s-why.

28   Eckhart Tolle, "A Quote by Eckhart Tolle," Goodreads (Goodreads), accessed April 2, 2023, https://www.goodreads.com/quotes/70003-plea-sure-is-always-derived-from-something-outside-you-whereas-joy.

On a podcast recently, Jane McGonigal, a futurist, discussed how hard it can be to effect change. "The brain normally assumes things will continue as they are. But what that means is it can be very hard to wake up and realize this thing that used to be true is no longer true, or this assumption I had is no longer helpful."[29]

One of the ways she helps herself and others better imagine a new future is through "journaling from the future." What does that mean? We call it vision journaling. Put yourself some three to five years from now, and then write a journal entry about your life *at that time*.

McGonigal explained how important it is to provide details when you journal, covering as much as you think you would write about in the journal in the future as if it were today. This means being able to cover each of the challenges that are a priority from your assessment and your intention plans, documenting them in detail. Be sure to answer the *who, what, when, where, how* and *why* questions, writing each vision journal entry as a story. Embracing this technique has been very helpful to better envision and begin to effect change.

Cover each of these:

- What you are experiencing—doing, seeing and feeling
- Where you are living
- Where you are working
- What your relationships look like, with your sons and daughters, friends, and partner (if you have one)

Now it is time to elevate—taking mindful, deliberate, and consistent actions to bring about the change needed to obtain what you have envisioned.

---

29 Jane McGonigal, "Predict the Future, Feel Ready for Anything and Prepare for the World Ahead" podcast, Impact Theory, April 11, 2022, https://impacttheory.com/episode/jane-mcgonigal/.

Body: Food and Drink

When it comes to improving your body, there are several elements you may want to address as part of your overall growth journey, examining the assessment and the priority challenges you indicated. Everyone has their own set of challenges. Here's a list to consider, but keep in mind that they will not happen all at once or be the same for everyone.

- Drink a glass of lemon water to start each day to boost metabolism.
- Give up alcohol completely or cut back to only occasional usage.
- Abstain from mind-altering substances, so you are present and lucid throughout the growth process.
- Implement intermittent fasting, eating one or two meals in the afternoon and early evening.
- Eliminate red meat, relying instead on organic chicken for meat-based protein.
- Reduce carbohydrate and sugar consumption. Watch those simple carbs!
- Give up too much coffee and almost all caffeine, converting to tea instead.
- Eliminate all carbonated drinks (to reduce saturated sugar and carbonic acid intake, and including diet sodas and sparkling waters).
- Take a high-quality age appropriate multivitamin each day.
- Conduct a gut biome test to further refine diet to understand specifically what your gut needs to reinforce the good flora and inhibit bad bacteria, viruses, and more.
- Use probiotics designed specifically for your body.
- Eliminate foods from the corn and nightshade families.
- Use apple cider vinegar supplements after meals.

- Use a pre-testosterone supplement (not testosterone itself) like Nutragenix to aid in building muscle.
- Add MCT oil to your diet to boost brain health, reduce inflammation, metabolism, as well as satiate hunger between meals (but be careful of adding too much, especially if you have a family history of heart disease).
- If sleep is a problem, begin to explore natural remedies like lavender oil to help with that.

Body: Movement and Exercise

Every journey begins with a single step, and the key for many to successfully start a growth mindset is to physically get moving. This was essential to Tom's own journey, which started with that first walk in the park the morning after his wife passed. Physical forward movement has been shown to reduce the impact of anxiety and quell PTSD. Research reports that just thirty minutes or more of exercise a day for three to five days a week may significantly improve depression or anxiety symptoms by as much as twenty-five percent compared to those who are inactive.[30] Here are a few key elements that can improve the body:

- Start every day with a meditative walk, listening to devotionals and growth podcasts or practicing being very present in nature, using all five senses.
- Go to the gym each day to exercise.
- Execute aerobic exercise at least three days per week.
- Practice yoga to improve and maintain mobility at least three days per week.
- Practice measured breathing.

---

30 Matthew Pearce, "Association between Physical Activity and Risk of Depression," JAMA Psychiatry (JAMA Network, June 1, 2022), https:// jamanetwork.com/journals/jamapsychiatry/fullarticle/2790780.

Mind

The mind needs to be exercised as well as it shifts from sadness and loss to growth and purpose. If you work out your body, but don't change your mindset, you may continue to struggle with your journey, falling back and failing to maintain positive gains and effect change. Again, a journey begins with a single step—something easy and simple performed first thing in the morning and every day:

- Make your bed every day first thing.
- Boost quality sleep time by retiring earlier every evening and get plenty of sleep.
- Use white noise while sleeping.
- Be mindful about the first and last thing you look at, controlling what you see first and last each day.
- Journal positive affirmation each day in order to lessen the power of negative thoughts.
- Listen to growth podcasts or read books to be inspired by others and learn their secrets to growth, joy, and success.
- Work on writing and art or something creative every day.
- Shift your goals from work and making money to finding your purpose and enjoying the new journey you are on.
- Create space for deep, meditative thought (usually during morning walks and yoga practice).
- Nurture and exercise faith every day.

Begin Again? Dating after Loss with Helen Keeling-Neal

KNOWING WHERE AND WHO YOU ARE, IS WHAT POINTS YOU IN THE DIRECTION OF WHERE AND WITH WHOM YOU WANT TO GO.
—HELEN KEELING-NEAL

Society has certain expectations about the proper mourning period and when a widow or widower should start dating again. What is the right time? Well, the truth is that everyone is different, and went through a different process of losing their loved one.

Some went through a very long disease process and had a partner who was not the same for a long period of time before they died. They experienced a really long time in which they felt lonely. Those often want to date sooner because they are craving connection with somebody. Someone else who had a sudden loss might be different, and would likely take more time to get over that sudden loss. Regardless, everyone's different.

Making it more complex, there are social rules and norms, which are not clear about this. Then there are family rules, which are not clear either, so each person has to do what works for him or her. Some avoid the grief at that moment in time and immediately get into a relationship. The challenging piece about diving head first is that those feelings of grief don't go away. They just compartmentalize and they'll come up and bite them in the ass later.

It's not uncommon to want connection, to know that you're attractive to someone and someone's attracted to you. It's normal to crave sexual intimacy and all that goes with it. Very normal. Sometimes a person needs to get into a relationship right away and it becomes part of their story, so they can grow. It's best to stay away from judging a timeframe or a time window, because everybody is so individual, and everybody brings their own story.

And not just the story of the process of a loved one passing away. But the story before that: how they were raised, their attachment styles, as well as any earlier trauma. It really is an individual journey, for sure.

There is a need to practice dating, and the dating world has changed completely. There are so many different avenues now. There are websites, community groups, church groups, all kinds of avenues.

Nevertheless, it's not easy. You go out with a person that is not the one you know and love because they're gone now. Just doing this can trigger you emotionally. Helen went out to dinner with a guy, and they had a nice talk over a good meal. At the end of dinner, they sat in the car and he hugged her good-bye. She went home and cried for three days because he didn't smell like David. He had cologne on, but it was the "wrong" cologne. The second she smelled that cologne, her emotional brain was triggered. It could be the wrong clothes, the wrong smell.

Snakes in a Bucket

But that's part of the process. She needed to get out there, sniff the wrong cologne, cry for three days, and then pick herself up and get back out again. The truth is that if that grief is not expressed and released, it will compound. Then, if that relationship ends, you've got another compound grief situation—especially if the person doesn't want it to end.

People hear about anger, sadness, denial, bargaining, and acceptance, but you have to remember that they are not linear. They are like snakes in a basket. You put your hand in and you never know which one will strike next. Grief comes in pockets and pods of feelings. You can't plan for it. It doesn't work that way.

Some of the greatest healing can be done in current relationship, as long as you're with someone who can understand and hold space for it. You see this even with a relationship that ends. Usually you finish up with a piece of grief that continues into the new relationship because the new one kicks up the stuff that's connected to the old relationship and your past.

Grief is a lifetime thing. It does get easier and more manageable the further from the time of passing, but it is still there. It's gonna pop up. There are going to be times when you become painfully aware of the gap, like a big hole in that special occasion. There's no stopping that.

There are some things to watch out for though. Before you date, make sure that you're comfortable with being alone, so that you don't need someone. You don't want to be looking for external validation. That's a codependent, fawn mode behavior which tends to happen once grief sets in.

The work each person must do to get to this stage is different too. Some people (because of their attachment styles) will never, ever be able to be alone. That would take much deeper work. You're not just looking at the grief. You have to look at the whole person, including hurts from those formative childhood years and all the way to the present, and how that informs the grief process, attachment styles, and dating journey.

What Are You Looking For?

Being alone can be an issue as well. Helen took not being in a relationship to the extreme, and just dodged relationships for years. She would meet someone and before too long find a reason why it wasn't right. She became really good at not being in a relationship.

This facet of a person's "new" life begins with mindfulness. You are looking for alignment. To find alignment, you must be yourself, so you must do the work you need to be yourself first. You need to develop a healthy attachment and know who you are. You need to be comfortable within yourself to the best of your ability. For many, this requires understanding your attachment styles, and talking with a therapist helps a great deal.

As you find your new self, you can create a list of values that you have. It's not a checklist for your date. We're not talking about that. You want to go on a mission to find out who you are, and how that informs what you are looking for in someone else. That order is essential.

The order is essential. Don't make a list of what you want in a partner until you've looked at your own values and know who you are, and identified some of the areas that you may want to work on. You should not be expecting your partner to check off all the boxes, and certainly shouldn't be looking for someone to fix and fill the holes that you have in yourself.

Nobody in the present can fill an unmet need from the past. You're the only one that can work on, heal, and fill your own unmet needs. It won't ever work if you're just looking for someone to fill those needs, something they can never accomplish for you.

When you do meet someone, you must practice radical acceptance of who they are. You should never think: *Well, maybe over time, they will … go to church, join my gym, whatever.*

That's just going to build resentment over time for both of you. They're going to resent you for trying to control and manipulate change in them, and you are going to resent the fact that they're not changing quickly enough or in the way that you want them to change. That is just irrational across the board. Do not expect changes.

On the other hand, sometimes you can fool yourself, "looking for the pony in the pile of manure," when it really is manure all the way down. There's not always a pony.

Maya Angelou said, "If someone shows you who they are, believe them the first time and act accordingly."[31]

You do need to hold space and compassion for a person, but after a certain amount of time doing that, it really can be time to get out. You want to help people rise up, but not at the cost of settling for less because you're putting their care ahead of your own needs and space. So it's really important to find a balance and establish boundaries without abandoning or deprioritizing your own needs. Seeing the best in someone, (and ignoring the reality) is a form of toxic positivity, while liking someone with a plan to change them is manipulative and unhealthy.

The bottom line is that you are making these choices. And it's hard at best. Let's face it, dating is basically haphazard. There are friends trying to set you up with their friends. And all the pressure in that. Then there are dating apps, and anyone who's done that has some stories. Oh, and then there's the bar scene which has a lot of alcohol involved. If you're drinking, you're not dating that person; you're dating someone whose frontal cortex is already offline—as is yours. So neither of you are making healthy, mindful choices or decisions in that environment.

It takes time and trial and error, and the inward growth part is paramount. On Helen's second date, nearly a year later, as she was driving to the date, she got herself mentally married, divorced, and pissed off before she even met the guy because she had this long internal narrative—a story that sabotaged the date before it happened.

---

31 Maya Angelou, "Maya Angelou Quote in Oprah Interview," Facebook, accessed April 2, 2023, https://www.facebook.com/MayaAngelou/posts/when-someone-shows-you-who-they-are-believe-them-the-first-time-people-know-them/10161350302994796/.

Finding quality people (and you don't know what that is until you find them) requires spending time with them and figuring out who they are. George Carlin had this whole comedy routine about how for the first six months you're dating, the other person is a representative of themselves, rather than the actual person. So you want to make sure that you are as authentic as you can be early in that relationship. That doesn't mean you parade all your baggage, take it or leave it. You don't want to scare them away or find someone attracted to the baggage. You don't want to do that, so that needs to come out in bits and pieces. It's going to be a dating forensic investigation to get past the person's representative, and find out who your partner really is.

Therefore, it's incredibly important that you first know who *you* are and what *you want*. Is it quality time together? Is it touch and affirmation? Is it gifts? Knowing your love language as you go out and date, and learning your partner's love language, and sharing that information with each other is a good practice.[32] Maybe not at the first coffee, but early on. In fact, a coffee or tea meetup is a good way to begin to practice.

You'll have ones that you want to have end in an hour, and others that are amazing, and could be the beginning of a longer-term relationship. At the very least, you meet a new face, but you could make a friend.

Dating Apps

Using dating apps can feel really weird. It's an uncomfortable process and can feel shallow, like scrolling through a catalog. However, with healthy limits, boundaries, and zero expectations, it can be an adventure. You're practicing.

---

32 Gary Chapman, "What Are the 5 Love Languages?," Discover Your Love Language® - The 5 Love Languages®, accessed April 4, 2023, https://5lovelanguages.com/learn.

Many prefer organic connections best—meeting people via the coffee shop, attending an exercise group, like yoga, tai chi, or spin cycling. These environments enable you to meet people, become friends, and learn more about them to see if there might be something more there.

Churches can also be great. You can meet some great people at worship gatherings. Meetings surrounding your hobbies (painting, dance, pottery, writing, etc.), and even starting a new one are also options, as is taking classes (which are often free if you're over sixty) at a college in your area. These all have the benefit of putting people who are already aligned in some way together.

And then there are your helpful friends and the blind dates they recommend for you. This can feel pressured, but it can also be a wonderful way to connect because they come "vetted."

There's no perfect way.

Personality style is also a factor in this. Those who are more introverted aren't going to want to be in bigger social situations. When the male is supposed to engage in the conversation first, this can be difficult for someone who's introverted to initiate.

An introvert might find apps more comfortable. For those with time and location restraints, dating apps can be helpful as well. The point with the apps is to not overthink things. Just go for the coffee. Because then you'll know within an hour or less. Don't be afraid to practice the ways you find. And remember, it's just coffee, and even after the third date, you don't have to be thinking about the rest of your life. Don't have any agenda other than to enjoy a coffee.

You want to be just as authentic as you can. If you're nervous, just be nervous. Just be yourself.

On the other side, when a widower comes "on the market," so to speak, they're now "available." There are people who would like to date this person, so they make overtures to get to know them.

That can be a little complex.

Discretion and Vulnerability

There is a vulnerability that often comes with the loss. Right afterwards, I think widowers can be particularly vulnerable when someone comes in through the side door of caring and helping and nurturing. This may not necessarily be conscious on that person's part. They may feel like they are caring and nurturing, but on some level, they may also recognize that this is an eligible person that fits a criteria or a lifestyle or a connection that they're missing. This is especially true of those known for being affluent, and who are now, at the same time, particularly vulnerable.

You have to have a lot of discretion in choosing who you're going to get connected with, just to make sure it's done from a place of integrity. I think one of the big things you have to check is this: "What part of your body wants this relationship? Where is it based?" If the answer is: "Hey, I would like to have sex, I would like to be sexually intimate with someone, I crave that…." Recognize that as a normal, human (and wonderful) thing to have in one's life. So here is a woman that wants to be with you. That's very engaging, very attractive, and very validating for someone who may have been with someone who was ill and not able to engage in that way, or for one that has had their self-esteem knocked down as a result of going through a really difficult loss. It can feel good to be found attractive, right?

Be wary of setting up a relationship based on these elements and finding that the relationship doesn't have the substance of the legs to go along with it. That will cause you more pain in the end. There's a need for discussion when you meet someone and when you start dating. Not right away, because right away would just be weird, but there's a need for discussion on what you want. What are you looking for in a couple-ship? Are you looking for a friend to hang out with and go to the movies with and have sex with, or are you looking to really develop a couple-ship?

(This is where knowing who you are and what you want is very important, by the way.)

Take it really slow. Go on those coffee dates. Intentionally, don't immediately go out on a romantic dinner, where A can lead to B can lead to C. You want to talk to each other over time and develop the relationship. Take your time and get to know each other and decide what is best as you go. You are in the healing process.

In regard to sex, everyone has to figure that out in their own time. Putting it off might make your partner feel like they're not attractive, but that's an opportunity to work through that. Again, the best thing is to talk about it. Have those conversations. So however long you wait for that, you come up with that timeframe *together*.

Your goal is to get to know each other and be mindful about the process. It's kind of fun. Here you are in a situation that builds delayed gratification and when it happens, you're in it together, and you've already spent this time getting to know each other.

That's why conversation is so important. Also, when you have sex, you start to find out whether you're compatible there too, because that's a process too. Not everybody is sexually compatible.

Another frank conversation prior to sex is over testing for sexually transmitted diseases (STDs). If you're someone who carries the herpes virus, you want to be able to have that conversation with your partner early on, before you've been sexually intimate. And do it without shame. And it's very, very common. There isn't the shame stigma around it like there used to be. You also want to discuss protection, and discuss birth control. There are a number of widowers who are of the age where pregnancy could be an issue.

The bottom line is that you have to be responsible. You really do need to bring up those conversations. You must ask if a person has any STDs, and when they last got tested. All of those things are really important. You just need to be frank. Talk about your sexual health and wellness for you and your partner. Both people in the partnership are responsible for their own sexual wellness.

Our culture does not promote this, so it's not just awkward, it's exceptionally awkward. Uncomfortable or not, you have to sit down and say, "Hey, let's talk about STDs. I'll start. How's your coffee?" Just start from there, speak sort of lightly, and begin. If you're talking with someone who is unable or unwilling to have those conversations, that's a bit of a clue. (Uncomfortable is fine. Of course, they're going to be uncomfortable, aren't you?)

The fact is that if someone is not able to open up and talk freely about subjects that need to be discussed in relationships, they may not be able to communicate well enough for that level yet.

Don't back off. You can circle back around to it. Just don't do anything until there's been resolution and clear communication about it. Sexual health is not necessarily about being STD free. It's about communicating and protecting oneself and one's partner by communicating.

Communication requires transparency and honesty. Talking about all this spurs on all kinds of factors that surrounds the subject of sex in general. Everyone wants different levels of commitment and commitment styles. One couple may choose to be exclusive, and not date anybody else. They want a monogamous relationship. Another couple may make a different arrangement. You have to decide your commitment levels in little steps.

There's also a difference for those that may have lost a spouse, never had any children and want them (or have very young children), compared to someone whose kids are almost or already out of the nest, or one that doesn't have kids and doesn't want to have any. So one person may want to accelerate a little bit and want to be exclusive: get engaged, get married (or move in) sooner because they want to raise a family, or they want to have a family unit to raise their kids. While others are working with a completely different scenario.

Being on the same page with the one you're dating is very important. Be up front step by step, and don't leave the other person guessing. Don't expect them to read your mind. There's many resources about communication and commitment that can help too. Everyone needs time and space to grow into commitment. You may be ready for it, but they may need to do some personal work to become ready for it. And vice versa.

The Next Level

When you consider the "next level" of commitment, you're looking at things like going on vacation together. You know, who pays for it, and how would you do that? Do the kids go along (if there are kids)? If so, where do you go? And how many rooms do you get? And so on.

You've got to have conversations about that. What works when you're dealing with children who have lost a parent is really, really important, especially when you're doing something like a vacation or a family event for the first time together in this new format with a new person.

This can be a very difficult thing for children because they can feel a loss or an absence of Mom very keenly, so you want to be mindful about that too.

One of the concerns is that the kids feel like they can lose you to this other relationship or maybe to the other family.

It makes everything different. If the new relationship brings with it a blended family with other children, the firstborn in one family may now be second in a blended family. There's a complexity to that. Once again, therapy can be really helpful for the kids in this. Therapy for grieving children and family can normalize the future for the kids.

It's a good idea to do this even with dating. Having some family sessions, even though you're not technically married, gives you some resources and allows you to talk through some things, and this can help.

About a year and a half after David died, Helen had a relationship with someone that had children. She never forgot that day at the beach when the little boy came to her, saying he didn't know if his dad had told her but he was having some very big feelings about this. Helen sat in the water with him and listened, telling him it made sense that he had some big feelings about this. It was kind of hard for the boy, but it was really good that he was expressing how he felt. Helen was blessed that he felt comfortable enough and safe enough with her to tell her that.

You really need to spend that extra time and be aware that your children are going to have those feelings, even if they don't express them. You don't want to indulge a child's feelings, but neither should they be dismissed or overlooked. You have to find a balance, and every child is unique. It works on both ends of the spectrum.

Finances are another issue altogether. It's like you need a forensic analysis of the finances. If a woman is moving into a widower's house, what can she change in the house, so that it's going to feel like her home...? This really does warrant a lot of question-and-answer sessions to get down to it and figure it out. It's messy and quite difficult, and it can feel very complex and overwhelming, but that's just an indication to not jump at it.

Take some time to engage in diligent communication. If you have done that from the beginning, you've been building toward mutual agreement and alignment. That will never be total, but that's okay.

It's really good for a couple to sit down and talk about how finances were handled in previous relationships, whether widowed or divorced. What worked from that, and what didn't work from that? What do you want moving forward? And vice versa too. How are your finances handled now? What do you think you want moving forward? A certain amount of autonomy, and then a certain amount of combined resources? Just have that discussion. You might have someone who saves, and another who is like, *carpe diem*, let's buy a ticket to Italy. Everyone lives differently and handles money differently too.

When you come up to the marriage line, you want to know the person emotionally, physically, financially, and spiritually—in all those areas. Additionally, remember that if you're in a relationship with someone who has been through a divorce, there is grief there that can be very difficult too. Widows and widowers don't have a corner on the market on grief and loss.

There's a specific kind of grief and loss experienced through death, but there is also grief and loss and a whole bunch of stuff that goes along with divorce. You have to be very mindful of what's inside someone's head. It's complicated.

Remarrying is the next topic. Everyone wants to live "happily ever after" and have a prince/princess future. So who do you invite to the wedding? Do you invite your in-laws? It's complex in that sense, but if you make a decision to remarry, you want it to be fresh for you as a couple. You don't want to do anything that is the same as in the past on either side of the relationship. You want to craft something that works for you. Plan it so you can honestly giggle with joy about eating cake, and really have fun. You want to avoid stress, and just make it completely about the two of you.

Remarrying will affect your children too, and trigger grief for all of you. If the person you marry is divorced or lost a spouse, you're going to be thinking about your previous marriage, but you're also going to be thinking about them completely differently. So grief might pop up.

You're creating something special and unique going forward. You're not trying to recreate what you had before. You're creating new and different memories, and all your memories are important. Every family is different. Younger children may want a new father or mother figure long before you do, while teenagers are completely different. They usually do not take well to that. The whole thing can be very difficult.

It's also not healthy to carry on a long-term relationship that you already know is not going to progress. You are setting yourself and your family up for further loss in doing that. There's an added factor if you bring someone into your family when you're still connected with your in-laws. They can struggle with accepting someone new, a replacement, and that kicks up their grief and possibly resentment too. Your kids have lost a parent, and now they have you alone. Once another person enters the mix, they must share your time and potentially adjust to yet another person's children, who then get a part of you as well. So kids can be really upset about that time-split.

Children of all ages need the reassurance that you are their dad and they are your priority—and will stay your priority. Blended families can be really difficult. When one parent is deceased and the new one is divorced, that makes it really difficult because this person over here still has both parents, maybe just in different locations. So this person over here is sharing time with somebody who still has both parents. You must manage the perceptions and the expectations along the way, talking with the kids about it. You must constantly check in on them and help them normalize their feelings, but still make your decision as an adult. You can't let a raging fourteen-year-old dictate your life. Once again, communication is key.

One son flat out told his mother this: "I never want to see you with another man. You are not getting married or dating again." There's something to watch out for in this. Sometimes a parent enrolls their child in the emotional role of co-parent, like an emotional spouse. They try to meet their needs through that child. This can happen especially with teenagers because they like the responsibility; they like to step up and be in charge; they want to be in control.

Once that adolescent has been enrolled in that role (as the parent or the adult or the surrogate spouse), there's going to be a fracture. The best thing is for a teenager to date someone themselves, so they can gain some perspective on relationships themselves.

The bottom line on beginning to date again after losing your spouse is this: know yourself first. Because knowing where and who you are points you in the direction you want to go. Then, get to know your other person and *take your time* with it.

Ask the hard questions and have the difficult conversations, even if you're afraid that will push the other person away. Do it anyway. If it doesn't work out, you will have more opportunities. Lastly, only introduce people to your children and family when you're sure there's going to be some continuity. Don't do it quickly. You don't want a revolving door. You want to make sure that this is someone you're going to be with for a chunk of time and manage the kid's expectations before you take that step.

The Top 6 Dating Errors for Widowers

- Not doing the personal work you need first: know yourself and heal first.

- Not leaving the house and getting out there (groups of any kind: sharing, exercise, hobbies).
- Not using a dating app to expand horizons and practices.
- Not meeting enough different women to figure out what you are looking for.
- Introducing women to the kids too quickly.
- Accelerating in the relationship too quickly (exclusivity, moving in together, engagement, and remarrying).

Chapter 7

FAITH

A Walk in the Woods - Quiet Time for Connection, Communication, and Answers with Tom Pisello

IT IS ONE THING TO PROCESS MEMORIES OF TRAUMA, BUT IT IS AN ENTIRELY DIFFERENT MATTER TO CONFRONT THE INNER VOID —BESSEL A. VAN DER KOLK, *THE BODY KEEPS THE SCORE: BRAIN, MIND, AND BODY IN THE HEALING OF TRAUMA*[1]

CAST YOUR CARES ON THE LORD AND HE WILL SUSTAIN YOU. (PSALM 55:22A)

TRUST IN THE LORD WITH ALL YOUR HEART, AND DO NOT RELY ON YOUR OWN INSIGHT. IN ALL YOUR WAYS ACKNOWLEDGE HIM, AND HE WILL MAKE STRAIGHT YOUR PATHS. (PROVERBS 3:5–6 RSV)

BUT THOSE WHO HOPE IN THE LORD WILL RENEW THEIR STRENGTH. THEY WILL SOAR ON WINGS LIKE EAGLES; THEY WILL RUN AND NOT GROW WEARY, THEY WILL WALK AND NOT BE FAINT. (ISAIAH 40:31)

---

1   Bessel A. van der Kolk, *The Body Keeps the Score: Brain, Mind, and Body in the Healing of Trauma* (New York: Penguin Books, 2014), 298.

Tom was searching, and knew that if he was ever going to get where he wanted, he'd need to look somewhere new. He couldn't just work out more or listen to more podcasts and read more books. He needed to get outside his comfort zone.

His friend Chris, a newly minted pastor, was hosting a Christian men's retreat for a new ministry he was establishing. He'd only known Chris for a couple of months and had attended a few of his monthly home church events. Tom had no clue who else would be attending the retreat, and no idea what to expect as it was his first retreat ever.

What would he have to admit to and share with strangers? Would they understand where he was coming from and the pain and journey that brought him there? Would they "grade" his faith, or expose the many shortcomings in his beliefs and practice?

Somehow he overcame these fearful questions, to not only say yes, but be one of the first to commit to the retreat. From what he did know of Chris, he knew it would be well worth spending a long weekend with him and his group. So away he went—flying up to the North Carolina mountains to join Chris and four other men, who were there to help each other improve their relationships with Jesus.

The four other men, besides Chris and Tom, included Pastor Omar, who was taking time away from his flock just to support Chris; Jed, the owner of a well-established faith-based retreat property called Strange Farms in the Atlanta area; Todd, a businessman who was so committed to his faith that he had bought the North Carolina property and cabin just to host such events (and who Tom had worked with thirty years before, but didn't recognize right away); and Chris's brother, Michael, who like Tom was young in his spiritual journey, but really committed to overcoming life's struggles and growing in his faith. Thank goodness for Michael, as he also became Tom's fishing partner for much of the weekend.

Together the men dove into the curriculum, an escape from the day-to-day noise to focus on their relationship with God and seek the Holy Spirit more deeply. They listened to Christian music, prayed together, reviewed Scripture, and assessed the pain they were holding onto (and that was holding them back). They took a personality test, a spiritual gifts assessment, and a love languages test as springboards to help them discuss who they were today, what made them tick, and what they had to offer. What was their purpose?

In between, they shared their personal stories, challenges, and faith journeys while prepping meals, grabbing a bite, or fishing. Despite an entire weekend of fishing whenever possible, Tom and Michael only managed to catch one small mouth bass, but they had a blast casting worms just as they were metaphorically casting crowns (throwing their egos, pride, accomplishments, achievements, and false sense of control at Jesus's feet).

All of the Scripture, songs, assessments, and prayer time intentionally led to one special morning on the last day of the retreat—a walk in the woods.

Chris had attended a retreat a few years earlier with his wife, Lori, at Jed's farm outside of Atlanta. This retreat had also culminated with a walk in the woods on Jed's property. As Chris and Lori took that walk, they asked God for direction and answers to several life-changing questions. Those answers were clear, leading Chris to take a 180-degree career change, leaving a great corporate marketing position with Expedia to become a pastor and counselor. As a result, Chris and Lori had created this retreat ministry.

So Chris knew the power of a walk in the woods as the exclamation point to the weekend. If executed properly, this walk could strip away all the noise of daily living, so you could peacefully converse, ask questions, and most importantly, *listen*. If the right questions were asked, the walk could help the hiker find himself, surrender to the next level, answer questions, instill purpose, and ultimately, change his life.

Tom needed guidance on what to do next in his life—as a person, as a parent, in his career, and in potential future relationships. As he walked the trail, he needed to find the path God wanted him to walk in his future.

Tom mapped out his plan for the walk the night before in a journal, using his growth through GRIEF model:

- Grace: This was a list of his sins and transgressions, and the forgiveness he needed to seek for himself or grant to others he felt had offended him, and not just recently, but for as far back as he could remember.
- Reflection: This was a tally of all the blessings he had and a time of gratitude before God.
- Intention: This was his present inventory of what he needed help with most, along with the questions he needed answered about his situations and challenges.
- Elevation: This was his intention to find peace in the natural world surrounding the walk. He simply wanted to lean into the quiet and the meditation to listen intensely and be sure he received the exact answers God was speaking to him without distortion and without missing anything.
- Faith: This was his commitment to follow the answers he received even if they didn't exactly match what he wanted or expected.

As they drove to the state park to hike through the rolling hills around Badin Lake near their cabin, Tom read through his journal, adding a note or two here and there, and sharing his sense of nervousness with Michael, as they both had extensive lists of questions to present to God, and no idea what to expect. Once they arrived and prayed for each other, they each took different trails to assure that they had plenty of space to be alone with God for the next three hours.

Journal in hand and one foot in front of the other, Tom marched past campgrounds and escaped civilization. It was extremely important for him to start the conversation humbly, asking God for forgiveness.

Applying Grace

First, Tom sought forgiveness as he looked back and saw his life and actions more clearly. Too often he had led with his ego and pride, so he recognized that as well as the disrespect and offense he had doled out to various people throughout his life. He also saw how he had made an idol of work and worldly success (and their distractions) and put them first. Then he zeroed in on the last years with Judy and owned the resentment he had felt and the unkind ways he had sometimes treated her, especially in the later years as the cancer took its toll on them both. Lastly, he recognized with shame how he had moved too fast in seeking a new relationship after Judy passed, as he looked for a refuge to cover his own pain and fear. He wrote about each and then walked through each one verbally with the Lord.

Confessing everything he could remember, he began to vocalize each one to Him, which led Tom to remember other issues he didn't have in his journal. As the list expanded (and it took a while), it was incredibly cleansing.

After asking forgiveness for himself, he moved on to forgiveness for others—anyone he felt had hurt him, abandoned him when he was in need, or made him feel inadequate. He brought each one to Jesus, saying, "I forgive … for.…"

It is within these past hurts that much of our self-doubt and pain resides. They are the source of many triggers, unhealthy behaviors, as well as harmful indulgences and addictions. Forgiving those who hurt you doesn't mean you are condoning their actions or erasing the boundaries that they crossed. It's good because it releases your anger and hurt, bringing you freedom.

Forgiveness is not about the offender. It's about you—your feelings and your mental health. As Tom let go of his heart's burdens over his own sin and the offenses he carried, he felt lighter and lighter with each step. It was marvelous. He was ready for the next step.

The Blessings of Reflection

Next, he went through all of the blessings bestowed upon him, recounting every element of his life for which he was thankful. Then he read them each aloud to himself, spilling out his gratitude for his beautiful daughters, career, health, and so much more. One by one he vocalized each, realizing as he did, just how many gifts Jesus had provided him. He remembered Jesus's words in Luke 12:48 that from those to whom much is given, much is expected. So once he was cleansed and had given thanks, he sought Jesus about His future plans for him, seeking His guidance.

Intentional Questions

Following the path through the hills, Tom made his way to the lakefront and walked along the beautiful shoreline, mentally centering himself before the Lord. Then he went through the list of questions he had prepared the night before. He verbally covered each troubling situation in his life, seeking guidance. The issues he had the most questions about included how to be a better father, his retirement and ministry and what that would look like, as well as future relationships. He sought God about the steps he should take next in life.

Elevation: Seeking God

As he asked each question, he sought quiet, trying to clear his mind by focusing on his breath, the sound of the birds, the waves and the wind, and the noise of each step on the path. He captured the beauty in his surroundings—the light through the trees, the sparkles crowning the water.

He listened, and didn't hear a thing.

Quiet before the Lord, he listened more intently. Still nothing. Not a single word.

Afterward Chris spoke about how he had received direct answers and confirmations to every question during his walk and the reinforcements afterward, so Tom was sure he wasn't doing the walk properly. Maybe his faith wasn't strong enough yet, or perhaps he wasn't approaching God the right way. What should he change about their conversation?

Fear and doubt were a cacophony in his head, so loud it assured him that he couldn't hear a dump truck driving through a nitroglycerin plant, so how could he ever hear the voice of God and what God wanted him to know? Inside Tom felt like a frustrated child, expecting answers right away, and struggling to understand that they would all come in God's timing.

Disappointed and questioning, he walked into a sudden opening on the path, and found himself on a large sunlit boulder on the water. Facing the sun, he breathed deeply. Hands at his sides and palms out, he quieted his mind and surrendered control. He became still and opened his heart.

Faith: Waiting Brings Answers

And then it happened. Words filled his head, and it was not the random noise of his own doubt anymore. There was a magic and wisdom in the phrases he was hearing, so he wrote them down as quickly as he could.

This book is part of the first direction God gave him that day as He encouraged Tom to help others through writing, videos, podcasts, and more. With a little patience, he received answers and guidance on everything he had brought to the Lord shortly after. All in His time, not Tom's.

Hearing God requires listening, not just for an immediate reply, but for delayed responses, subtle nudges, and winks in the right direction. His voice is sometimes provided via words in your own head. God gave Tom His message as a poem. At other times you hear God in a Scripture that comes alive, or through the words of other people. He speaks through events, in art, in music. God can literally speak through anything.

You just have to be listening patiently. The answer may not be the one you want, which may be why so many people are afraid to ask God for guidance on the tough questions. However, God's direction will always be the best plan for your life. And you know the answer is from Him when it is surrounded with peace, joy, and clarity, and *not* a source for amplified anxiety, confusion, and chaos.

Once He speaks to you, act on it. And continue to speak to Him, spending quality time with Him and walking with Him. Tom's walk in the woods was exactly what he needed at the time, providing the necessary space to deepen his spiritual connection, and hear from God. It was life-changing.

A Walk in the Woods

Moving amongst the trees, slowly climb
I seek, the Holy Spirit to find.

Pledging surrender,
God, I am in Your hands,
You have my body, my mind, my soul.

Your instrument,
I am under Your control.

I walk this path to find You,
Show me the way.

Do You walk with me?
I see Your guiding steps before me.

Do You forgive me?
I taste Your salvation wash over me.

Do You love me?
I feel Your healing touch grace me.

Do You have the answers I seek?
I listen for Your voice.

I hear the leaves rustling song,
Water flow rhythm,
Crow call chorus:
Peace, joy and clarity surround.
Your answer given, Your words are a gift.

TIM + DIANA

Helplessness: A Cause of Grief and Trauma?

> WHEREVER YOU ARE, BE THERE TOTALLY. IF YOU FIND YOU'RE HERE-AND-NOW INTOLERABLE AND IT MAKES YOU UNHAPPY, YOU HAVE THREE OPTIONS: REMOVE YOURSELF FROM THE SITUATION, CHANGE IT, OR ACCEPT IT TOTALLY.
> —ECKHART TOLLE, *THE POWER OF NOW: A GUIDE TO SPIRITUAL ENLIGHTENMENT*[2]

---

2   "A Quote from the Power of Now," Goodreads (Goodreads), accessed April 17, 2023, https://www.goodreads.com/quotes/8877732-if-you-

LOSS IS WHAT HAPPENS IN LIFE, BUT MEANING IS WHAT YOU DO AFTER THAT LOSS OCCURS. SO THE MEANING IS NOT IN DEATH; THE MEANING IS SOMEHOW IN US AND WHAT WE DO NEXT. —TIM OHAI

Tim Ojai is the founder of Kupu Solutions, a strategic effectiveness expert and coach. Tim lost his wife, Diana, in 2020, and is now a single father of a twenty-two-year-old son and a twenty-year-old daughter.

He and Diana met in the 80s during his freshman year of college. Diana was a sophomore and they overlapped for a semester, and then she graduated. Even though Tim knew her brother and cousin and had many shared friends, they didn't really know each other.

Everyone Saw It

And so fast forward, Tim was originally from Kona, Hawaii. Diana wound up moving to Kona years later, and mutual friends always encouraged them to meet. Both of them felt pushed and resisted the pressure. They were both teachers. Tim taught elementary school, and Diana, preschool. Soon even the families from the same neighborhoods with kids at both schools suggested they meet each other. One even told Tim that this was a marriage quality relationship. He really backed off at that one.

So they knew each other, but just weren't getting together until an Ironman activity where they both volunteered. Tim was one of the main folks doing security, and Diana was on the finish line security team. Late at night during a twenty-four hour shift, they were waiting for midnight as the last athletes

find-your-here-and-now-intolerable-and-it#:~:text=%E2%80%9CIf%20 you%20find%20your%20here%20and%20now%20intolerable%20 and%20it,Then%20accept%20the%20consequences.

straggled in. There wasn't a lot of activity and they were just sitting there, talking. And it was nice. It was pleasant.

A little while later. Tim saw Diana in the grocery store. As he walked down aisle three, she came around the corner. He never forgot that moment. They started talking again, and for the first time, there was this energy. They wound up checking out in the same line, which wasn't planned. She was a person in front of Tim with somebody between them. He just waited his turn, looking at candy bars and magazines and just trying to stay in his own space. She noticed him and let the guy between them go. In the end, she invited him to a barbecue that Saturday. He had already been invited, but she didn't know, so it was all too easy for him to say yes.

Tim got there early, and she showed up late as she was working weekends at a different job. It turned out that they were the only two single people at the party. Tim was sitting in the backyard, on a big, big blanket on the grass by himself. When Diana looked for a spot, her friends all said, "Tim has space!" She nearly left at that, but decided to join him instead.

They talked, and the best part was that now there was no pressure. Even though their friends had nudged Diana that day, nobody was trying to push them. The next thing they knew, the party was over and everybody gone. Since they were still talking, their hosts invited them to go for ice cream. Diana went but Tim stayed behind.

It wasn't until this point that Tim asked his buddies who Diana was and discovered she was the one they had been trying to set him up with for a really long time. He felt like an idiot.

They married in 1999. Since Diana got pregnant on their honeymoon, they went from being a newlywed couple to a family of three in nine months. Their son was born in 2000. At the time, they were both teaching, but there's no money in teaching in Hawaii. There was also the time factor. Their present positions really only gave them one day a week to hang out. After a lot of prayer and soul searching, they realized they should move to California where Diana's family lived and where Tim's mom had also just moved.

After moving to northern California, Tim looked at some teaching jobs, but landed in sales instead. He had no intention of ever doing that, but enjoyed it. He worked as a sales coordinator and then worked with regional marketing strategy, helping with business development. He learned so much that he wanted further training.

Changing Lanes

Since he did so well in sales and support, his company was going to make him a sales rep out of Reno, but it didn't work out. As Tim and Diana were now expecting their daughter, they decided to make a change. Tim wound up starting over as a trainer in Houston. Their daughter was born there, and Tim rose through the ranks very quickly, and eventually, was in a global role working for Shell Oil, living on planes and in hotels, home only on the weekends.

This was brutal on Diana and their marriage was getting hammered. They were on vacation back home in Hawaii and sitting on a friend's lanai watching the sunset, when Tim asked her, "Did you think your life was gonna look like this when you were growing up? Because no way, not at all, I didn't."

At that point, they asked each other what living according to their values looked like, and that basically erased nearly every obligation they had, so they started over. Diana wanted to be a stay-at-home mom so she left her job. They had two littles, and wanted to be as much a part of their life while they were young as possible. Tim left corporate and started his own consulting company.

Their Six-Year Battle

The first customer he landed was Walmart! He led his own company for twelve years before going back to corporate in 2019. There was also an opportunity to do a transformation for a sales enablement function at a software company called Workday.

Diana was diagnosed with acute lymphoblastic leukemia (ALL), where "acute" means it hits hard. She almost died right when she was diagnosed, but they were able to get some new blood in her body as it was collapsing. Tim held her hand and thought she was gone right then.

Instead they started a six-year journey. Diana went into remission and kept the cancer in remission. She had a bunch of chemo and other treatments. It was brutal. But she was able to get to that five-year mark. They were told that after five years, you were good to go. Fantastic.

However, it came back very aggressively a few months later. She started feeling weird around Christmas of 2019. Tim was in London on a business trip when she called and told him the cancer was back. She was at Stanford Hospital, a great, great hospital. COVID-19 hit by February and they were locked down in California, as the Bay Area was getting hit.

Tim returned on Valentine's Day and they spent their first day together by getting Donna checked in to the hospital. She had a bone marrow transplant, which turned into a bone graft, and she died from that rejection on July 4, 2020.

As you can see, Tim now has these two holidays burned into his head in a way they're not supposed to be.

Dealing with the Disconnect

Their daughter graduated high school right before Diana passed. She went to college, but basically ruined that first semester.

She had nothing left. Tim's son was going to school too, and also just got his black belt. He was an instructor, and going to school for business because he wanted to run his own academy. The hardest part of COVID-19 for him was the shutdown of the academy. He went from being able to work out regularly, no matter what was happening inside of him, to sitting in the house and just going sideways.

Tim had to figure out how to help him open up physically. They started training the neighborhood kids because the parents were going nuts with their kids stuck at home. No running. No sports—nothing. Some of Tim's son's Jiu Jitsu buddies said to him "I'm gonna kill my kids. Would you please give them a private lesson?" It was perfect. They converted their garage into a miniature academy. This fixed his son's personal space and the neighborhood need simultaneously.

Eventually, Tim sent his son to Hawaii because Hawaii didn't have the shutdown that California had. He got him a job with his cousin, so he could go to Jiu Jitsu at a regular place, and that really helped him.

Physical movement is important. Something powerful happens when you tap into that mind/body connection. When we shut down for COVID-19 and then opened back up, all of a sudden, things started to unlock again.

Grief brings a fuzzy sort of disconnect between the mind and the body because we're living in the mind differently. Our mind is telling us not to be in the present. It's too hard and overwhelming, but when you connect with your body and start doing things, it resets that clock, and brings a person into the present. Physical activity is vital.

Tim started walking, eventually joining the gym as well.

He found that whenever he got tense, going for a walk didn't just clear his head, it actually unlocked his brain. It helped him process his grief. He began to do different things, feel different things, think different thoughts, and eventually feel differently too. His walking was helping him to reconnect his brain, when his grief left him locked in his limbic system. His brain relaxed through physical movement, which allowed him to come out of the emotion and into logic and thinking again.

Self-Expression

He also got a tattoo. The word *tattoo* is Polynesian. In Hawaii, you get a tattoo when something significant happens in your life, so it's not just a form of art, it's actually part of the life process. Traditionally, people get tattoos as part of the grieving process because getting the tattoo itself hurts. Tim's tattoo took three separate sittings to complete and goes all the way around his forearm up to his elbow. It hurt in a powerful way, because that pain coincided with Tim's grieving for Diana.

When you see somebody with a Polynesian tattoo, you're not supposed to ask what it means. You can comment on it and if they want to share, they'll share because there's more involved in their tattoo than just the art. There's actually a historical and powerful evolutionary story in the ink.

Tim co-created this with his nephew in Hawaii, who gave him the tattoo. It was wild how it worked out. Tim asked to do something on his forearm that really told the story of his immediate family. Each part is significant and symbolic. The little, tiny arrows on the top are a headrest to represent the wooden headrests his family used as pillows long ago. A weaving pattern like cords of rope is above the olonā plant, a native of Hawaii used for centuries to weave together a really strong cord.

Since Tim also has a strong European heritage, he blended his Celtic roots into it too. The head, the legs, and the tail of an Irish hound represents his son, Connor, named after King Connor, which means "lover of hounds." Next, there's little rectangles that go around the outside. That's a Polynesian pattern that represents the octopus. Connor loves the octopus because it speaks of tenacity and strength.

A Celtic heart represents his very creative daughter. He had different knots embedded in the harp, including a pattern of birds that goes from the harp all the way out, and back to his elbow. Hard, thick lines go over the art and hold it all together; that's called framing. The frames are like the beams of your house or the ribs of your boat, providing strength. Tim has a lot of frames in that section, but the birds leave the frame. The birds are not in the frame. The headrests represent good thoughts and good dreams, and the cord represents a marriage that came out of their dreams. This beautiful woman produced two beautiful children until she left them, and the birds represent the fact that she left, leaving the frame. The tattoo was a combination of telling his story and giving meaning to his experience.

Having been raised in a culture that had strong traditions surrounding death and grief helped Tim. American culture, and Western culture in general, struggles with grief. Most are just grief illiterate.

When Diana passed, the company he worked for graciously gave him time off, but very quickly expected him back. It was like, "Okay, it's time to get back to work. It's time to get stuff done now." But grief doesn't work like that. There is no on-and-off switch. You can't just experience grief for a season and walk away. You'll grieve forever. The question is: How much of your capacity is it going to consume?

One out of nine people in the U.S. were affected by losing someone to COVID-19. That's just one disease. That's not including anyone else who died for other reasons during this time. Grief is more common now than ever before, but it's hard to explain to people.

A Heart Filled with Grief

A good way to do it is to draw a box and fill the box with a heart. That's the whole heart filled with grief. Over time, you draw a bigger box around the first box as you grow, and the grief looks smaller. However, it's not the grief that gets smaller. It stays the same size, but you have enlarged your heart to make your life bigger.

Grief is a trauma. And trauma is driven by helplessness. Anytime you feel helpless by losing a job, losing a spouse, losing a child, anything that makes you feel helpless, that trauma needs to be grieved. If we don't really understand how to do that, we're going to relive our grief. It will never stop, so to speak, and we will never grow past it. So we need to process it. Every Fourth of July, every Valentine's Day, every birthday, every park you drive by—all kinds of things can become triggers. It takes time to navigate that stuff. And American culture doesn't have a lot of help and guidance in grief.

Tim tried to explain to people that he was different now. Number one, his "give a damn" was broken. He just didn't care. He was literally holding Diana's hand as she died, so he was the one who called the time of death when the physician came in. So when people complained about a missed deadline, or discussed the importance of some business strategy, he thought, *Why are we doing that?* He tried to wear his veneer, but he didn't care. On top of that, he had his own family stuff. Each of his kids had their own journey. He had no idea how to help them. His daughter is a lot like him, so she got super angry. Her warrior spirit came right to the surface, and she was ready to fight anything because she didn't know who to fight.

Tim's son took his warrior spirit to the mat, because the academy opened back up. The people there and his professor came alongside him and helped him. They didn't have to necessarily explain everything, but his body was able to process what his soul was going through. Tim, however, went through a time where he was sitting at home alone. Eventually, he started watching TV, all kinds of stuff he'd never watched before. He started binge watching *Breaking Bad*. It was really good, but it was so dark that about halfway through season two, Tim thought, *Why am I watching this?* It was making him feel more dark, more depressed. That was when he started walking. He had to get out of his house and walk, and watch different content, feeding himself better stuff. Following that journey was the only way he was able to keep paddling and keep moving forward.

During the COVID-19 lockdown in California, Tim walked and walked. He didn't talk to anyone. He was all icy, cold stares, sending a strong "just leave me alone" message to anyone he met. He was in his head a lot and needed that space. There's no right way to grieve. You just grieve. You just let it go. Walking allowed his thoughts to wander. As he got his heart rate up, his thoughts flowed again, and he could think more clearly.

Then he could begin to find meaning again, and that was the key. You're trying to make meaning out of this? It's not that some wonderful thing had happened. There were questions that assaulted Tim and his family. He told the kids that this hadn't happened because God wanted Mom to die. You don't find this idea in Christian theology. Tim says *scoob* a lot. It is based on the Greek word *skubalon*[3] in the Bible—and it means poop. Excrement. It's worthless. God doesn't want anyone to die. He doesn't want anyone to suffer. He doesn't want anyone to be sick. All of that is the result of living in a fallen world, and death is part of the impact of living in a fallen world. So not God's fault.

---

3   James Strong, "4657. Skubalon," Strong's Greek: 4657. σκύβαλον (skubalon) -- refuse (Biblehub), accessed April 24, 2023, https://biblehub.com/greek/4657.htm.

Tim was still working and became a workaholic, and in time, a borderline alcoholic. He just threw himself into extra stuff. The busyness he didn't really care about didn't help him, but it kept him in motion. Lockdown was slower than normal already without the usual distractions. Eventually, he was forced to slow down. It was not intentional, but it became a blessing to have that time alone.

Tim's work was reduced to back-to-back Zoom conferences all day. When that turned off, the house was silent. His kids were around, but he didn't feel able to share with them because they were dealing with their own grief. It was all too much to share.

Sitting in his house by himself in silence was a super easy atmosphere for drinking. He'd pour one glass, and then make it a double pour, and then do it again, and then figure out how to go to sleep. He knew it wasn't healthy. He was eating whatever he wanted, drinking whatever he wanted, but at some point realized that this was not how he wanted to live. If he took this route he was not going to live to a decent old age. He had to make some changes.

He found that the more he walked and moved, the more he started listening to podcasts and audiobooks that were about grief. That's when he recognized that grief was a journey, and he needed to be on it instead of avoiding it. His was a year and a half after she died. So he started to get on that path. Since then he's made real health gains and lost sixty pounds. He didn't eliminate alcohol completely, because he likes red wine, whiskey, and bourbon, especially when he's smoking a cigar. God bless a good cigar. So he curtailed it and moved it to weekends only.

On business trips, he doesn't drink at all. That demonstration of discipline and the effort created the capacity for healing. He tried and he feels like his soul, spirit, and body met him halfway and started opening up. That really changed things.

One method for him was doing dishes, a job he'd always disliked. Now he's learned to love it. It's become his space. It's a ritual that grounds him and brings him to the present. That's a big thing. Instead of trying to relive the past or obsess over the future, he focuses on maximizes the moment. When you're washing dishes, it's very much about what's in your hand right now. You have to pay attention because you don't want that dish or glass to slip out of your hand. You have to make sure it gets clean and rinsed. Washing dishes became as healing for him as going for a walk. That work allows his brain to calm itself down.

Bringing Your Kids with You

Eventually he ventured into a dating app where he met a beautiful lady he has been dating for the last three months. He wasn't going to do this initially, but a friend told him he had to get "back in the saddle." His reply was, "What does that even mean?" The friend recommended a dating app. He wasn't ready.

Then another good friend told him that a third of today's relationships start online. He asked, "Would you rather walk into a club and meet somebody, or let an algorithm help you?" That was how he met his wife, so Tim decided to give it a go.

Initially, Tim and his girlfriend were both nervous. She had been divorced for eight years and wasn't too comfortable being the first one dating someone who lost their wife. Her kids had gone through a divorce journey. They had watched their parents split, and saw that tension, so they wanted their mom to meet someone who would take care of her and make her happy. Tim's kids didn't have that attitude. They sat down and had a moment to discuss the next steps.

Tim's relationship with his late wife Diana hadn't been perfect. Goodness gracious, no marriage ever is, but they had a great marriage nevertheless. If she were still alive, they'd still be married. So his family's journey has been very different from the woman he is now dating. At first, his son told him he didn't even want to know about it. Then he said something really powerful: "I don't know if it's because it's not Mom. I don't know if it's because it's too soon, even though it's been a couple of years. I don't know what it is. But how I feel has no bearing on whether or not I want you to be happy. As long as you're doing the right thing, I will support you." That was incredible for Tim.

His daughter didn't use the same words, but was ready to meet her, so he's setting up an online meetup at this writing.

Unless you're dating a widow, they're going to need to learn what you're going through. Tim talks about Diana and their relationship, and his loss and grief, but also holds back on some things. There are definitely some things that she's not ready to talk about yet. It's a little overwhelming for his girlfriend to hear some of these things. She just feels intimidated. She'll say, "Oh my gosh, you know, if Diana were alive today, you'd still be married to her, and you and I would not be talking." That's the truth.

However, it's also true that she's been gone for a few years and you can't just stop living. Even so, if you're a widower and you're looking to get back in the game, it's best if it is on your own terms. Everyone has their own personal journey, and you choose your timing. For Tim, this has been great. He's clicking and getting along really well. He feels like he has met somebody really special. Because of that, he talked to his kids about timing too. He didn't want to go too fast in the relationship for them.

He asked them how fast is too fast. His son answered, "You're experienced and mature, and you know what you want. I don't think you need what I need at 22, but take your time. Get to know each other, and even if it's working, give it at least one year before going any further. Basically, the truth is that I need a year to adjust to this, Dad."

If you've got kids, you have to bring them along with you. They need a chance to deal with it. Not every kid will be behind their parents moving forward. They may be stuck. Subsequently, they will keep the widower stuck because they can't get past their own trauma.

Something True

Tim had always had faith in a Creator. This universe and life didn't just happen because of random math. It's too complex to be random. However, Tim's also a nonconformist, so when his give-a-damn meter broke, he needed something authentic and real and true and pure.

He had a friend who had lost her husband, and her faith got rocked. The two of them had lots of discussions about truth. How did you know what was really true? The only answer he could come up with was that he knew Jesus is Truth. Jesus said, "I am the way, the truth, and the life" in John 14:6, so Tim believes there is something in the person and character of Christ that resonates so deeply that it defines truth. This doesn't go against logic; it simply goes beyond it. So it transcends the rational.

That's why we call it faith. If it wasn't a mystery, and there was no unknown, you wouldn't need faith. It would just be science. Tim locked onto the idea of Jesus being Truth, and went back and started re-reading his Bible, looking at the original language. He found that what Jesus actually taught was not the same as what he had been taught. For instance, Jesus told people to repent using the word *metanoia*.[4] Tim didn't really

---

4   James Strong, "3341. Metanoia," Strong's Greek: 3341. μετάνοια (Metanoia) -- change of mind, repentance (Biblehub), accessed April 24, 2023, https://biblehub.com/greek/3341.htm.

understand that term so he studied it further. When Jesus said to repent, He was telling people to *change the way they thought*, so they could then change their direction. The two are connected. The Bible also said that Jesus spoke with *exousia*[5] (or authority). He had the authority of heaven behind Him in everything He said and did, speaking from a 100% position of love. Today Jesus makes that same authority available to everyone.

Even the word Jesus used for evil (*poneros*[6]) is not referring to evil in the way people usually think. It's more about oppression and sickness, the natural results of sin in the world. So when Jesus was casting away evil and healing people, His miracles were also a metaphor. Through His actions, Jesus was communicating this: "I'm touching people, and whatever's afflicted in them is going away. That's who I am and that's what I do. I have authority over all evil, so repent and follow Me, and I'll show you a better path and help you overcome evil too."

This is the faith journey: to have our affliction, our brokenness, and disease that hits us from all different angles throughout life be healed, so we can be the best versions of ourselves. More importantly, we can then extend that same love and healing to others and rejuvenate them.

The truth is that the fear that had been injected into what Tim had been taught earlier in his life isn't in the Bible. Tim was taught a hard gospel: you better do this, or else. So he believed that if something bad happened, it was because he did something wrong. That's not how it works.

Life happens the way it happens because mankind lives in a broken world. Because of that, we need love more than

---

5   James Strong, "1849. Exousia," Strong's greek: 1849. ἐξουσία (exousia) -- power to act, authority (Biblehub), accessed April 24, 2023, https://www.biblehub.com/greek/1849.htm.

6   James Strong, "4190. Πονηρός (Ponéros)," Strong's Greek: 4190. πονηρός (ponéros) -- 79 occurrences (Biblehub), accessed April 24, 2023, https://biblehub.com/greek/strongs_4190.htm.

anything else. And when you lose the love of your life, where do you find that love again? That's the moment you realize your faith is more important than the person. That's when you realize that whether that person is there or not, you are still connected to pure love, which means you are able to extend pure love to others.

That doesn't mean you'll immediately be an expert at showing and extending love, but it does mean that through a connection with Jesus, a person will become a better, deeper, and simpler human being. Letting go of everything else does that.

The other ingredient is hope. In your grief, it is all too easy to lose your hope. When people go through the grieving process, they often fall into this: *How am I ever going to get through? This is the worst thing ever. Now everything is going to be broken forever. It'll never be better.* Eventually a person gets past this and realizes, *Wait a minute, I still have hope because I still have love, and I have peace because I still have love.* Love is central to living. Everyone wants hope and peace, but without love, they can get lost. When the love of your life is ripped away from you, your peace and hope get ripped away with it. That's why it's so important to find meaning in your grief. It helps you find love again.

Loss happens in life, and everyone must find meaning in what has happened to them. The meaning is not in the dying; the meaning is somehow in us and what we do next. We try to lessen the pain of grief with the meaning we give it. This builds a foundation not to move on—because you don't—but to move forward.

A great example of this is Candace Lightner, the woman who lost her thirteen-year-old daughter to a drunk driver and started Mothers Against Drunk Driving (MADD). She turned the loss of her daughter and that grief into something that was powerful and transformative and, literally, went on to save millions of lives through education and tougher legislation for

DUIs across America. Her loss became her own personal crusade to prevent other mothers from experiencing the same pain she had.

Full

Heartful—Overflow warmth
Mindful—Echo shout praise
Soulful—Shaken to my knees
Joyful—Peace my purpose

Strength from His love
Power in surrender, full and complete.

Angry with God? Finding Faith through Your Healing Journey with Joseph Thompson

WHERE THERE IS ANGER THERE IS ALWAYS PAIN UNDERNEATH. —ECKHART TOLLE, *THE POWER OF NOW*[7]

I SOUGHT THE LORD, AND HE ANSWERED ME; HE DELIVERED ME FROM ALL MY FEARS. (PSALM 34:4)

---

7   Eckhart Tolle, "A Quote from the Power of Now," Goodreads (Goodreads), accessed April 18, 2023, https://www.goodreads.com/quotes/990129-where-there-is-anger-there-is-always-pain-underneath.

YOUR STORY IS ABOVE THE JOURNEY. YOU REAL-
IZE THAT GOD IS TRUSTING YOU TO TELL A STORY
WITH YOUR GRIEF JOURNEY THAT CAN NOW IM-
PACT AND MAKE A DIFFERENCE IN OTHER PEOPLE'S
LIVES. —PASTOR JOSEPH THOMPSON

MAY THE GOD OF HOPE FILL YOU WITH ALL JOY
AND PEACE AS YOU TRUST IN HIM, SO THAT YOU
MAY OVERFLOW WITH HOPE BY THE POWER OF THE
HOLY SPIRIT. (ROMANS 15:13)

Pastor Joseph Thompson founded Light the Nation in Lagos, Nigeria, in 1986, and later served for over thirty years at some of the fastest growing congregations in the United States, including Action Church in central Florida, Primal Church in Johnstown, Colorado, and New Life Church in Colorado Springs. Also an entrepreneur and business leader, he and his wife, Sola, founded Rehoboth Home Care Services in central Florida. Joseph has counseled thousands of people experiencing grief over his past forty years in ministry.

Many widowers are angry over their loss, and often blame God for what they're going through, but would you blame the Minister of Transportation for all the traffic accidents? If a drunk hit you and killed your family members, you don't blame yourself. It's the drunken person's fault—the one that was irresponsible. Every individual makes choices that affect others. It's certainly not the Minister of Transportation's fault.

The Big Picture

It's interesting how even Christians blame God when something doesn't go the way they want. They turn their anger upwards. There's a lot of reasons for that, but the important thing to remember is that God is writing a macro story about His creation and humanity. He's the God of the Big Picture.

There's a quote that says, "You may not agree with the way God runs His world, but you are not God, and you don't have a world." It's His story, not ours. The point is this: God is writing a macro story. All of our lives are micro stories within the macro story He's telling. Every good story includes intrigue, suspense, loss, pain, hurt, joy, and celebration. All of those emotions are embedded in the macro story God is writing.

Sometimes our smaller part of the story is in that chapter of pain and grief. But you don't walk out of the movie theater twenty minutes into the movie when the protagonist is in trouble and his life is falling apart. You stay until the end.

Since God is the macro Storyteller, there's a lot you don't see. Life is on a continuum with a beginning, middle, and end to it. You show up somewhere in the middle of the continuum, so all you know is this part, the now, and the past what you've experienced. However, God sees from here to the end of time, and knows exactly what you must experience to get to the next part effectively and successfully.

Five years ago, Tom lost his precious wife after nineteen years of marriage. She was his soulmate. Since then, Tom has touched many lives because of the purpose God directed him into through his grief. However, if God had asked him if he would be willing to lose her so he could get to this place, he would have said, "Absolutely not."

But God is telling His macro story, and in it your story intersects with the stories of many others who need healing and restoration from their pain, the same pain you have walked through. The Bible says God comforts everyone in their troubles, so they may, in turn, comfort others with the same comfort they received from God when they went through their journey. That's the macro story.

Everyone's micro story is fraught sometimes with pain, and hurt, and loss, but the key is to embrace the fact that God is telling a bigger story, and that He has trusted you with pain.

Why is it a trust? God is trusting you to handle it in him. He knows you have two options: you can turn away from Him and curse and deny Him, or you can turn deeper into Him. God trusts people with loss.

God is sovereign, the ultimate Source of all power, authority, and everything that exists, but He has also given us a free will. You are not a mannequin or a puppet on a string. Normally, you get to make your own choices, but in the case of grief, God saw your full story, including where He desired you to change from the experience of loss. For Tom, God saw the healing of other men, and He knew that He had to allow the loss of his wife to bring Tom to that place, but God had no guarantee that Tom would allow his pain to shape him as it has. Tom may have turned to drinking and drugs and illicit sex and more instead, but through his own free will, Tom chose the better path.

That is the key of faith. Faith is the bedrock, the foundation, the jumping off point into navigating grief. Without it, navigating grief seems impossible. Grief is cyclic and full of anger, depression, bitterness, and despair. But it's a journey.

There's an ancient Chinese proverb that declares that "a journey of 1,000 miles begins with a single step." So to deal with grief, you have to be willing to take a step in a different direction than you've been going. This is hard to do because pain makes you nearsighted. It gives you tunnel vision. All you see is your pain, and the fact that you are a victim. It can be very difficult to take a step outside of that, which is why people need real help with it.

You really need to talk to someone, ideally a mental health professional. It can also be a fellow widower who has walked the same road to help give you a better perspective than you have at the moment, but down the road, a professional can be of great help and relief.

Your first step is being willing to talk and open up honestly. The male ego can get in the way of this. Western culture has taught men that strong men don't cry. Strong men take care of themselves and don't need help. Strong men can't show (and certainly don't share) how they feel. That's a lie from the pit of hell.

If you're not crying, you're not a strong man. You're a weak man because you're hiding your true feelings. It takes strength to be vulnerable. Being vulnerable means you're willing to acknowledge you're not right, you're willing to weep, you're willing to feel pain, and you're willing to seek counsel to grow into a different direction. It takes strength and vulnerability to even recognize that the road you've been on is not the right road and you need to turn onto a different path.

That's why talking to someone is the first step. Another person can help you understand the road you are on, and help guide you onto a different, and better, path for you.

Dealing with Pain

The second thing that is critical is journaling. It is a huge player in healing. Here's why. Joseph's sister passed away tragically in a plane crash several years ago, and although he rarely posted anything about his own life on social media, he started to keep a public journal. Every day for thirty days following her death, he shared his raw emotions, his feelings, and his hurt on social media. At the end of thirty days, he felt like he didn't need to do it anymore.

About day twenty-four, two different friends reached out to him, one from London and one from Nigeria. Both wrote, saying, "You have no idea how the last twenty-something days you have been writing has brought tremendous healing for us." These were people who had also lost loved ones in the same flight in which his sister was killed. In total, 166 people were killed. They were reaching out to tell him that his writing became their catharsis, that process of navigating through their pain. His words helped them understand it and turn it back to Jesus. They suggested he write a book, so he compiled all of it and wrote a book entitled *Imagine*, meaning imagine that this was your journey. Imagine what you would do if you had to walk through this.

The point is this: Joseph experienced incredible healing through his writing. He likened it to emptying poison out of his system. He poured the buildup of pain and grief and anger out of his heart. Because he did it publicly, many people reached out to him.

So the first step needs to be that pouring out: pour out your heart to a friend, a confidant, a mental health professional, a pastor. Pour out what you're feeling. Pour out via pen and paper, social media, or a blog. The medium is up to you, but take the time to pour out what you're feeling. Otherwise the loss and sadness will overwhelm you. When you are filled with grief, if you don't get it out, it will just stay there, well up, and drown you.

Here's the best part. That pouring out isn't just healing in that moment. It helps later on too. Joseph's sister was killed over ten years ago, but from time to time, he opens that book, and reads it and weeps anew. It's easy to forget emotions, but it's important for your personal growth that they are revisited.

A woman forgets the pain of childbirth because of the joy she feels as she holds her baby in her arms. Grief is completely different. From this kind of pain you are able to build strength and walk through your healing.

It's similar to working out in a gym. Pain helps build muscles. It's not when you're lifting those weights that you're gaining muscle. That's when you're tearing the muscle, and it's painful, but the end result is that when you're resting, your muscles are rebuilding. All those fibers are reconnected, which is why you get stronger and develop muscle. "No pain, no gain."

Suppressing pain can send a person into a self-destructive path marked by addiction, largely because they have lost their sense of identity and purpose. Joseph was born in Nigeria and grew up in England, so he's lived on just about every continent. He's spent the last thirty odd years in America. Overall, he's been exposed to a large variety of cultural responses to the challenges of grief.

In the West, people see themselves as the hero in their own story. Like in our fairy tales. The princes and princesses are always good people that are treated badly, but in the end they triumph and are successful. Then life is good. Happily ever after. Joseph calls this Fairy Tale Theology and the Western church is largely built on it. Since people see themselves as the hero, they are never the one that made poor choices that were ultimately destructive and caused them pain. So because their expectations have not been realized, they blame God. He did not meet their expectations. He did not give them a happily ever after in the way they thought He should. They suppress their emotions and often their faith as well. The truth is that people need to express their emotions and sort them out *with* God.

This goes back to the macro story that God is telling. Since people are in small stories within the larger one, the critical key is obedience. Obedience to God, faith in God, trust in Him. Since He is the Writer of the story, People need to trust that He can see the entire vista, beginning to end, the complete picture.

So God says, "This is how I want you to respond to your loss," and He gives you help and direction and comfort. In the moment of pain, it's very hard to respond when God says to take a leap off a cliff covered by cloud. You don't know what's under those clouds. That jump might be just two feet off the ground. It might be further. You don't know because you can't see the ground. The thing is that even if it's not two feet, even if it's 200 feet, God is underneath those clouds with everlasting arms. He's there to catch you and support you.

The key to navigating through the compelling sense that you should suppress your feelings and keep it all together is obedience. God says this:

> POUR OUT YOUR HEART BEFORE ME, FOR GOD IS A REFUGE FOR HIS PEOPLE. (PSALM 46:1)

Obedience means to do what He says, and He beckons to people and says, "Pour out your heart. I can help you with this." The Bible also says this:

> TRUST IN ME, AND I WILL SHOW YOU GREAT AND MIGHTY THINGS HIDDEN, THAT YOU DO NOT EVEN KNOW. TO PROSPER, NOT TO HARM YOU, BUT TO GIVE YOU A FUTURE AND A HOPE. (JEREMIAH 29:10–11)

Ultimately, there is a way out of loss and sadness, even if you don't see it. Giving it all to Him in the middle of those clouds and expressing all the feelings and pain inside is a counter-culture leap through those clouds. And He is beneath them.

And part of God's direction will be to talk to Him and to other people. That's the secret.

God Reaching through People

When Joseph's sister died, and as he subsequently started writing every day, many people left comments. Most of them were kind and considerate, but didn't help him. However, others were wholly different. Those who had experienced loss themselves really helped him.

One wrote saying that they could "not pretend to understand what he was going through" and went on to tell him that "pain and grief are real." They knew this because they had lost their daughter. Joseph remembers thinking, *Wow! No parent should bury a child. My sister, yeah, that's painful enough, my sister, but a child. And yet this person says I can't pretend to understand your pain. Yes, you do.*

And that's the point: people who have walked through grief and pain really understand how to encourage and comfort others. There were statements like that from many, and they were the ones that made him feel better. Each one of them had a strong faith and had navigated their own loss, so Joseph thought, *If they can do it, so must I. I must be obedient too. God took care of them, so He can do the same for me.*

He revived his faith by talking to people who had walked a similar journey. So sharing is key—with a mental health counselor, a church family, and/or a group of people who have experienced something similar to what you've experienced. All of these are sources of communication and connection.

The other thing that helps in this process tremendously is exercise. Joseph exercises six days a week, and he's almost sixty years old. He's committed to not only being physically healthy, but also healthy mentally and emotionally, and exercise helps with all three. It's brilliant. Exercise influences neural growth in the brain. Did you know that if you run for fifteen minutes a day or walk for an hour a day, you reduce the risk of depression by twenty-six percent? That's a twenty-six percent reduction for around fifteen minutes a day.

So sharing, faith, and exercise are all critical to dealing with all the pain and everything. That's the story that God is telling through your life. That's the story that's impacting people. Your loss wasn't your destination. It's part of your journey. It's a catalyst for a shift, so you can now make a difference in other people's lives.

So overall, it's hugely important to remember that your story is part of God's story, His Big Picture. God is trusting you to tell a story with your grief journey that can now impact and make a difference in other people's lives. And that's, frankly, absolutely and exquisitely wonderful.

Words

Words I needed to hear
To let me know I'm on the right path, when that path wasn't clear
Moving in the direction You want me to go
Restrain me, too fast
Nudge me, too slow
Clarity, purpose revealed

Chapter 8

THE BOTTOM LINE

God made people in His image: spirit, soul, and body. People's lives are made stronger by these intricately interwoven strands of body, mind, and spirit. In the alignment, optimization, and binding of these three comes promise, power, and peace. However, in our grief, each of these strands has been pulled, strained, frayed, and sometimes even broken. Gloom, despair, and anxiety result.

For many, it's overwhelming. Often feeling like a failure because of what they just experienced, as has been explored, widowers are challenged in every one of these areas. In this shattered state, it's hard to see that their life is not over, *but it isn't.* This is not their destination. *This is not the end of their story.* It's the beginning of a brand-new journey. Just not one they would have chosen.

That's why you have to slow down, write, talk, and learn from professionals. As you ascend, step by step in your journey, brokenness becomes rebirth. You take one small step at a time toward new heights and purpose, but you never lose what you had with your loved one. God doesn't waste anything. He sorts it out.

He uses it to motivate you further and rebuilds your heart, renewing your faith and even healing old wounds in the process. He's not done with you, no matter what. Following each element of GRIEF—Grace, Reflection, Intention, Elevation and Faith—will go a long way to helping with this journey. It's non-linear and messy at best, but relying on this process works.

People aren't supposed to forget the past and all their beautiful memories and just move forward. Instead, God embraces people in their grief relationally, so that every experience is brought forward. You can achieve growth through GRIEF, navigating your journey with more peace from what you have learned, remembering most of all, that you are not in this alone.

The Now, a Note from Tom

As I write this, I am over five and a half years into my grief journey.

I remain sober. I remain spiritual in my faith. I remain fit, although I did suffer a big setback, and needed bypass surgery to remain alive. (The body indeed keeps score.)

I finally found a partner and am now engaged to be married. Literally an answer to my Walk in the Woods prayers. The relationship is a fulfilling, caring, and different kind of love, as it should be.

My daughters are both doing well: the oldest is now a registered nurse, and the youngest still in college.

We all still have moments of fond memories and joy mixed with random tears and sadness. This last Mother's Day was a sh** show, but that is the journey—non-linear, random, sad punctuations still hit us from nowhere.

But we know we've grown through our grief journey, transcending the clouds that blocked our vision and got in our way. We have all three been inspired by the experience, choosing a life of purpose, never forgetting Judy's mantra, inspiring us to do better each day in our new lives without her: "Only a life serving others is a life worth living."

These are some of the titles Tom and his brotherhood found helpful through their own journey, and hope these can help you in yours:

- *Man's Search for Meaning* by Viktor E. Frankl
- *The Body Keeps the Score: Brain, Mind, and Body in the Healing of Trauma* by Bessel van der Kolk M.D.
- *The Power of Now: A Guide to Spiritual Enlightenment* by Eckhart Tolle
- *The Grieving Brain: The Surprising Science of How We Learn from Love and Loss* by Mary-Frances O'Connor
- *The Gifts of Imperfection* by Brené Brown
- *Beyond Boundaries: Learning to Trust Again in Relationships* by John Townsend
- *Getting to Commitment: Overcoming the 8 Greatest Obstacles to Lasting Connection (and Finding the Courage to Love)* by Steven Carter
- *No More Mr. Nice Guy: A Proven Plan for Getting What You Want in Love, Sex, and Life* by Robert A. Glover
- *Think Like a Monk: Train Your Mind for Peace and Purpose Every Day* by Jay Shetty
- *The Laws of Human Nature* by Robert Greene
- *Built through Courage: Face Your Fears to Live the Life You Were Meant For* by Dave Hollis
- *Can't Hurt Me: Master Your Mind and Defy the Odds* by David Goggins
- *Overcome: Crush Adversity with the Leadership Techniques of America's Toughest Warriors* by Jason Redman
- *Game Changers: What Leaders, Innovators, and Mavericks Do to Win at Life* by Dave Asprey
- *Super Human: The Bulletproof Plan to Age Backward and Maybe Even Live Forever* by Dave Asprey
- *The Myth of Normal: Trauma, Illness, and Healing in a Toxic Culture* by Gabor Maté M.D.

- *My Utmost for His Highest* by Oswald Chambers
- *The Widower's Journey: Helping Men Rebuild after Their Loss* by Herb Knoll
- *The First 365* by Terrell L. Whitener
- *Widower to Widower: Surviving the End of Your Most Important Relationship* by Fred Colby
- *The Group: Seven Widowed Fathers Reimagine Life* by Donald Rosenstein
- *Lack or Success: A Step-by-Step Guide for Aligning Your Purpose, Raising Your Consciousness, and Transforming Your Experiences to Turn Failure into Success!* by Brian Rassi
- *Surrender to Your Adversity: How to Conquer Adversity, Build Resilience, and Move Toward Your Life's Purpose* by Rob Swymer

IF THIS BOOK HAS HELPED YOU, WILL YOU HELP ME SPREAD THE WORD?

There are several ways you can help me get the word out about the message of this book...

- Post a 5–Star review on Amazon.
- Write about the book on your Facebook, Twitter, Instagram, LinkedIn, – any social media you regularly use!
- If you blog, consider referencing the book, or publishing an excerpt from the book with a link back to my website. You have my permission to do this if you provide proper credit and backlinks.
- Recommend the book to friends – word-of-mouth is still the most effective form of advertising.
- Purchase additional copies to give away as gifts.

Tom Pisello

GROWTH THROUGH GRIEF

A Widower's Guide to Healing and Renewed Purpose